# CHALLENGING GENDER STEREOTYPES IN EDUCATION

## KAREN JONES

Sara Miller McCune founded SAGE Publishing in 1965 to support the dissemination of usable knowledge and educate a global community. SAGE publishes more than 1000 journals and over 800 new books each year, spanning a wide range of subject areas. Our growing selection of library products includes archives, data, case studies and video. SAGE remains majority owned by our founder and after her lifetime will become owned by a charitable trust that secures the company's continued independence.

Los Angeles | London | New Delhi | Singapore | Washington DC | Melbourne

# CHALLENGING GENDER STEREOTYPES IN EDUCATION

## KAREN JONES

Learning Matters
A SAGE Publishing Company
1 Oliver's Yard
55 City Road
London EC1Y 1SP

SAGE Publications Inc.
2455 Teller Road
Thousand Oaks, California 91320

SAGE Publications India Pvt Ltd
B 1/I 1 Mohan Cooperative Industrial Area
Mathura Road
New Delhi 110 044

SAGE Publications Asia-Pacific Pte Ltd
3 Church Street
#10-04 Samsung Hub
Singapore 049483

Editor: Amy Thornton
Senior project editor: Chris Marke
Project management: Swales and Willis Ltd,
Exeter, Devon
Marketing manager: Lorna Patkai
Cover design: Wendy Scott
Typeset by: C&M Digitals (P) Ltd, Chennai, India
Printed in the UK

**Library of Congress Control Number: 2020933774**

**British Library Cataloguing in Publication Data**

A catalogue record for this book is available from the British Library

ISBN 978-1-5264-9454-2
ISBN 978-1-5264-9453-5 (pbk)

At SAGE we take sustainability seriously. Most of our products are printed in the UK using responsibly sourced papers and boards. When we print overseas we ensure sustainable papers are used as measured by the PREPS grading system. We undertake an annual audit to monitor our sustainability.

# THIS BOOK

THIS BOOK IS FOR **ANYONE** WORKING WITH OR ASPIRING TO WORK WITH CHILDREN AND YOUNG PEOPLE IN EDUCATION.

IT IS **PARTICULARLY SUITED** TO TRAINEE TEACHERS AND EDUCATION STUDENTS.

IT **FILLS A GAP** IN KNOWLEDGE, IDENTIFIED IN RESEARCH, FOR TEACHERS AND EDUCATION PRACTITIONERS.

THIS BOOK **HELPS** YOU TO DEVELOP YOUR KNOWLEDGE OF HOW AND WHEN GENDER STEREOTYPES FORM AND HOW THEY CAN BE PERPETUATED IN VARIOUS WAYS DURING A CHILD'S EDUCATION.

IT **SUPPORTS** YOU TO CHALLENGE THESE STEREOTYPES, HELPING YOU TO TACKLE THE PROBLEM.

THIS BOOK WILL **SUPPORT** YOU WITH RESEARCH INFORMED PRAGMATIC SOLUTIONS TO IMPROVE PRACTICE AND TRANSFORM THE SCHOOL OR LEARNING ENVIRONMENT.

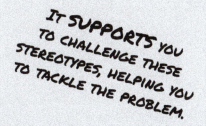

# CONTENTS

Contents

# ACKNOWLEDGEMENTS

We would like to credit and thank Severine Wilken, Jenny Brown and Joanna Leach, as well as all the anonymous contributors who kindly allowed case studies for this book.

# ABOUT THE AUTHORS

**Karen Jones** is Associate Professor of Educational Leadership and Management at the Institute of Education, University of Reading. Her main responsibilities include leadership and teaching of postgraduate programmes, as well as doctoral supervision. Adopting feminist and critical perspectives, she explores issues of gender, equity and power in her research.

**Marina Della Giusta** is Professor in Economics at the School of Politics, Economics and International Relations, University of Reading, where she was awarded her PhD in 2001. Her research interests include behavioural and labour economics, with a particular focus on gender, stigma and social norms.

**Yota Dimitriadi** is National Teaching Fellow and Associate Professor at the Institute of Education, University of Reading, where she undertakes doctoral supervision, leadership and teaching of TEL and computer science. This includes the initial teacher education (ITE) secondary computer science, PGCE primary education, BAEd and MA education programmes.

**Catherine Foley** is Associate Professor of Mathematics Education at the Institute of Education, University of Reading. Previously a leading mathematics teacher and local authority consultant, she now leads the school-based Primary School Direct programme and mathematics teaching within primary postgraduate initial teacher training.

**Carol Fuller** is Professor of Sociology of Education at the Institute of Education, University of Reading, with a particular interest in identity construction. She is particularly interested in the role of meaning in making sense of self, aspirations and confidence/self-efficacy. Her particular specialisms are social background and gender.

**Rebecca Harris** is Professor of Education at the University of Reading, with responsibility as School Director of Teaching and Learning. Their research explores the nature of the history curriculum, how young people engage with it, and the decisions history teachers make about what the curriculum should cover.

**Maria Kambouri-Danos** is Associate Professor of Early Years Childhood, Education and Care at the Institute of Education, University of Reading, with a particular interest in child development, gender and parental involvement. Her research explores how children learn and develop particular concepts, especially through play-based learning and adult interactions.

**Nasreen Majid** is Lecturer in Primary Mathematics Education at the University of Reading. She has taught in primary schools and was an advanced skills teacher for mathematics. She is interested in teacher identity and how this is shaped over time. Her current research interests lie in how primary teachers shape their mathematics identity.

**Cecilia Muldoon** is a PhD student at the Institute of Education, University of Reading, focusing on stigma in class and gender and educational practice. She is also involved in community projects that address social inequalities related to class and gender.

**Anna Tsakalaki** is Lecturer in Education at the Institute of Education, University of Reading. She is Director of the PG Certificate in Special Educational Needs Coordination and Inclusion Pathway Leader at the MA in Education. She is an active researcher of literacy difficulties in different languages.

**Meilun Yan** is a PhD student at the University of Reading. Her research explores the impact on Chinese children who are left at home by their migrating parents, in relation to their self-confidence and sense of efficacy. The ways that gender influences these areas is of particular interest to her.

# 1

# INTRODUCTION

## KAREN JONES

## KEYWORDS

- **PURPOSE**
- **CONTENT**
- **FEATURES**
- **CHAPTER OUTLINE**

### THIS CHAPTER

- sets out the purpose of the book;
- outlines the content and key features of each chapter;
- gives tips on how to engage with the content features and apply ideas from the book in practice.

## PURPOSE OF THE BOOK

Gender stereotypes are prevalent across all spheres of society, not just education, but because the formation of gender stereotypes coincides with a child's progression through education, and education is a key site for the perpetuation of gender stereotypes, practitioners at all stages of a child's education can help children develop a positive image of their gender and neutralise negative gender stereotypes and bias.

This book has been written for anyone working with or aspiring to work with children and young people in education. It is particularly suited to trainee teachers and education students, but also fills a gap in knowledge, identified in research, for teachers and education practitioners (e.g. classroom assistants, early years practitioners). The purpose of the book is to help you develop knowledge of how and when gender stereotypes form, as well as how they can be perpetuated in various ways during a child's education, so that you can help tackle this problem. This book will support you with research-informed pragmatic solutions to improve practice and transform the school or learning environment.

## OVERVIEW OF EACH CHAPTER

Chapter 2 explores sex-based differences between females and males, as well as looking at how and when gender identity forms and gender stereotypes take root. In Chapter 3, we will build on this by exploring non-binary ideas about gender in more detail. Chapter 4 will examine the intersection between gender and social background/ethnicity. Chapter 5 examines the impact of gender stereotypes on children's subject and career choice, as well as the longer-term economic implications.

Following that, we will explore how gender stereotypes manifest and may be perpetuated in specific curriculum and subject areas, beginning with Chapter 6, which looks at early years and children's play, followed by Chapter 7 (primary and secondary mathematics learning), Chapter 8 (the national history curriculum for primary and secondary schools) and Chapter 9 (ICT).

Next, we will turn to contemporary issues in education, beginning with Chapter 10, which examines dyslexia from the perspective of gender stereotypes. Chapter 11 examines sexism, sexual harassment and sexual violence in schools.

Chapter 12 advocates a whole-school approach to working with parents, communities, colleagues and school leaders. Chapter 13 focuses on how to work with mums in disadvantaged communities. Finally, Chapter 14 will consider a future without gender stereotypes, as well as suggesting further activities to prompt reflection and action planning.

## CONTENT FEATURES

Embedded within each chapter of this book are prompts for self-reflection, practical exercises and activities. You will be given tips on how you can engage with different types of material embedded in those chapters to help your reflections and action planning. The reflection questions and activities in this book have been developed to help link theoretical ideas and learning with classroom practice. Each chapter in the book includes activities that you can do to evaluate your practice or activities that you can do with children in class. There are also suggestions for curriculum and lesson planning, topic selection, and task selection. We hope that these activities provide practical ways to transform the learning environment. Some involve working with parents, colleagues and school leaders.

There are many more ideas for classroom-based activities to follow in this book. As you read each chapter, you can use Table 1.1 to plan ways that you can challenge gender stereotypes in education. This will help you to make the best use of this book to transform practice.

## ACTIVITY

Jot down some bullet-pointed notes on what you would like to learn from this book and how you hope to use this in practice (you might like to use Table 1.1). We suggest that you set yourself some achievable goals to test out ideas from the book in your practice. For example, you might want to introduce children to more counter-stereotype role models in storybooks or do more to encourage children to consider a broader range of careers. This might involve planning a time when you can explore why girls and boys are steered towards certain careers. This could include reading Chapter 5 on subject and career choice and setting yourself the goal to complete an activity with children in class. This might include initiating a discussion to deconstruct what makes a good nurse, doctor, electrician, bus driver, care worker, and so on. This could be followed with a discussion to deconstruct why these roles have traditionally been dominated by women or men (e.g. why there are more female nurses than male, more male electricians than female, etc.).

Table 1.1   *What future action will you take?*

| Examples of action you could take | How? | When will you begin? |
|---|---|---|
| Neutralise children's gender stereotypes by making more counter-stereotypes visible. | Read stories with women who are heroes or men who are caring for children. Use examples of female historical figures or scientists in class. | |
| Expose learners to counter stereotypical career role models. | <ul><li>Read Chapter 5.</li><li>Conduct classroom activity – children to draw pictures of people in different professions.</li><li>Initiate discussion on gender stereotypes relating to careers.</li><li>Invite a female scientist or firefighter or a male nurse to give a talk to children about the work they do.</li></ul> | |
| Use more positive examples of counter-stereotypes in class/school. | <ul><li>Consider the messages conveyed about gender in the pictures/posters displayed.</li><li>Ensure gender balance of scientists, historical figures, ICT specialists, etc.</li></ul> | |
| Campaign to challenge gender stereotypes. | <ul><li>Read Chapter 11.</li><li>Speak to colleagues about ideas.</li><li>Involve children and their families in actions to counter gender stereotyping.</li></ul> | |

## CHAPTER SUMMARY

This book will address a serious issue that is currently highly topical, which has to date received little attention in education courses, initial teacher training courses, or published literature. We hope that you find this book a unique resource for understanding gender stereotypes in education, whether you are currently working with or aspiring to work with children and young people. This introductory chapter provided tips on how to engage with the content features in this book to transform your practice.

# 2

# THE FORMATION OF GENDER IDENTITY AND GENDER STEREOTYPES

## KAREN JONES

## KEYWORDS

- SEX-BASED DIFFERENCES
- SEX
- INTERSEX
- GENDER

- SOCIAL COGNITIVE THEORY
- SOCIAL LEARNING THEORY
- SOCIALISATION
- GENDER IDENTITY

- GENDER STEREOTYPE DEFINITION
- GENDER STEREOTYPE FORMATION

### THIS CHAPTER

- defines and explores terms of reference, including sex, gender and gender stereotypes;
- explores key theories that explain the development of a gendered self;
- examines when gender stereotypes form and how they shape our experience in life.

# INTRODUCTION

*Men really DO have bigger brains: the amazing image that reveals just how male and female brains are wired differently.*

This is the title of an article published in the *Daily Mail* (Prigg, 2014). There are many more articles like this that illustrate just how much attention is given to differences between the sexes. Think for a moment about how many times you have heard phrases such as 'battle of the sexes' or 'the opposite sex', or even 'men are from Mars and women are from Venus' – a throwback to the relationships book by John Gray (1992). Have you ever commented or heard someone else refer to girls/women as more patient, considerate, empathetic or considerate to the needs of others than boys/men? Or have you heard or joked yourself that women are better at multitasking than men? Or perhaps you have heard someone grumble about 'women drivers'! You will have seen many examples that relate to children in education and in everyday life (see Table 2.1).

Table 2.1   Gender stereotypes

| Girls | Boys |
|---|---|
| Pink | Blue |
| Dolls | Lego |
| Playing house | Playing outdoors |
| Princesses | Superheroes |
| Caring | Tough |
| Quiet | Loud |
| Gentle | Rough |

At the root of these stereotypes is the idea that girls/women and boys/men possess innate characteristics that stem from their biological make-up and distinguish them not only as different, but as complete opposites. The idea that people can be divided into two discrete groups – females and males, each group with characteristics that go beyond physical differences – has been the subject of a great deal of debate. Some people question the extent to which females and males are different, while others argue that any differences which do exist stem from cultural influences, and they are not biologically determined. We will explore these debates and binary assumptions surrounding gender in more detail in this chapter, then in Chapter 3 we will turn to non-binary gender and explore the experience of transgender children and young people.

Your personal experiences will have a strong influence on how you make sense of this topic, so we have included questions to help you reflect on your own experiences, values and ideas throughout the chapter. To get started, pause now to reflect on your own views on sex differences.

## REFLECTION

- In what ways do you think females and males are different?
- Apply the differences you have identified into categories (e.g. physical differences, personality differences, cognitive differences).
- In your view, are these differences natural or innate - something we are born with - or do you believe there might be social or cultural reasons for these differences?

You can return to your answers to these questions after reading this chapter to see if your views have changed in any way, or perhaps your ideas will be confirmed!

## WHAT DO WE KNOW FROM RESEARCH?

### Sex-based differences

Research can help to establish the facts so that we can make informed judgements. Let's look at some of the evidence from three studies based on medical research, neuroscience and biobehavioural studies into sex-based differences (Blair, 2007; Ruigrok et al., 2014; Nostro et al., 2017). These studies show:

- Females have two X chromosomes but no Y chromosome. Males have one Y chromosome and one X chromosome. Some genes on the Y chromosome have no counterpart on X chromosomes. By contrast, in some cases, genes on the X chromosome can be found at higher levels in females than males.
- There are many differences relating to physiology and pathophysiology, meaning the physiological processes associated with disease or injury, such as the cardiovascular, musculoskeletal and immune systems, as well as the cellular mechanisms of sex steroid hormone actions on non-reproductive tissues.
- Receptors for sex steroid hormones (androgens, oestrogens and progestins) are present in many tissues that do not have a reproductive function, such as the heart, bone, skeletal muscle, vasculature, liver, immune system and brain.
- The male heart has a significantly greater left ventricular mass and chamber size than females.
- Males tend to have a larger skeletal and muscular structure and are, on average, larger than females.
- Females tend to have a wider pelvis for giving birth.
- Males have larger overall brain volumes than females, and differences have also been found in regions of the brain.

*(Continued)*

(Continued)

- Some of these differences are associated with different mental health conditions. Differences in the amygdala, hippocampus and insula are areas implicated in sex-biased neuropsychiatric conditions.
- Female brains are nearly four years younger than males, in terms of how they age.
- Tests to assess whether differences in grey matter volume relate to personality traits have found no significant correlations between personality scales. However, significant associations have been found for neuroticism, extraversion, and conscientiousness in males, which may be due to interplays between hormones or differences in brain organisation.

As these examples from studies of sex-based differences show, there are many physiological differences between females and males that have important implications for understanding health conditions and healthcare (Blair, 2007). However, this does not tell us that men are from Mars and women are from Venus! Personality–brain relationships remain unknown (Nostro et al., 2017), and there is no evidence that brain size or structure is linked in any way to brain function (Ruigrok et al., 2014).

## REFLECTION

- List some differences that you have observed between different males that you know.
- Now repeat this exercise, focusing this time on females that you know.
- Consider what these females and males have in common.
- Refer to your previous reflections to see if your views have changed in any way.

One of the problems of focusing on biological differences is that insufficient attention is paid to what we have in common. Many people argue that the distinction made between females and males polarises relations between women and men in ways that subordinates or marginalises women by assigning them an inferior status (Knights and Kerfoot, 2004). One way to overcome this is to deconstruct sex-based differences, to examine what men and women have in common as opposed to ways that they might be different. Another way is to view masculinities and femininities as a continuum rather than in bipolar ways.

Thus far, we have only considered two sex categories – females and males – when in fact some people are classed as having intersex traits. This means they are born with physical or biological characteristics that do not fit with traditional definitions of female or male. It is difficult to know how many people are born intersex in the UK because under the Births and Deaths Registration Act 1953, the law in England, Wales and Northern Ireland requires the sex of a baby to be given on the birth certificate as female or male. Births are normally registered within 42 days, but the guidance for an intersex child is that registration is deferred until medical investigations are complete. Even though this may take longer than usual, there is still no intersex category of registration, so the child is assigned a sex based on medical advice. Because of this, published records on the proportion of the population that is born intersex are difficult to find in the UK. However, one UK charity estimates around 150 children born in the UK each year undergo tests into their sexual assignment (DSD Families, 2019). The Intersex Initiative in the US estimates that 1 in 2,000 children are born visibly intersex (Intersex Initiative, 2008). Reports from the Office of the High Commissioner for Human Rights estimate that between 0.05 and 1.7 per cent of the population is born with intersex traits (OHCHR, n.d.).

Research with intersex persons plays a crucial role in understanding gender identity formation. One study of 24 intersex people found that with two partial exceptions, the sex given at birth corresponded to the gender identity of the participants. The author of the study concluded that gender identity is not determined prenatally by biology, but learnt postnatally through socialisation into the sex we are assigned at birth (Lev-Ran, 1974). The author appears to be overly ambitious with their claims, since recent work suggests that children with intersex traits suffer from shame, stigma, abuse and many human rights violations (OHCHR, n.d.).

# WHAT IS GENDER?

The term 'gender' is so widely used today that it is easy to think it has always been in common use. In fact, it seems to have first appeared in this context in the 1950s in the work of John Money, a psychologist specialising in sexual identity and the biology of identity (Ehrhardt, 2007). The term 'gender' became more widely used in the 1960s, mostly due to Robert Stoller, who is credited with being the first person to distinguish between sex and gender. The writer and sociologist Ann Oakley drew on Stoller's work in her own account of gender in the 1970s, and her work remains influential today.

Put in its simplest form, Oakley (1972) argued that sex is biological whereas gender is learnt through processes of socialisation. According to Oakley, it is not our biology that determines who we are, how we behave or what we become; it is society that makes girls/women and boys/men as different as they are. Proponents of socialisation theory argue that while sex distinguishes us as women or men, according to the make-up of our chromosomes, reproductive systems, genitalia and other physiological features, it is society that creates much greater distinctions between the sexes. It is through socialisation that we learn socially constructed notions of femininity and masculinity. These distinctions are reinforced through girls' and boys' toys, books, games and activities, such as dolls, prams and playhouses for girls and action toys for boys. The process of learning social rules and norms that govern appropriate behaviour for a girl or boy begins at birth, and is reinforced through the family, school, peers and the media, as well as religion and the culture of the society in which we grow up. From this perspective, gender is defined as a 'system of social practices' (Ridgeway and Smith-Lovin, 1999, p192). While there are many different forces of gender socialisation, the family has the most profound and lasting effect (Bradley, 2007). We would like you to consider these ideas as you read the following case study.

## CASE STUDY

### The beauty queen

*I recall becoming acutely aware of my gender at a very young age, around the time when I was 2-3 years old. While I did not spend all of my time thinking that, significant experiences have stayed in my memory. The first was a beauty competition I was entered into when I was around 2 years old. I recall a flurry of activity and preparation leading up to the day, my mum's excitement deliberating over what I should wear and what to do with my unruly hair. Nothing seemed to be more important in the lead-up to the big day!*

*I recall arriving at the summer fayre where the beauty competition would take place. Pretty stalls lined the green and I distinctly recall there was a donkey derby race taking place. It was a lovely hot sunny day. I was ushered into a marquee full of mothers who were busily dressing their little girls. I sensed their anxiety as they gazed at the other little girls and compared them with their own. Even at that age, the pressure to be beautiful and compete with other little girls on terms of beauty seemed wrong. I don't recall the pageant itself – I was probably too frozen with fear to remember it! What springs up next in my memory is hearing that I had won first prize, and the horrible realisation that I'd be on show again. I wriggled, squirmed and scrunched up my eyes when the trophy was handed over, and photographs were taken with local dignitaries. I felt like a terrible fraud. I hated every moment of it, but Mum was ecstatic all the same.*

As this story illustrates, society creates rules and norms that shape what we view as appropriate activity for girls and boys, but this can change over time and space. Today, it is likely that a mother would be criticised for entering her daughter into a beauty competition. Indeed, she would probably struggle to find a beauty competition for children in the UK in the first place, since such events are no longer considered socially acceptable.

## REFLECTION

- Pause and reflect on your own experiences growing up. When did you first become aware of your gender? How did that happen, and how did you feel?
- How did your gender shape your experiences growing up? What activities did you do? What toys did you play with? Were you expected to behave in a particular way (e.g. quiet, tough)?
- If you had been born a different sex, do you think your childhood experiences would have been different? If so, in what ways?

# THE FORMATION OF THE GENDERED SELF

The question of how and when we form a gendered self has intrigued researchers for many decades, and there is now a large volume of research that can help us to understand aspects of children's thinking, as well as how that relates to their gender development.

Bandura's (1977) social learning theory focuses on the context of socialisation. Bandura claimed that people who act as models in a child's environment, such as family, peers, teachers and characters on television, provide examples of behaviour that children observe, encode and may imitate. Although a child may imitate behaviour that is not considered appropriate for their gender, they are more likely to imitate a person with whom they identify who is therefore of the same sex. However, identification is more than a simple process of imitation; it involves the adoption of values, beliefs and behaviours. People in the child's company may respond by rewarding the child (e.g. 'Aren't you a good girl playing quietly with your dolls') or say something to curb unwelcome behaviour (e.g. 'Big boys don't cry'). Thus, responses from others can reinforce gender-appropriate behaviour. Children internalise those responses and behave in ways that earn approval. As part of a cycle of vicarious reinforcement, children learn by observing what happens to other people when they are rewarded or punished for particular behaviour. We would like you to consider these ideas when reading the following case study.

## CASE STUDY

### 'Oh no, I'm a tomboy!'

*I was around 3 years old, walking down the street one day; the conversation about tomboys started quite casually. Mum explained that tomboys were girls who exhibited the characteristics and behaviours of boys. Tomboys liked playing outdoors and getting dirty, she explained. I was very curious and puzzled about this. I asked lots of questions: How would I know if a girl was a tomboy? Did tomboys have short hair? Did tomboys wear boys' clothes? Why were tomboys bad children? What should I do if I met a tomboy? With each answer, it gradually dawned on me that she was saying I was a tomboy! I loved playing outdoors, digging up earth in the garden, exploring insects and worms, and even collected them in jam jars. In that vivid moment, I realised that I didn't behave in an appropriate manner for a girl. I needed to behave more like a girl!*

Although people hold different views on sex and gender, most agree that gender identity is much more complex than it being a reflection of a person's biological sex. The problem for many people is that society places different rules and values on forms of femininity and masculinity. This fosters beliefs about what is appropriate behaviour for females and males, hence the idea that playing in mud is OK for boys, but not for girls, in this case study. However, as this case study also shows, children are not passive recipients of socialisation; they have the cognitive ability to question the forces acting upon them. This brings us to the role of cognition in gender identity formation.

# SOCIAL COGNITIVE THEORY

Although Bandura's social learning theory has been very influential, and is still discussed widely today, critics argue that it places too great an emphasis on the role of the environment and does not adequately acknowledge cognitive processes that are at play. Bandura recognised this himself, and provided a more detailed consideration of cognitive learning processes in his later work, which he renamed social cognitive theory (Bandura, 1986). Another well-known writer on cognitive perspectives is Lawrence Kohlberg. His account provides the foundation on which many other studies are built (Kohlberg, 1966). Kohlberg was interested in the cognitive judgements made by children about their gender identity, and he was particularly influenced by Piaget's (1961) idea that children are active learners, capable of interacting with their environment to construct mental models of the world. According to social cognitive theory, children are not passive recipients of environmental cues; they make their own judgements. Kohlberg applied these ideas to a study of gender identity. He believed that children learn gender roles and come to enact them through their cognitive understanding of the social world in terms of sex-role dimensions. According to Kohlberg, gender identity is a cognitive process, and it is that which influences behaviour, not biological instinct or cultural norms. Although the environment provides many opportunities for a child to learn about gender roles and cultural norms and values, children self-socialise because they actively seek out and organise information and act in accordance with that information. From this perspective, children only adhere to specific gender roles if they have developed an associated gender identity.

## WHAT DO WE KNOW FROM RESEARCH?

### Key themes from social learning and cognitive perspectives

Perry and Bussey (1979) studied 48 female and 48 male 8-9-year-old children. They found that the children's imitation of adult behaviour was strongly influenced by how strongly they believed the adult displayed behaviours appropriate to the child's sex. This suggests that children evaluate adult behaviour rather than simply absorbing it. It suggests that there is an interplay between environmental factors and cognitive processes.

Ideas from social learning and cognitive perspectives were merged in the 1990s into social constructivist approaches. It is thought that female and male children differ in terms of their behaviour, interests and/or values for three key reasons:

1.   children are shaped by adults;

2.   peers shape each other in accordance with the way they have been socialised;

3.   once children have developed a firm gender identity, they socialise themselves according to stereotypes for their gender.

(Bussey and Bandura, 1999)

Current thinking draws together ideas on gender development to suggest that the degree to which children will differ in the extent to which they align with gender stereotypes will depend on the strength of socialisation pressures, as well as the nature and coherence of gender schemas (cognitive frameworks that help us to organise and interpret information) relating to children's knowledge of characteristics and social expectations stereotypically associated with each sex (Maccoby, 2000).

# When do gender stereotypes form?
## *What do we know from research?*

Research shows that from around the age of 2 young children begin to develop concepts of gender (Aina and Cameron, 2011).

Between the ages of 3 and 5, young children develop their understanding of what it means to be a girl or a boy and develop their own gender identity. At the same time gender stereotypes begin to emerge. During this period, idealised stereotypes and expectations about motherhood and work professions are often fostered. Children may begin to feel constrained by societal pressures to fit in with narrow roles for their gender.

2 Years

5 Years upwards

Most children are able to identify whether they are a boy or a girl by the age of 3 years (Martin and Ruble, 2004).

By the age of 5 gender stereotypes are well formed and by 5 to 7 years they are rigidly defined (Martin and Ruble, 2004).

## During primary and secondary education negative gender stereotyping can escalate into profound sexism.

**References:**
Aina, O.E. and Cameron, P.A. (2011) 'Why does gender matter? Counteracting stereotypes with young children', *Dimensions of Early Childhood*, 39(3): 11-20.
Martin, C. and Ruble, D. (2004) 'Children's search for gender cues: cognitive perspectives on gender development', *Current Directions in Psychological Science*, 13(2): 67-70.

The research we have explored so far has focused on how children develop a gendered self. Next, we will explore when this takes place in a child's development, as well as the impact of gender stereotypes on children and young people.

## WHAT DO WE KNOW FROM RESEARCH?

### When do gender stereotypes form?

Kohlberg (1966) suggested that gender identity develops in three stages:

1.  *Gender labelling*: Children can label themselves or other people as a girl or boy, mummy or daddy, but this is not stable over time. It can be influenced, for example, by a person's hairstyle or clothing.

2.  *Gender stability*: Children form stable ideas about gender. For example, the notion that girls will become mummies and boys will become daddies is now stable over time. It does not change because of a person's physical appearance.

3.  *Gender consistency*: Children develop a consistent view of gender that remains fixed over time and in different situations.

## WHAT DO WE KNOW FROM RESEARCH?

### Phases and ages of gender stereotype formation

- Research shows that from around the age of 2, young children begin to develop concepts of gender (Aina and Cameron, 2011).

- Most children are able to identify whether they are a boy or a girl by the age of 3 (Martin and Ruble, 2004).

- Between the ages of 3 and 5, young children develop their understanding of what it means to be a girl or a boy, as well as developing their own gender identity. At the same time, gender stereotypes begin to emerge. During this period, idealised stereotypes and expectations about motherhood and work professions are often fostered. Children may begin to feel constrained by societal pressures to fit in with narrow roles for their gender (Martin and Ruble, 2010).

- By the age of 5, gender stereotypes are well formed, and by 5–7 they are rigidly defined (Martin and Ruble, 2004).

- During primary and secondary education, negative gender stereotyping can escalate into profound sexism. Evidence of this is seen in research conducted with 1,634 teachers at primary and secondary schools in England and Wales:

    *Gender stereotyping is a typical feature of school culture .... Sexual harassment is highly prevalent in schools. It is also gendered, overwhelmingly involving boys targeting girls .... Sexism and sexual harassment in schools has been normalized and is rarely reported .... The use of misogynistic language is commonplace in schools.*

    (NEU and UK Feminista, 2017)

The research report calls for consistent and ongoing action from schools, government and education bodies to tackle problems, and recommends that the Department for Education (DfE) urgently makes tackling sexism and sexual harassment in schools a policy priority. Further, it recommends training for Ofsted inspectors to enable them to take action. This includes inspections of initial teacher training (ITT) providers to assess whether the training course adequately equips trainees with the skills they need, as well as compulsory training for all trainee teachers. We will explore these issues in detail in Chapter 11.

# HOW DO GENDER STEREOTYPES SHAPE OUR EXPERIENCES IN LIFE?

Gender stereotypes are a result of deeply rooted attitudes, values, norms and prejudices. Although they are often viewed in relation to girls and women, they shape the experiences of everyone. The gender stereotypes children encounter can profoundly influence:

- expectations of appropriate gender-based behaviour;
- academic preferences;
- perceptions of ability;
- perceptions of status and worth;
- access to equitable educational opportunities;
- interpersonal and intrapersonal relationships;
- physical and psychological wellbeing;
- career choice;
- access to equitable work opportunities and economic wellbeing;
- regard for self and others.

Thus, gender stereotypes can squash talent, limit educational experiences and achievement, and corrode aspirations, which in turn can limit professional opportunities and prospects.

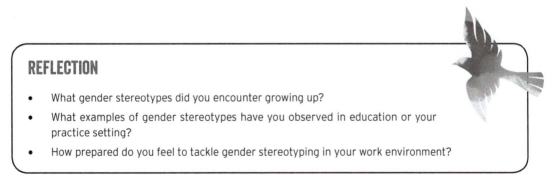

## REFLECTION

- What gender stereotypes did you encounter growing up?
- What examples of gender stereotypes have you observed in education or your practice setting?
- How prepared do you feel to tackle gender stereotyping in your work environment?

We don't expect you to have the answers to these questions, but by understanding our own knowledge and confidence gaps we can begin to think about acting to close those gaps.

# CHAPTER SUMMARY

This chapter examined when and how gender identity forms and gender stereotypes take root. Some of the terms we have looked at so far include:

- *Sex*: Described in the *Oxford Dictionary* (2019) as 'Either of the two main categories (male and female) into which humans and most other living things are divided on the basis of their reproductive functions'.

- *Intersex*: The condition of having both male and female sex organs or other sexual characteristics.

- *Gender*: By contrast, viewed as 'Either of the two sexes (male and female), especially when considered with reference to social and cultural differences rather than biological ones. The term is also used more broadly to denote a range of identities that do not correspond to established ideas of male and female' (Lexico, 2020). Following Ridgeway and Smith-Lovin (1999), this book defines gender as a 'system of social practices' (p192).

- *Gender identity*: Refers to a person's sense of their own gender, regardless of whether this corresponds to the sex they were given at birth or if they are female or male.

- *Gender stereotypes*: Defined as 'preconceived ideas whereby females and males are arbitrarily assigned characteristics and roles determined and limited by their gender' (GEC, 2015).

# FURTHER READING

**Fawcett Society** (2019) *Gender Stereotypes in Early Childhood: A Literature Review*. Available at: www.fawcettsociety.org.uk/gender-stereotypes-in-early-childhood-a-literature-review

**Zero Tolerance** (2013) *Just Like a Child*. Available at: www.zerotolerance.org.uk/resources/Just-Like-a-Child.pdf

# REFERENCES

Aina, O.E. and Cameron, P.A. (2011) Why does gender matter? Counteracting stereotypes with young children. *Dimensions of Early Childhood*, 39(3): 11–20.

Bandura, A. (1977) *Social Learning Theory*. Englewood Cliffs, NJ: Prentice Hall.

Bandura, A. (1986) *Social Foundations of Thought and Action: A Social Cognitive Theory*. Englewood Cliffs, NJ: Prentice Hall.

Blair, M.L. (2007) Sex-based differences in physiology: what should we teach in the medical curriculum? *Advances in Physiology Education*, 31(1): 23–5.

Bradley, H. (2007) *Gender*. Cambridge: Polity Press.

Bussey, K. and Bandura, A. (1999) Social cognitive theory of gender development and differentiation. *Psychological Review*, 106(4): 676–713.

DSD Families (2019) *About Us*. Available at: www.dsdfamilies.org/charity

Ehrhardt, A.A. (2007) John Money, Ph.D. *Journal of Sex Research*, 44(3): 223–4.

Gender Equality Commission (GEC) (2015) *Gender Equality Glossary*. Available at: https://eige.europa.eu/rdc/thesaurus/terms/1222

Gray, J. (1992) *Men Are from Mars, Women Are from Venus*. London: HarperCollins.

HM Government (1953) *Births and Deaths Registration Act 1953*. Available at: www.legislation.gov.uk/ukpga/Eliz2/1-2/20

Intersex Initiative (2008) *Intersex FAQ (Frequently Asked Questions)*. Available at: www.intersexinitiative.org/articles/intersex-faq.html

Knights, D. and Kerfoot, D. (2004) Between representations and subjectivity: gender binaries and the politics of organizational transformation. *Gender, Work & Organization*, 11(4): 430–54.

Kohlberg, L. (1966) A cognitive-development analysis of children's sex-role concepts and attitudes. In E.E. Maccody (ed.), *The Development of Sex Differences*. Stanford, CA: Stanford University Press.

Lev-Ran, A. (1974) Gender role differentiation in hermaphrodites. *Archives of Sexual Behaviour*, 3(5): 391–424.

Lexico (2020) *Gender*. Available at: www.lexico.com/definition/gender

Maccoby, E.E. (2000) Perspectives on gender development. *International Journal of Behavioral Development*, 24(4): 398–406.

Martin, C.L. and Ruble, D.N. (2004) Children's search for gender cues: cognitive perspectives on gender development. *Current Directions in Psychological Science*, 13(2): 67–70.

Martin, C.L. and Ruble, D.N. (2010) Patterns of gender development. *Annual Review of Psychology*, 61(1): 353–81.

National Education Union (NEU) and UK Feminista (2017) *'It's Just Everywhere': A Study of Sexism in Schools and How We Can Tackle It*. Available at: https://neu.org.uk/sites/neu.org.uk/files/sexism-survey-feminista-2017.pdf

Nostro, A.D., Müller, V.I., Reid, A.T. and Eickhoff, S.B. (2017) Correlations between personality and brain structure: a crucial role of gender. *Cerebral Cortex*, 27(7): 3698–712.

Oakley, A. (1972) *Sex, Gender and Society*. London: Maurice Temple Smith.

Office of the High Commissioner for Human Rights (OHCHR) (n.d.) *Fact Sheet: Intersex*. Available at: www.unfe.org/wp-content/uploads/2017/05/UNFE-Intersex.pdf

*Oxford Dictionary* (2019) *Sex*. Available at: https://en.oxforddictionaries.com/definition/sex

Perry, D.G. and Bussey, K. (1979) The social learning theory of sex differences: imitation is alive and well. *Journal of Personality and Social Psychology*, 37(10): 16699–712.

Piaget, J. (1961) *The Child's Conception of Number.* New York: Norton.

Prigg, M. (2014) Men really DO have bigger brains: the amazing image that reveals just how male and female brains are wired differently. *Daily Mail*, 11 February. Available at: www.dailymail.co.uk/sciencetech/article-2557051/Men-really-DO-bigger-brains.html

Ridgeway, C.L. and Smith-Lovin, L. (1999) The gender system and interaction. *Annual Review of Sociology*, 25: 191–216.

Ruigrok, A.N., Salimi-Khorshidi, G., Lai, M.C., Baron-Cohen, S., Lombardo, M.V. and Suckling, J. (2014) A meta-analysis of sex differences in human brain structure. *Neuroscience & Biobehavioral Reviews*, 39: 34–50.

# 3

# CHALLENGING THE GENDER BINARY: EXPLORING THE EXPERIENCES OF TRANSGENDER CHILDREN AND YOUNG PEOPLE

## REBECCA HARRIS

## KEYWORDS

- **GENDER**
- **STEREOTYPES**
- **GENDER NORMS**
- **TRANSGENDER**
- **TRANS**
- **INCLUSION**
- **DIVERSITY**

## THIS CHAPTER

- explores issues relating to gender norms and gender identity, as well as challenging the notion of gender being seen as a simple male-female binary divide;
- focuses on the challenges for children and young children who identify as transgender;
- explores the ways in which schools and practitioners can work to provide an environment in which gender-nonconforming youngsters can flourish.

# INTRODUCTION

*For the first few months after I came out, entire classes would chant 'chick with a dick' at me, in PE people would pull down my shorts and pants, groups positioned to ban me from using the toilets and changing rooms and joining PE lessons.*

(Stonewall, 2017, p14)

This quote, reported in Stonewall's *School Report* from a young person, illustrates the experiences that many of those who identify as transgender can encounter in schools in the UK.

This chapter will explore matters relating to the experiences of young people in education who are transgender. We will discuss terminology, our understanding of gender, and how people develop a sense of identity. We will also examine how the way schools operate impacts on children and young people who identify as transgender. As part of this exploration, we will also look at what practitioners in educational environments can do to create a safe, inclusive environment for those that do not fit into traditional gendered identities.

We must acknowledge that for some, this is a deeply controversial issue. Trans issues attract an increasing amount of media coverage, reflecting growing awareness of trans-related matters, but also arguments about trans rights and debates about gendered identity.

# THE 'PROBLEM' WITH 'GENDER'

Problematising gender seems to be an odd thing to do. After all, when we are born, it is obvious whether a child has female or male reproductive organs (unless someone is born with ambiguous genitalia, which is one sign of someone being intersex). Yet this conflates sex and gender. Sex refers to an individual's biological condition, sexuality reflects to whom someone is romantically attracted, and gender refers to how a person identifies.

Gender-specific stereotypical roles and expected standards of behaviour are often generated through society and used to 'police' what is seen as 'normal'. In this way of thinking, there are two genders, male and female, and people are either one or the other; this is what we call a binary construction of gender. In turn, this creates what is referred to as a 'cis-normative' culture (see below for a definition of 'cis' or 'cisgender'). This culture then becomes firmly established and any behaviours or expressions of gender identity beyond the norm are seen as 'odd', 'weird' or 'deviant'. This is at the heart of the challenges facing those who do not identify comfortably within this binary perception of male and female.

# TERMINOLOGY

In my experience, the terminology associated with people who do not identify with their assigned gender at birth is an issue that can generate confusion and discomfort for those who are happy with their birth gender. As soon as people remove themselves from the label of 'male' or 'female', it then becomes difficult to define them without using another label.

This means other labels or terms are used to define someone who identifies as transgender, and although this is useful, it can also be contentious. For example, the term 'transgendered' has been frequently used in the past, but nowadays there is a growing preference for the term 'transgender' (hence the use of the term in this chapter). The reason for this is that 'transgendered' implies something happened to someone that made them trans, rather than being an identity with which they were born. Similarly, it could have been possible in this chapter to talk about transgender and non-binary people; 'trans' or 'transgender' are broad umbrella terms, but are often used specifically to describe people wanting to be the opposite gender, whereas non-binary people may feel uncomfortable with the notion of being labelled 'man' or 'woman', so may reject such labels outright, or embrace aspects of both. However, in this chapter, 'transgender' or 'trans' are used in their broadest sense. The following are terms that are often used:

- *Trans*: This is an 'umbrella' term to describe people who are uncomfortable with or reject the sex they were assigned at birth. There are a wide variety of terms used by trans people to describe themselves, including (but not limited to) *transgender, transsexual, genderqueer (GQ), gender-fluid, non-binary, gender-variant, cross-dresser, genderless, agender, non-gender, third gender, two-spirited, bi-gender, trans man, trans woman, transmasculine, transfeminine* and *neutrois*. (*Note*: The term 'transvestite' is not used; this is because of the negative connotations associated with this term, which is generally used for someone who dresses in the clothes of the opposite gender for sexual excitement.)

- *Transgender man/trans man and transgender woman/trans woman*: These are probably the most commonly used terms to describe someone who is assigned female/male at birth but identifies and lives as a man/woman. This may be shortened to trans man/woman, or *FTM/MTF*, an abbreviation for female-to-male/male-to-female.

- *Transsexual*: This is another term for someone who is transgender but is increasingly seen as a more medical term to refer to someone whose gender is not the same as, or does not sit comfortably with, the sex they were assigned at birth. This term is still used by some, although for many the terms 'trans' or 'transgender' are preferred.

(adapted from Stonewall, n.d.)

Alongside issues around labels is the use of pronouns. Some people prefer to adopt the pronouns used for the opposite sex (i.e. a trans woman may well use she/her). However, this implies that someone is simply switching from one end of the binary scale to the other, whereas some people, who may be more fluid or ambiguous in their gender identity, or still trying to make sense of their identity, may prefer gender-neutral language and use pronouns such as they/their and ze/zir.

In addition, there are other terms associated with understanding non-binary experiences. The following provides an explanation of some other common terms and ideas:

- *Cisgender or cis*: Someone whose gender identity is the same as the sex they were assigned at birth. An alternative is 'non-trans'.

- *Deadnaming*: This is calling someone by their birth name after they have changed their name, often affecting trans people who have changed their name as part of their transition.

- *Gender dysphoria*: This is when a person experiences discomfort or distress because there is a mismatch between their sex assigned at birth and their gender identity. This is also the clinical diagnosis for someone who doesn't feel comfortable with the sex they were assigned at birth.

- *Gender expression*: This is how a person chooses to express their gender outwardly. A person who does not conform to societal expectations of gender may not, however, identify as trans.

- *Gender identity*: This refers to a person's innate sense of their own gender, whether male, female or something more fluid, which may or may not match the sex assigned at birth.

- *Gender reassignment*: This is a term for describing a person's transition. Gender reassignment usually means to undergo some sort of medical intervention (e.g. hormone treatment, surgery), but it can also mean changing names and/or pronouns, dressing differently, and living in their self-identified gender. Gender reassignment is a characteristic that is protected by the Equality Act 2010. It is seen as a contentious process by some; for example, some argue that it has medicalised transgender issues, while others reject the notion that you can physically change gender.

- *Gender Recognition Certificate (GRC)*: This enables trans people to be legally recognised in their affirmed gender and to be issued with a new birth certificate. Not all trans people will apply for a GRC, and a GRC is not required to change your gender markers at work or to legally change your gender on other documents such as your passport. (*Note*: At the time of writing, the government had consulted on reforms to the Gender Recognition Act 2004 with a view to making it easier for people to obtain a GRC. At present, only those over 18 can obtain a GRC, and it requires medical diagnosis/proof for one to be issued.)

- *Passing*: If a trans person is regarded, at a glance, to be a cisgender man or cisgender woman, then they are seen as being able to 'pass'.

- *Transitioning*: This is the process a trans person may follow to live in the gender with which they identify. This is likely to vary from individual to individual. Medical transition involves treatments such as hormone therapy and surgeries, but not all trans people pursue this route. Transitioning can be purely social, involving telling friends and family, dressing differently, working in the preferred identity, and changing official documents.

# IDENTITY FORMATION

Transgender matters are largely about identity, and in this instance whether someone identifies as female, male or something alternative. Debates about identity often reflect the nature versus nurture model of human behaviours (i.e. we are either born how we are or we learn to become how we are). In terms of identity formation, this would mean our identity is either shaped and determined by ourselves or by the society in which we live. An alternative idea is sociocultural theory (Schachter, 2005), or the socioecological model (Eisenberg et al., 2012), which present identity formation as the interaction between the self and the wider social and cultural context. For example, the socioecological model, although it is generally used to provide a framework to examine behaviours and human development, offers a useful means of conceptualising identity development (see Figure 3.1).

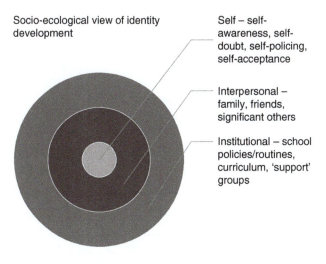

Socio-ecological view of identity development

Self – self-awareness, self-doubt, self-policing, self-acceptance

Interpersonal – family, friends, significant others

Institutional – school policies/routines, curriculum, 'support' groups

*Figure 3.1    Socioecological view of identity development*

At the centre is the 'self'. This requires a person to be self-aware of who they are. For someone who is transgender, this can be confusing and uncomfortable if they do not fit into the usual binary notion of gender. As one of the young people who responded to the Stonewall survey said:

> *If I knew what trans meant at an earlier age, I might have had an easier time at school. I went through a period of being very anxious and depressed because I was so confused about my own gender identity, and didn't feel I had anyone to talk about it. I couldn't figure out why I was so uncomfortable in my own skin.*

(Stonewall, 2017, p24)

As this quote illustrates, self-awareness can become self-doubt and/or self-policing as the person tries to work out how best to fit in and what might be deemed 'acceptable'. This can result in finally accepting themselves for who they are. As you can imagine, this can be a very isolating experience – many transgender people do report being aware they were 'different' from a very young age, often 4 or 5, and struggled to understand their feelings and the implications of these.

The 'self' then interacts with others (i.e. family, friends and peers). These interpersonal relationships impact with a person's sense of self as they negotiate what to reveal about their identity. A transgender person faces the fear of potential rejection from those they love, and ridicule from those with whom they interact on a regular basis. This interaction will in part determine whether a transgender person is willing to 'come out'.

Both of these layers, then, are influenced by the wider institutional or social context (e.g. whether there are role models or policies clearly in place to support those who identify as transgender). The absence of these can make it more challenging for some to accept themselves or to feel comfortable being open about who they are.

## REFLECTION

- How important is gender to your sense of identity?
- How comfortable would you feel doing something you considered to be an activity for the other gender?
- Have you ever had your sense of identity challenged? If so, how did this make you feel?
- What helps you feel secure in your identity?

## WHAT DO WE KNOW FROM RESEARCH?

### The experiences of transgender children and young people in schools

Research helps us to understand why this matters. In 2017, Stonewall carried out a survey of the experiences of LGBT+ youngsters in secondary schools. Although Stonewall have carried out similar surveys in the past, this was the first that sought to include the experiences of transgender young people. There were nearly 4,000 responses in total, and of these nearly 500 came from those identifying as trans.

Overall, the report showed that the experience for LGB youngsters was improving compared to previous surveys, but there were still significant issues, and those who identified as transgender generally experience more challenges than their LGB peers. Nearly two-thirds of transgender young people reported being bullied and around half experienced transphobic language. More worryingly, 84 per cent reported self-harming, 45 per cent had attempted suicide, and around 10 per cent had received death threats from their peers. Needless to say, such experiences have significant mental health and wellbeing issues, which in turn impact on academic engagement and performance for these young people in schools, with potentially significant lifelong repercussions. For anyone to find themselves in such a position is appalling, especially when it is possible to provide support.

DePalma's (2013) work has shown that gender norms become established early in primary schools, in part because of the way teachers and schools work. She found that many teachers conflated ideas of sexual orientation and gender identity, seeing them as interchangeable rather than distinct issues facing particular groups of children. Sexual orientation is a question for students who identify as lesbian, gay or bisexual (LGB), whereas gender identity is applicable to those who are transgender (although questions about sexual orientation may occur at some point). Through DePalma's project, teachers worked with children to help them recognise gendered assumptions, so they were shown pictures of people and were asked to identify who was male/female, and then asked to look at a series of objects and explain whether they were 'girlish' or 'boyish' objects. This latter activity in particular opened up a lot of discussion and helped the teachers and children realise that our ideas about boys and girls are often socially constructed. This then led into some work where the children were asked to create a collage around the question, 'Who am I?' The aim of this project, which is known as 'No Outsiders', was not to encourage children to think of themselves as transgender, but to recognise that there are different ways of being male and female (i.e. boys may like some 'girly' things, and vice versa), and also that being different should not be seen as an issue. It is designed to remove the stresses and stigma that many young trans people experience by normalising variance in gender identity and expression.

As explained above, through the socioecological model of identity formation, children and young people will struggle with their self-identity if there are no visible role models or positive affirmation of their transgenderism. Interviews I have conducted with young people show that often a little support can go a long way in developing the confidence of these youngsters in who they are.

As part of this, policy documents are important. Where schools have clear policies on supporting trans students, which are adhered to, and where teaching staff are aware of trans issues, it is evident that trans students feel safer in school. However, this is not common, and issues that affect trans students on a day-to-day basis are frequently ignored. According to Stonewall's *School Report*, 58 per cent of trans students are not allowed to use the toilet of their preferred gender, 67 per cent are not allowed to use the changing room for PE that aligns with their gender identity, 64 per cent are not allowed to play in sports teams that align with their preferred gender, 33 per cent are not allowed to use their preferred name, and 20 per cent are not allowed to wear the uniform in which they feel comfortable (Stonewall, 2017).

For non-trans people, these might appear unimportant matters, but as Ingrey (2018) explains, issues such as which toilet can be used sends out a message about who we are and where we do and don't belong. Having separate gender toilets regulates where students can go and can force them to fit into a cisgender norm. Having to ask for approval to use a designated toilet space is, according to Ingrey (2018), 'humiliating, pathologizing and alienating, and ultimately transphobic' (p781). Having gender-neutral toilets and changing facilities would be the ideal, but in the interim schools need to talk to young trans students about what they want and would be comfortable with.

Similarly, although policies are important, there can be a tendency to portray trans students as needing 'support' or 'protection'. This actually reflects the way in which cisgender norms are embedded in everyday practices, so that people have to go out of their way to provide additional support for trans children and young people, whereas ideally being transgender needs to be normalised, so it is no longer seen as an issue. This means acknowledging that being transgender is part of the diversity of life.

## REFLECTION

How inclusive do you feel your school is of transgender students? Consider the following:

- Do you believe that young people in your environment might feel the need to hide they are - or think they are - trans?

(Continued)

(Continued)

- Do you believe that your colleagues might feel the need to hide they are trans?
- Do you believe that young people in your environment feel comfortable disclosing they are trans?
- Do you believe that trans youngsters in your environment would receive verbal abuse from peers (e.g. name-calling, derogatory comments)?
- Do you believe that trans young people in your environment would receive physical abuse from peers (e.g. pushing, shoving, thrown objects)?
- Do you believe that trans youngsters in your environment would receive death threats from peers?
- Do you believe that trans young people you work with would contemplate or actually self-harm?
- Do you believe that trans youngsters in your environment would receive positive encouragement from peers when they come out to them?
- Do you believe that trans young people you work with would receive positive encouragement from staff when they come out to them?

What makes you believe that your workplace provides a positive/negative environment for trans youngsters?

This means that beyond physical things such as toilets, trans issues need to be encountered in the normal day-to-day existence of all young people in schools. The absence of trans issues in the curriculum means transgender students do not see themselves as part and parcel of society, and to be absent from the curriculum can lead to a sense of alienation, marginalisation and not belonging. This also means that the wider school community does not encounter trans-related issues, and so they come to appear abnormal. At present, there are few research studies into the impact that the lack of visibility in the curriculum has on transgender students, but it is likely that the issues are the same as those experienced by minority ethnic students – there are many studies which show that the absence of minority ethnic figures and culture in the curriculum has a detrimental impact on such students.

# DEVELOPING PRACTICE

Some areas of the curriculum could incorporate aspects of transgender culture. There is a growing body of literature and storybooks that could be used in literacy and English lessons. For example, David Walliams' book *The Boy in the Dress* offers a way into discussing issues about difference and how being different is perfectly normal and acceptable. The writings of Tyler Ford could easily be used as the basis of English lessons, exploring the experience of someone who identifies as non-binary. History is another possible area. Although transgender histories are only really starting to be studied in academia, there are opportunities to bring aspects naturally into the curriculum. For example, many primary schools teach about the Ancient Greeks, and the story of Hermaphroditus shows that gender identity is not just a modern concern. The history of many ancient periods across the globe reveal an acceptance of transgender individuals or recognition of a third sex, such as the *hijra* within Indian culture.

Perhaps the most obvious place in the curriculum for trans issues is within personal, social and health education (PSHE) or an alternative variation of this. There is no prescribed curriculum for this subject, although it is a compulsory part of the school curriculum. However, the PSHE Association do provide helpful guidance (see **www.pshe-association.org.uk**). They provide a coherent programme of study that schools can use and adapt. As part of their proposals, they focus on nine overarching concepts; of these, 'identity', 'relationships', and 'diversity and equality' would seem to align comfortably with a focus on developing an understanding and acceptance of transgender individuals. The programme is also built around three core themes: 'health and wellbeing', 'relationships', and 'living in the wider world'. Each presents opportunities to engage with transgender issues, and at Key Stage 2 children are expected to learn that:

> *differences and similarities between people arise from a number of factors, including family, cultural, ethnic, racial and religious diversity, age, sex, gender identity, sexual orientation, and disability (see 'protected characteristics' in the Equality Act 2010) [and] about the difference between, and the terms associated with, sex, gender identity and sexual orientation [as part of our] relationships.*

> (PSHE Association, 2017, p15)

At Key Stage 3, young people are also expected to learn:

- about the difference between assigned/biological sex, gender identity and sexual orientation;

- the terms associated with sex, gender identity and sexual orientation, and to understand accepted terminology;

- about the unacceptability of sexist, homophobic, biphobic, transphobic, racist and disablist language and behaviour, as well as the need to challenge it and how to do so;

- to recognise bullying and abuse in all its forms (including prejudice-based bullying both in person and online/via text, abuse, exploitation and trafficking) and to have the skills and strategies to manage being targeted or witnessing others being targeted.

> (PSHE Association, 2017, p25)

As a guide for schools, this offers a useful sense of direction. The Department for Education (DfE) has also recently introduced new guidance specifically on relationships education (RE) for primary schools and relationships and sex education (RSE) for secondary schools. This guidance emphasises the importance of teaching about equality and respect, and schools are told when they 'consider it appropriate to teach their pupils about LGBT, they should ensure that this content is fully integrated into their programmes of study for this area of the curriculum rather than delivered as a standalone unit or lesson' (DfE, 2019, p15). However, the guidance is less specific on the expected outcomes in relation to LGBT+ matters in comparison to the work published by the PSHE Association. Nonetheless, it is clear that there is a requirement on schools to provide appropriate education for all students around transgender issues.

As practitioners, we need to recognise the role we can play in normalising transgender issues, and this is something lacking in many school curricula. The following comments from students who were part of Stonewall's *School Report* show that if we, as practitioners, do not engage with these issues, young people will turn elsewhere to find out what they see as necessary:

> *I truly believe that the lack of education on LGBT issues is not only wrong but also dangerous, as we have to turn to the Internet to educate ourselves on topics relevant to us.*

(Stonewall, 2017, p23)

> *The only LGBTQ+ stuff we were taught was if we asked a specific question about it in PSHE lessons. Other than that, the school hasn't talked to us about LGBT stuff, me and my friends learnt everything we know from the Internet or from other LGBT people.*

(Stonewall, 2017, p23)

## TRANSFORMING PRACTICE

At present, there is little robust evidence about good practice in supporting children and young people whose gender identity and expression is at variance with their gender assigned at birth. However, we are increasingly aware of the challenges facing these students; these are overwhelmingly to support them in appreciating, understanding and becoming comfortable with their gender identity. Besides working with the individuals, it also requires schools and other educational environments to educate the wider population, both young people and adults.

Stonewall's *School Report* identifies ten key recommendations for supporting LGBT+ youngsters, which are summarised below:

1. *Get the basics right*: Have clear policies and procedures to deal with bullying and the use of inappropriate language.

2. *Show clear leadership*: Senior staff need to give a strong message about unacceptable behaviours and promote a positive learning environment for all.

3. *Create an inclusive curriculum*: LGBT+ people and experiences should be reflected in the curriculum, and students should have appropriate PSHE education.

4. *Equip your staff*: All staff should be aware of the challenges facing LGBT+ students, especially around the factors that can adversely affect mental health and wellbeing. Staff need to feel confident in tackling problems and providing support as appropriate.

5. *Celebrate difference*: People and societies are inherently diverse, and this needs to be reflected in the school ethos and physical environment.

6. *Provide information and support*: Schools should have LGBT+ resources in libraries and be in a position to signpost young people to other resources and organisations that can support them.

7. *Provide specific support for trans students*: Besides the points above, schools need to be explicit in supporting the needs of trans students, as well as working with them to discuss issues around confidentiality (as trans students may not be 'out' at home), uniforms, activities and facilities.

8. *Protect health and wellbeing*: Being aware of the particular challenges for trans students means pastoral staff should be able to offer support or signpost students to external support.

9. *Involve LGBT+ young people*: Schools should involve young people in the creation of policies that affect them, as well as supporting students who wish to establish their own LGBT+ groups.

10. *Work with parents, carers and local organisations*: Schools should engage with the wider community so that they understand the work schools are trying to do to address bullying and inappropriate language.

(Stonewall, 2017)

In many ways, the need to create an inclusive curriculum that addresses the needs of transgender youngsters is the same as the impetus to create a more inclusive curriculum for other marginalised groups in society. Diversity in the curriculum should reflect the diversity that exists generally in society. However, the situation for young trans people is complicated by the general lack of understanding that these students face within a system that has been constructed on cisgender norms. It is only by becoming aware that these norms exist that we can start to question them and their appropriateness. However, as various research studies show, this needs to be done quickly if we are to address the serious issues that these students face. If we get things wrong, there can be serious negative consequences, but if we get things right, we can make a positive difference to the lives of these young people.

# CHAPTER SUMMARY

We need to:

- be aware of our own assumptions about gender being based around a male–female binary, as well as how this informs the way we see the world;

- become more knowledgeable about the challenges facing young people who do not fall into society's neat gender categories, as well as appreciating the significant mental health and wellbeing issues that can accompany someone who identifies as transgender;

- look at the steps we can take as individual practitioners to make educational settings a safe and welcoming space for young transgender people in order to create an environment in which they can flourish and be respected.

## FURTHER READING

**Mitchell, M. and Howarth, C.** (2009) *Trans Research Review*. Manchester: Equality and Human Rights Commission.

**NASUWT** (n.d.) *Trans Equality in Schools and Colleges*. Available at: www.nasuwt.org.uk/uploads/assets/uploaded/085066bb-c224-40de-b79e2a1358801ee9.pdf

## REFERENCES

DePalma, R. (2013) Choosing to lose our gender expertise: queering sex/gender in school settings. *Sex Education*, 13(1): 1–15.

Department for Education (DfE) (2019) *Relationships Education, Relationships and Sex Education (RSE) and Health*. Available at: www.gov.uk/government/publications/relationships-education-relationships-and-sex-education-rse-and-health-education

Eisenberg, M., Madesn, N., Oliphant, J. and Resnick, R. (2012) Policies, principals and parents: multilevel challenges and supports in teaching sexuality education. *Sex Education*, 12(3): 317–29.

HM Government (2004) *Gender Recognition Act 2004*. Available at: www.legislation.gov.uk/ukpga/2004/7/contents

HM Government (2010) *Equality Act 2010*. Available at: www.legislation.gov.uk/ukpga/2010/15/contents

Ingrey, J. (2018) Problematizing the cisgendering of school washroom space: interrogating the politics of recognition of transgender and gender nonconforming youth. *Gender and Education*, 30(6): 774–89.

PSHE Association (2017) *PSHE Education Programme of Study: Key Stages 1–5*. Available at: www.pshe-association.org.uk/system/files/PSHE%20Education%20Programme%20of%20Study%20%28Key%20stage%201-5%29%20Jan%202017_2.pdf

Schachter, E. (2005) Context and identity formation: a theoretical analysis and a case study. *Journal of Adolescent Research*, 20(3): 375–95.

Stonewall (2017) *School Report: The Experiences of Lesbian, Gay, Bi and Trans Young People in Britain's Schools in 2017*. London: Stonewall.

Stonewall (n.d.) *Glossary of Terms*. Available at: www.stonewall.org.uk/help-advice/glossary-terms

# 4

# CONSTRUCTING SELF: GENDER, SOCIAL BACKGROUND AND ETHNICITY IN DEVELOPING EDUCATIONAL IDENTITIES

## CAROL FULLER, NASREEN MAJID AND MEILUN YAN

## KEYWORDS

- **REINFORCEMENT**
- **SELF-IDENTITY**
- **ETHNICITY**
- **GENDER**
- **LABELS**

### THIS CHAPTER

- highlights how schools can inadvertently reinforce both positive and negative understandings of self;
- considers the ways that this self-identity impacts on educational confidence and narratives of educational 'success' and 'failures';
- explores the role of educators in supporting the development of the confidence and resilience needed to succeed.

# INTRODUCTION

This chapter explores how the education system could be argued as reinforcing, as well as 'interacting' with notions of, a gendered, social and ethnically defined self. Experiences of schooling also provide a powerful framework that young people use to form a sense of themselves, in this case educational 'success' or 'failure'. The consequences of these will be considered in relation to how they can impact on educational confidence, engagement and aspirations. Ideas and suggestions are then offered as to how educators can support a reframing of identities so as to support young people to develop the levels of resilience and self-confidence that are arguably the key skills for success in the twenty-first century.

The question of who we are is a central one and key to broad existential questions that, in one form or another, underpin our everyday life. Yet unpicking and defining what and who we are is far from easy, and can very often be compounded by uncertainty as to whether who we think we are is the result of innate qualities and traits, or more the result of our lived experiences. Despite this, however, it is important to consider this area given that so much of what we do in life is framed by an understanding of our answers to these questions. For example, within education, we generally have some understanding of where we sit in terms of our 'ability', whether through the grades we get, the sets we are in or the informal feedback we get from those around us. These messages then become a framework on which we base assessments of ourselves when considering our future pathways and plans. If we take this educational example as our starting point, it helpfully provides us with an underpinning framework for understanding the profoundly social nature of identity construction. This is particularly important when we consider the ways that gender, social background and ethnic understandings of ourselves also shape and inform the identities we construct for ourselves within an educational context.

# SEEING OURSELVES THROUGH THE EYES OF OTHERS

If we work on the principle that at least some of how we see ourselves is a reflection of the messages we receive (Fuller, 2009, 2018), then it is useful to focus in more detail on the role of culture within the development of our identity. For writers such as Ortner (1996), culture is indeed extremely important in defining who we are, consisting as it does of rules, norms and expectations. She considers culture as a means to organise social life, to define actors and their social roles, as well as setting the parameters of social expectations. For Ortner (1996), culture is therefore a 'serious game … [where] power and inequality pervade the game of life in multiple ways' (p12). She argues that while there is some agency in constructions of self, there is not a great deal of autonomy, meaning that identity construction is embedded within power structures. Culture, then, is not just about values, norms and practice, but also about dominance. Power becomes much more meaningful when we think of the ways that culture exerts distinctive influences on different groups. Gender, for de Beauvoir (1997), is one such group where notions of cultural norms and values are pervasive and very evidently embedded in culture. For de Beauvoir (1997), this is an important issue, and one on which she is keen to be clear: women's behaviour is not dictated by hormones or biology, but is firmly 'moulded by her situation' (p608). The nature versus nurture debate surrounding gender has already been addressed earlier in this book, so in the rest of this chapter we will consider the ways that some of the stereotypes which emerge via these cultural assumptions manifest in education, in both the ways in which students may frame their understandings of themselves as well as the ways in which teachers may see them.

## REFLECTION

- Consider the following question: If a newborn child was placed in a white room, with no windows or toys, and no interaction with anyone or anything, who would that child consider themselves to be? That is, how would they see themselves?
- Think about the students in your class. Do you believe that girls and boys learn differently? How much of your answer can be explained by biology, and how much from learnt behaviour and cultural norms?

While placing a newborn child in such a white room would likely never happen, the point of the exercise is to encourage us to recognise that so much of how we see ourselves is informed by our environment and our interactions with others. What we do and what we introduce to that environment can shape how we play, what we play with, how we view ourselves, how we view others in relation to ourselves, and so on, which we come to believe as normal and natural.

## CASE STUDY

### Siobhan

Siobhan grew up with parents who had been raised in care. She went to a school in a large working-class area where students tended to leave and go straight into work or motherhood. She performed badly in her final exams in school, and she too left to go into low-paid care work. While at school, she was described by one teacher as 'a disruptive element' and was assessed as 'being very likely to have her first baby by 17' by another. In short, she grew up in an environment where expectations and aspirations for her were not very high at all. While working in care, she was encouraged by the senior nurse to study, having taken a keen interest in her. Despite reluctance and resistance, with support she completed her first course and passed. Then began a love of learning. Thirteen years later, with three children and a husband, she completed an Access to Higher Education course and went on to university, completing a PhD in 2008. Eleven years later, she now works as a professor. What this example shows is that without encouragement and aspirations for them, young people can simply leave education to go into low-paid, low-status work that is often very gendered. The earlier experiences providing a frame for self meant this was all that was imagined.

## WHAT DO WE KNOW FROM RESEARCH?

### Gender and education

The role of gender in education is pervasive in discourse around subject choices, attainment gaps and future aspirations. The nature of the causal relationship between these areas in terms of the role of self and that of culture is ongoing. However, it is important to address the ways that education can – however unintentionally – reproduce notions of gender 'difference' via complicity and inertia. A clear example is in the ways we seek to understand how students learn. For example, research suggests that boys and girls have different preferences for learning (Wehrwein et al., 2007) and there are gender differences in how teachers' language is used in the classroom, as well as how teachers are prone to interact with boys and girls differently, which can lead to conflict in the classroom (Koepke and Harkins, 2008). While there may be many reasons for these findings, the teacher is a key variable, central as they are to the educational experience. This is also exemplified in research that explores gender bias in teacher expectations. In maths learning, for example, research highlights that even in the earliest years of schooling, girls are much more adversely affected than boys by negative biases from teachers (Gentrup and Rjosk, 2018). There are also numerous studies that look at ideas of 'boys being boys', which resonates very strongly with the idea of gendered identity constructions within education. As Skelton et al. (2007) note, different theories and ideas to explain gender differences in education, such as 'natural differences between the sexes; gender differences in learning styles; the "feminisation" of schooling and gender-based assessment procedures' (p5), have been challenged, discredited or dismissed entirely. For these authors, a key explanatory factor emerging from a range of studies that they explored was the notion of gendered normativity (i.e. ideas about gender which impacted on the way that girls and boys 'performed' their gender). These ideas influenced not just behaviours in the classroom, but achievement as well. Skelton et al. (2007) also found that schools and peer groups were highly influential in determining what type of 'girl' or 'boy' is appropriate in particular settings, highlighting the important influence of expectations and norms on the self.

Given the powerful ways that gender is enacted in schools – as a structure of practice and a site of identity construction – a focus on gender within one's educational practice is key to challenging some of the assumptions around gender. By confronting stereotypes, we hopefully begin to promote a shift in at least one of the axes on which students frame an understanding of who they are.

## SOCIAL BACKGROUND, GENDER AND EDUCATION

When we consider gender and its role in identity construction, it is important to recognise that in terms of influence, gender is a continuum; while aspects of gender can be understood and experienced as universal, there are significant differences in the influences of being male and female, depending on one's socio-economic status (SES) and background. In the context of this chapter, we understand SES to be a combination of education, occupation and income. While social groups can exert differing influences on the norms, values and practices of its members, gender also interacts with these social spaces, clearly highlighting that gender is a multidimensional conduit of power, exerting differing levels of influence both within and between groups.

Within education specifically, we can see clear gender difference between the social groups, as well as between the males and females within these groups. For Bourdieu (1986), gender and SES is a powerful praxis within education, with schooling being a potent site for the reproduction of many social inequalities. For Bourdieu, notions of 'habitus' and 'cultural capital' are central to the ways that social background is enacted in school. In short, 'habitus' relates to the values, dispositions, tastes and preferences into which we are socialised via our family and the environment in which we live. Given its social nature, habitus is thus structured, framed as it is by our social background and where the role of family is key. 'Cultural capital', in a Bourdieuian sense, reflects our habitus, and is thus the manifestation of the skills, education, language, dispositions and tastes that we have acquired (Bourdieu, 1986). Levels of cultural capital differ between different social groups and are the means by which we can create a sense of belonging – as well as distinction – between members of different social groups. Cultural capital is key to educational success, given that the 'culture' of the institution of education is that of the middle classes. It is in this way that education – however unintentionally – is a 'structuring structure', reinforcing social differences through the distribution of educational rewards to the cultural capitals it recognises.

For Bourdieu, and the writers who use his ideas, 'habitus' is also gendered, meaning that behaviours, dispositions, values, and so on, differ based on one's social space and whether one is male or female. For Bourdieu (2001), writing on the notion of masculine domination, gender is a form of symbolic violence and the means by which gender inequalities and access to power are most profoundly embodied. The idea is that notions of gender differences are so entrenched as to be neither questioned nor recognised. Hull (2002) suggests that the symbolic representations of gender seek to confirm and reproduce a status quo that is accepted and rarely challenged. This is evident in the behaviours we see when we look at gender differences and social space, such as – using stereotypes to make a point – the aspirations to work in the beauty industry or for fame as a sports star, compared to those who aspire to go to university to become teachers or scientists. It is therefore important to recognise that gender inequalities are also 'classed' inequalities. In the classroom, then, there are a number of forces shaping and influencing a student's aspirations, interest in learning, and how they see themselves. To illustrate, UK government data on progression rates to university in England highlight clear differences, first by social group, with pupils living in the most advantaged areas more than twice as likely to go to university, at 56 per cent, compared to only 26 per cent of the most disadvantaged, in 2016/17 (DfE, 2018). Females are also more likely than males to go on to higher education across the social groups. What explains these differences is something of a chicken-and-egg scenario. Our social class background predisposes us to our aspirations for higher education, which are then often reinforced in school, often because schools believe they know what their students want for their futures. What we have, though, is a process of gendered and social reproduction, however devoid of deliberate intention it is. In understanding how young people construct their identities, it is important to recognise the often-unconscious influences of gender and social background on what, and who, a young person believes themselves to be.

**REFLECTION**

- Who are the students in your class? How might their gender and social background influence the way they interact in the classroom? How alike or different do you feel to your students, in terms of your experiences?

- Have you ever heard a teacher say, 'Students in this school never want to go to university' or, 'None of our students would consider a vocational course'? Is this real or a consequence of the social make-up of the school?

- Can all students access your vocabulary? How do you know?

- Encourage students to consider the role that their family and environment may have in shaping their aspirations by providing opportunities for students to make connections between them.

- What opportunities can you offer to enable students to recognise and challenge their stereotypes?

# ETHNICITY, GENDER AND EDUCATION

So far in this chapter, we have considered the role of gender and social background on the development of identity, as well as the ways that our multifaceted sense of self can influence the aspirations we then have for ourselves and the aspirations others have for us. In this final section, we look at the way gender and ethnicity also powerfully interact, and how this occurs within educational spaces. It is important to be clear that gender is not experienced as a universal, meaning, for example, that 'a white male's masculinity … is constructed not only in relation to white women but also in relation to black men' (Connell, 1995, p75). Similarly, ethnicity is not experienced universally.

Put simply, the word 'ethnicity' derives from the Greek word *ethnos*, which translates to 'peoples' (Baumann, 2004). However, defining ethnicity within a highly complex social structure and melting pot of nationalities in modern society is complex and contested. According to Cohen (1978), attempting to define ethnicity is challenging because it is not only how an individual identifies themselves, but also how they are perceived within the society in which they live. Many scholars and researchers who write about ethnicity, however, refer to it as a sociological construct, a construction of reality, which historically was created in shallow and crude ways. Ethnic categories have arguably been created with little consultation with the minority groups they are intended to serve. Very often they are also based on stereotypes and assumptions (Chavez and Guido-DiBrito, 1999). The Office for National Statistics (ONS) is the UK's largest independent producer of official statistics and the recognised national statistical institute of the UK. In a discussion on the complex nature of collecting data that are in any way meaningful, they highlight the problematic nature of representing minority populations in the UK by their ethnicity, because ethnicity is complex, subjective and personal (ONS, 2019). Since ethnicity consists of many layers of understanding and meanings, it is extremely interpretive. Notwithstanding this, as the ONS data are used extensively to compare, contrast and draw conclusions on social issues, they have suggested a 'harmonised' approach to ethnicity. This is to encourage consistency over agreed definitions for collecting and analysing ethnic minority data. Although this does not come close to defining the term 'ethnicity' or overcome the limitations acknowledged by the ONS regarding the subjective nature of ethnicity, it is still important to attempt to create an approach for data collection that enables some comparisons of different ethnic group experiences. Drawing on these ideas in this chapter, then, ethnicity is understood as a form of social grouping in which there is a shared national and/or cultural tradition, with some associated norms and values. These can also be gendered and classed.

## WHAT DO WE KNOW FROM RESEARCH?

### Ethnicity and education

We live in increasingly multilayered societies where culture not only defines, but engages, our social consciousness, as well as how we interact and make sense of the society in which we live. The classroom should be, first and foremost, an equitable space of learning for all. However, research has shown time and again that educational outcomes are driven by gender, social background and ethnicity. Studies such as Kleen and Glock (2018) demonstrate that teachers held implicit negative stereotypes of ethnic minority students, associating them with poorer learning attitudes and behaviour. Literature in the field (see Dee, 2005; Rubie-Davies et al., 2006; Tenenbaum and Ruck, 2007) also further highlights how teacher stereotypes can play a key role in how they perceive minority pupil learning outcomes. Research has demonstrated that teachers can often rate minority pupils lower than their white counterparts (Burgess and Greeves, 2009) or hold stereotypes around perceived natural aptitudes. For example, research has revealed that Asian students are often viewed by teachers as possessing a natural ability in maths, whereas Chinese girls are viewed as prone to 'overstudy' (Francis et al., 2017). Research also reveals examples of teachers viewing Pakistani and Bangladeshi girls as lacking interest in continuing their education due to an assumption that they are preoccupied with marriage (Fuller, 2009). Students are not oblivious to these ideas, and the consequences can be pronounced in relation to their confidence in the education they receive.

As noted earlier, the expectations of others are central to the expectations we have for ourselves. It is therefore important for educators to recognise that learning spaces are social places. The knowledge and spaces we, as educators, create will inevitably have an impact on how students shape their identity, reflecting both implicit and explicit personalised ideas that come together to define our individual and shared experience.

## REFLECTION

- What assumptions might you make about different ethnic groups?
- Ethnicities are categories that suggest a degree of homogeneity, but consider, as an example, that Africa is a continent with different languages, religions and colonial histories. How useful is it, then, to consider categories of students using terms such as 'black African'?

You might have reflected on your assumptions about different ethnic groups and how the ethnic group 'black African' can never capture the vast range of countries, religions, histories and experiences of individuals. This is true of all other ethnicities. For example, Asian or Asian British ethnicities consist of Indian, Pakistani, Bangladeshi, Chinese and any other Asian backgrounds according to UK government population facts and figures for 2019 (Cabinet Office, 2019). The subcontinent of India alone includes countries as diverse as India, Pakistan, Bangladesh, Nepal, Bhutan, Sri Lanka and the Maldives. It comprises of four major religions: Hinduism, Buddhism, Jainism and Sikhism. This means that although in the UK the Indian ethnic population is the largest minority ethnic group in the country, there is evidently considerable heterogeneity across this group, as there is for all other ethnic groups.

## TRANSFORMING PRACTICE

- Be reflective and consider honestly your own ideas about gender and ethnicity.

- Consider the subjects that you teach. Do they capture the diversity of a student's social and ethnic background? In particular, think about the examples, scholars, writers and resources you use. Can you mix these up to offer a more diverse range?

- Consider how you group students and, where appropriate, ask students how they like to be grouped. Consider where there are opportunities for students to exchange ideas and learn from each other's ethnic backgrounds and religions, and provide opportunities for open discussion and reflection on gender perspectives.

- Celebrate a range of holy days, festivals and national events. Examples include the International Day of the World's Indigenous Peoples, World Ethnic Day, Chinese New Year, Parinirvana Day or Nirvana Day, St Patrick's Day, and Passover.

- Engage students in activities. One popular activity is to make a calendar of special days with students. This can include special days such as Eid al-Adha (Islam), Krishna Janmashtami (Hindu), US Independence Day, the summer solstice, and so on. Consider splitting up the task so that different groups of students work on a particular month of the year. Encourage students to come up with special days that represent a diversity of ethnicities, nationalities, religions, genders, and so on. Perhaps the group producing a month with the greatest variety of special days could be awarded a prize!

- Another simple activity is to ask students to pair with someone they don't normally mix with in class. Ask them to share thoughts about what they have in common. Depending on the age of the children, they could draw things they have in common (e.g. a pet, brother or sister, hobby) or write them on a flip chart or sticky notes. Ask students to call out all the things they had in common with their partner. Ask the following questions: What have you learnt about perceived differences? Are we all more alike than different? What aspects of difference can we celebrate, and why is it important to do that? What does this have to do with diversity and inclusion? Then ask students to reflect on what they have learnt.

- To learn a little about students' lives and family backgrounds, ask them to bring an item from home to talk about in class. Group students with people they do not normally mix with. Ask them to talk to the group about the item they have brought to class. For instance, they could explain what the item is and why they have chosen it. Ask students to reflect on what they have learnt about the backgrounds, interests and lives of other students in their class. You could use some of the questions from the previous activity to prompt discussion of how this relates to diversity and inclusion.

# CHAPTER SUMMARY

This chapter has considered how education systems could be argued as reinforcing, as well as 'interacting' with, notions of a gendered, social and ethnically defined self. The reflections offered, we hope, are designed to encourage us, as educators, to be aware of, and so support, a reframing of identities – where possible. If we can understand and highlight the ways that social life shapes how we see ourselves, as well as how we are seen by others, then young people can be encouraged and supported to challenge the stereotypes that disempower them. To develop the levels of resilience and self-confidence that are arguably key to skills for an individual's success in a twenty-first-century workplace, it is important that all students start from a place of equity in relation to who they think they are and what they hope for themselves.

# FURTHER READING

**British Council** (2010) *Inclusion and Diversity in Education: Guidelines for Diversity and Inclusion in Schools.* Available at: www.britishcouncil.es/sites/default/files/british-council-guidelines-for-inclusion-and-diversity-in-schools.pdf

**Fuller, C.** (2009) *Sociology, Gender and Educational Aspirations: Girls and Their Ambitions.* London: Continuum.

# REFERENCES

Baumann, T. (2004) Defining ethnicity. *The SAA Archaeological Record*, 4(4): 12–14.

Bourdieu, P. (1986) The forms of capital. In J. Richardson (ed.), *Handbook of Theory and Research for the Sociology of Education.* Westport, CT: Greenwood.

Bourdieu, P. (2001) *Masculine Domination.* Cambridge: Polity.

Burgess, S. and Greaves, E. (2009) *Test Scores, Subjective Assessment and Stereotyping of Ethnic Minorities.* CMPO working paper series, no. 09/221.

Cabinet Office (2019) *List of Ethnic Groups.* Available at: www.ethnicity-facts-figures.service.gov.uk/ethnic-groups

Chavez, A.F. and Guido-DiBrito, F. (1999) Racial and ethnic identity and development. *New Directions for Adult and Continuing Education*, 84: 39–47.

Cohen, R. (1978) Ethnicity: problem and focus in anthropology. *Annual Review of Anthropology*, 7(1): 379–403.

Connell, R.W. (1995) *Masculinities*, 2nd edn. Cambridge: Polity.

De Beauvoir, S. (1997) *The Second Sex*. London: Vintage Classics.

Dee, T.S. (2005) A teacher like me: does race, ethnicity, or gender matter? *American Economic Review*, 95(2): 158–65.

Department for Education (DfE) (2018) *Widening Participation in Higher Education, England 2016/17 Age Cohort – Experimental Studies*. London: DfE.

Francis, B., Mau, A. and Archer, L. (2017) *The Construction of British Chinese Educational Success: Exploring the Shifting Discourses in Educational Debate, and Their Effects*. Available at: https://discovery.ucl.ac.uk/id/eprint/1549042/1/Francis_Template%20Copy%20Francis%20Mau%20Archer%2031102016.pdf

Fuller, C. (2009) *Sociology, Gender and Educational Aspirations: Girls and Their Ambitions*. London: Continuum.

Fuller, C. (2018) The existential self: challenging and renegotiating gender identity through higher education. *Gender and Education*, 66(2): 131–47.

Gentrup, S. and Rjosk, C. (2018) Pygmalion and the gender gap: do teacher expectations contribute to differences to achievement between girls and boys at the beginning of schooling? *Educational Research and Evaluation*, 24(3): 295–323.

Hull, K. (2002) Masculine domination (review). *Social Forces*, 81(1): 351–2.

Kleen, H. and Glock, S. (2018) A further look into ethnicity: the impact of stereotypical expectations on teachers' judgments of female ethnic minority students. *Social Psychology of Education*, 21(4): 759–73.

Koepke, M.F. and Harkins, D. (2008) Conflict in the classroom: gender differences in the teacher–child relationship. *Early Education and Development*, 19(6): 843–64.

Office for National Statistics (ONS) (2019) *Ethnic Group, National Identity and Religion*. Available at: www.ons.gov.uk/methodology/classificationsandstandards/measuringequality/ethnicgroupnationalidentity-andreligion

Ortner, S. (1996) *Making Gender: The Politics and Erotics of Culture*. Boston, MA: Beacon Press.

Rubie-Davies, C., Hattie, J. and Hamilton, R. (2006) Expecting the best for students: teacher expectations and academic outcomes. *British Journal of Educational Psychology*, 76(3): 429–44.

Skelton, B., Francis, B. and Valkanova, Y. (2007) *Breaking Down the Stereotypes: Gender and Achievement in Schools*. Equal Opportunities Commission working paper series, no. 59.

Tenenbaum, H. and Ruck, M. (2007) Are teachers' expectations different for racial minority than for European American students? A meta-analysis. *Journal of Educational Psychology*, 99(2): 253–73.

Wehrwein, E.A., Lujan, H.L. and DiCarlo, S.E. (2007) Gender differences in learning style preferences among undergraduate physiology students. *Advances in Physiology Psychology*, 31: 153–7.

# 5

# SUBJECT CHOICE, CAREER DECISIONS AND GENDER STEREOTYPING

## MARINA DELLA GIUSTA

## KEYWORDS

- **GENDER**
- **STEREOTYPING**
- **IMPLICIT BIAS**
- **SUBJECT CHOICES**

**THIS CHAPTER**

- describes how gender stereotyping affects subject and career choices, and the important consequences of this;
- focuses on the role of different stakeholders in education;
- explains how teachers can help combat stereotyping so that both girls and boys can be helped to make choices that reflect their talents and passions.

# INTRODUCTION

In this chapter, we will explore the gendered causes of the subject choices made by girls and boys, as well as suggesting ways to combat them in both self-reflection on our own practice and in the context of the classroom. Although the story of girls' success in education is everywhere in the news and the international evidence on educational attainment generally highlights a closure of the gender gap in education (WEF, 2016), as well as girls systematically reporting more positive educational attitudes and aspirations than boys (Rampino and Taylor, 2013), there are key differences in the subjects that boys and girls choose to study. In particular, the UK, which already has one of the lowest shares of 15-year-olds intending a STEM career among the OECD countries, actually lags behind most OECD countries in women's aspirations to study a STEM subject and engage in a STEM career (see OECD, 2014). Apps et al. (2012) show that the UK ranking of 15-year-old pupils in mathematics and science in the OECD's PISA tests has been falling from 2000 to 2009, and was just below the OECD average in mathematics and only slightly above the average in science. A key contributing factor to the UK's deficit is the very low GCSE performance at 16 in science and mathematics subjects. High-level passes in these subjects at this level are a prerequisite for further study in these same subjects, so understanding what happens at GSCE level is clearly important, but it is not the whole story!

In fact, what is really striking is that after GSCEs, girls select *out* of STEM, even when they actually do better than boys in these subjects (IOP, 2013; Reuben et al., 2014; Smith and Golding, 2015). So, why do girls then opt out of maths, even when they do well in exams, and why does it matter? Of course, we should be concerned if someone does not exploit their talent per se, but we may respect the fact that this reflects their preferences. However, things turn out to be more complicated than this: research suggests that maths skills play an important role in determining earnings, even controlling for educational attainment in general (Joensen and Nielsen, 2009), and opting out of maths affects the selection of women out of STEM subjects at university as well as in the labour market, with important effects on pay gaps (STEM jobs pay better!), career and pension gaps, and individual and household outcomes later on (Olivetti and Petrongolo, 2006; Ceci and Williams, 2010). Being better paid affords a different negotiating platform for the division of household chores, as well as giving better opportunities to children. Chavatzia (2017) reported that women represent only 35 per cent of all students enrolled in STEM-related fields of higher education, and only 28 per cent in the critical information and communications technology (ICT) field, which means that any support to these critical fields unintentionally benefits men more than women. Another problem is that, as neuroscientist Gina Rippon explains so well in *The Gendered Brain*, science itself is all the poorer for not having enough women in it, given that they bring not just more talent, but different perspectives and directions of research (Rippon, 2019).

In this chapter, we will look at the research in the gendered factors that affect subject choice, as well as offering both research insights and suggestions to inform teaching practice, focusing in particular on combating the effect of gender stereotypes on subject choice and enjoyment, with the aim of helping pupils choose more freely across the wide range of subjects they are offered. We will focus primarily on girls and maths, but as you will see from the suggested activities, we will also consider boys and arts, as well as thinking more broadly about what can make pupils flourish outside gendered straitjackets. Much of what we will discuss will be important to the context of stereotyping more generally on the basis of other characteristics: not just gender, but also ethnicity, class and many other social markers, influence decisions in similar ways, and each of us sits at the intersection of these markers and negotiates our life, whether we are aware of it or not, in our context. We hope that the chapter will help you to think about your personal experience of these issues when reading the research and the examples, as well as enabling you to help pupils challenge unhelpful stereotypes and increase your own enjoyment of your job!

# WHAT DOES GENDER HAVE TO DO WITH PUPILS' DECISIONS?

There is a very substantial amount of research into the factors affecting the decisions of adolescents, including their beliefs about labour markets and many related choices (e.g. education, occupational aspirations, views regarding when to start a family), and questions are routinely asked in surveys to youngsters on matters ranging from their views and beliefs to the activities in which they engage, including their time use. The factors that have been investigated include general social expectations and views of the society in which children grow up, parental and peer characteristics and views, teachers' views, and, of course, the characteristics and experiences of children themselves. Children's expectations are strong predictors of attainment and of dropping out of education (Tan and Yates, 2011), even after controlling for demographic characteristics, family background and grades (Chowdry et al., 2013). In what follows, we will look at each in turn, starting with social attitudes, and in particular the extent to which gendered attitudes are related to educational choices and outcomes.

Attitudes surveys around the world reveal that people hold very gendered views regarding professions and the skills required by them. The latest available data on gender norms in the UK collected in the British Social Attitudes (BSA) Survey (NatCen Social Research, 2019) indicate that around half (47 per cent) of respondents in this national representative survey think that men and women are equally suited to all or almost all jobs. And although around three-quarters of the public think that neither girls nor boys are naturally better at maths or computing (72 and 73 per cent, respectively), computing is seen as more male (12 per cent think that boys are naturally more able to think than girls are), with men (16 per cent) more likely than women (9 per cent) to say that boys are naturally better, and – worryingly – younger people aged 18–34 (19 per cent) are more likely than all older age groups to take this view! When asked about gender differences in mathematical abilities, women (76 per cent) are more likely than men (67 per cent) to say that neither girls nor boys are naturally better at maths.

There are many routes through which such views held by adults can affect children. The most obvious ones are parents and teachers, but social media, and media exposure in general, have been studied as important sources of influence.

Parents matter in several ways, and not just for their time and financial investment. So, it is not only the case that the amount of parental time invested in children affects achievement (Zumbuehl et al., 2013), and that children from wealthier families are overwhelmingly represented in higher education (Anders, 2012), but attitudes of parents matter more directly too. In fact, even controlling for these factors, it is found that parental attitudes and preferences are themselves strongly transmitted to children. The literature on the intergenerational transmission of beliefs, preferences and attitudes (Bisin and Verdier, 2001; Della Giusta et al., 2017) identifies several possible channels: direct parental influence through education, location and school choices that affect the environment, and emulation (an effect extensively discussed in developmental psychology). These effects are found across many life choices, including education and labour market participation. For instance, recent work by Johnston et al. (2014), making use of the 1970 British Cohort Study (CLS, n.d.), found that gender role attitudes of mothers and children measured 25 years apart are strongly correlated, and that both the human capital as well as whether and how much female respondents work (and the partners of male respondents) are strongly affected by their mothers' hours of work. So, children do repeat a lot of choices, and not necessarily because they are promoted explicitly by the family; some of these things, as we all know too well, occur quite unconsciously, and we become aware of the similarities only in hindsight. It is not just the parents that matter, but teachers too, of course, and the teachers influence children's actual cognitive (attainment) and non-cognitive (behaviour, character, engagement) outcomes, as well as their expectations, both directly through teaching feedback and monitoring and indirectly through learning environments. Rosenthal and Jacobson (1968) found that teachers' expectations in American primary schools had a powerful impact on students' achievements. More recently, research has shown that teachers' diminished expectations of children with names associated with low socio-economic status affect student's cognitive performance (Figlio, 2005), and teachers can unconsciously rate children differently on aspects of performance that are subjective. This has been shown in essays designated with either German or Turkish names (Sprietsma, 2009), or assessment of African American children's behaviour, which was rated as more disruptive and inattentive by teachers from a different ethnic group (Dee, 2005). Conversely, optimistic teachers' expectations have been found to particularly benefit the achievement of students from minorities in the US (Jussim and Harber, 2005). Teachers, as if we needed reminding, have a powerful influence!

Turning to peers, the effects flowing from friends and classmates have also been extensively studied across many undesirable behaviours (e.g. crime, drinking, smoking) but also in desirable ones. A review of the literature on peer effects in education by Sacerdote (2014) finds that although some of these are highly context-specific (notably, test scores and exam performance), significant and strong peer effects have consistently been found in studies of educational and career choices. In the UK, Favara (2012) has made use of sex-segregated schools data from the national pupil database (the register of all pupils enrolled in state-maintained schools in England) to show how gender stereotyping affects educational choices from the age of 14, and this effect is larger for girls than for boys, and attenuated for those attending a sixth form single-sex school.

Ultimately, the children themselves make these decisions, of course, and their own characteristics and expectations are crucial too. The actual process of expectation formation seems to be an important channel in that expectations change quite a lot during teenage years, as found in analysis using the Longitudinal Study of Young People in England (LSYPE) (Anders and Micklewright, 2015). Expectations have been found to be strong predictors of educational attainment, even after controlling for demographic characteristics, family background and grades (for the US, see Jacob and Wilder, 2010; for the UK, see Strand, 2007; Chowdry et al., 2009; Jerrim, 2011; for Australia, see Khoo and Ainley, 2005; for Mexico, see Attanasio and Kaufmann, 2009; for Canada, see Looker and Thiessen, 2004). Rampino and Taylor (2013), making use of the British Household Panel Survey (BHPS), show that while girls have more positive aspirations and attitudes than boys, the impacts of gender on children's attitudes and aspirations vary significantly with parental education level, parental attitudes to education, child's age, and the indirect cost of education, and girls systematically report more positive educational attitudes and aspirations than boys, even after controlling for unobserved differences between children.

Personality matters too: a variety of studies have shown that personality traits are relatively malleable, at least over the early life cycle, and then tend to be stable during adult life (Cobb-Clark and Schurer,

2012). There is some evidence that policy interventions can promote useful traits and suppress harmful ones early in life, and while cognitive skills (e.g. IQ) are believed to be relatively stable by the age of 8, other aspects of personality might be easier to change at a later age (see Carneiro and Heckman, 2003). Mendolia and Walker (2014) have studied this specifically for a large cohort of English children born in 1990 and followed for seven years, starting in 2004. They found that children with external (as opposed to inner) locus of control or with low levels of self-esteem are less likely to have good performance in test scores at age 16 and to pursue further studies at 17–18, especially in mathematics or science. The effects of lower inner locus of control or self-esteem can be more acute for children from disadvantaged families, since they are less likely than advantaged families to be able to provide or access support. Interventions aimed at supporting the development of positive traits, such as growth mindset, have been trialled in a number of schools (EEF, n.d.). The evidence indicates that they improve cognitive outcomes, particularly for children who come from disadvantaged socio-economic backgrounds, while the effect on advantaged children is limited. In a related study, Bettinger et al. (2018) showed how secondary schools in Norway could increase students' perseverance in maths by shaping students' beliefs in their abilities to learn using an intervention based on Dweck's (2008) 'growth mindset'.

All in all, these studies indicate that there is a lot we can do: expectations are malleable, and they change quite a lot during teenage years as a result of interactions with the wider environment, so working positively on them can make an enormous difference!

## REFLECTION

- Do you think that gender views matter to pupils' choices?
- Would you say they mattered in your choices of field of study, or those of your friends?
- Can you think of an example of challenging a gender stereotype in the context of your work?

## WHAT DO WE KNOW FROM RESEARCH?

### Gender norms, choices and achievements

Worldwide, the achievements and choices in maths by girls have been found to be strongly connected with:

- the gender of professors (Carrell and West, 2010);
- teachers' gender views (Alan et al., 2018; Carlana, 2018);
- parental beliefs (Eccles et al., 2000; Johnston et al., 2014);
- wider gender norms of society (Guiso et al., 2008).

## STEREOTYPING

The psychology of stereotyping (Schneider, 2005; Jussim et al., 2015) is fundamentally based on the fact that we are 'wired to be social' (Lieberman, 2013): our brains continuously work out extremely fast predictions on who to interact with and how, as well as using fast shortcuts when doing so, which may or may not then be discarded when more careful observation is conducted (Rippon, 2019).

Stereotypes can be described as shortcuts that our brain can use to make decisions in absence of accurate information, providing shortcuts that incorporate a range of expectations of how someone else will behave. This is also true of self-expectations, which incorporate social rules of what is expected by someone like us. Given the vast amount of decisions we make in everyday life, a lot of our interactions are driven by fast, rather than slow or deliberate, thinking (Kahneman, 2011), as well as incorporating the biases that stereotyping generates. Unconscious biases arise from stereotypes about particular groups that are not challenged, and can drive decisions based on unverified information about the group to which an individual belongs, rather than specific information about them.

Gender is one important dimension along which stereotypes are formed (and interacts, of course, with other dimensions intersectionally), affecting expectations and actual behaviours (Rippon, 2019). The evidence from the literature on psychological traits suggests that women, on average, are expected (both by men and other women) to be more conscientious and compliant (Carter, 2014). When it comes to evaluations of own ability, men, on average, perceive their general intellect as higher and they tend to overestimate it, while women, on average, tend to do the opposite (Karwowski et al., 2013). Parents also perceive their sons' intelligence to be higher than their daughters', while children perceive the intelligence of their fathers to be higher than that of their mothers (Karwowski et al., 2013).

### REFLECTION

Would you say your performance was ever affected by expectations related to your gender being made salient to you?

## STEREOTYPES AND PERFORMANCE

Stereotype threat influences performance both positively (e.g. when girls are shown data suggesting they are more able than boys in maths, they perform better) than negatively, and for this it is enough to remind girls of their gender for them to underperform in maths (Johns et al., 2005; Jussim et al., 2015). This effect has been found in girls as young as 4, whose performance in a spatial cognition task worsened if they were asked to colour in a drawing of a girl playing with a doll before completing a task (Shenouda and Danovitch, 2014).

Gender stereotypes emerge in early childhood (Bian et al., 2017), and exposure to bias towards one's group affects effort, self-confidence, productivity and pupils' performance (Johns et al., 2005; Schmader, 2010; Devine et al., 2012; Campbell, 2015; Phelan et al., 2015; Gilliam et al., 2016;

Atewologun et al., 2018; Carlana, 2018). It is therefore important for teachers to understand that what may be driving the performance in a subject is linked to many more variables than pupils' ability; accounting for differences in test anxiety and maths anxiety, recent studies find that there is practically no difference in the maths scores of boys and girls (Devine et al., 2012). Intervention therefore needs to consider assessment forms and ways of teaching that encourage girls and minimise the fear of making mistakes. Evidence suggests that problem-solving, class discussions and research improve girls' maths performance (Boaler and Greeno, 2000; Boaler, 2002; Zohar and Sela, 2003; OECD, 2014), and they are less result-oriented, and more deep learning-oriented, than boys (Ajello et al., 2018).

# TEACHERS

Through your role in the learning environment, the selection and organisation of learning spaces, and the formation of groups, evaluation methods and feedback, there is a lot that you can achieve in challenging gender stereotypes. The first step is acknowledging them and learning to identify them, and pupils may be happy to join in!

## WHAT DO WE KNOW FROM RESEARCH?

### Teachers' and pupils' expectations

An original study by Rosenthal and Jacobson (1968) in American primary schools found that teachers' expectations had a powerful impact on students' achievements. Bias is also incorporated into teaching materials (Blumberg, 2015) and school environments, and providing tools for teachers to contrast it in the environment in which they work can have very important effects.

## EVIDENCE FROM PRACTICE

This video by Inspiring the Future shows how soon children associate jobs with gender: **www.inspiringthefuture.org/redraw-the-balance/**

Teachers ask children to draw a surgeon, a pilot and a firefighter, and most of the class draw men in these roles. The teachers then invite three women who are real surgeons, pilots and firefighters, and the children are initially bewildered. They then, of course, forget all about what they expected and enjoy spending time hearing about the actual jobs, and even trying some of the instruments they use to perform them.

Evidence from schools shows that showing children images of real people doing non-gender-stereotypical jobs and then asking them to think about their own future can really help them to see themselves in a different way!

## TRANSFORMING PRACTICE

### Activity 1

With the help of groups of pupils, conduct a gender stereotype audit of teaching materials. How would it work to swap around female and male characters? Would they do different things? Would they do the same things differently? Why?

### Activity 2

For mathematics teachers, there is evidence that girls enjoy more hands-on teaching of maths. Try some of the activities at: **https://mathandmovement.com/activities/**

### Activity 3

The campaign Let Toys Be Toys has come up with a range of school activities aimed at challenging gender stereotyping. See their website for more information: **http://lettoysbetoys.org.uk/ten-ways-to-challenge-gender-stereotypes-in-the-classroom/**

# CHAPTER SUMMARY

- Gender stereotyping affects subject choice through a variety of channels: society's expectations, parents, peers, and learning environment all play a role.

- The consequences of girls accepting gender stereotypes regarding their maths ability are very serious in terms of future earnings and many other outcomes.

- Teachers can do a lot to help recognise and mitigate the impact of stereotyping with their own awareness and their daily practices.

# FURTHER READING

**Bohnet, I.** (2016) *What Works: Gender Equality by Design*. Cambridge, MA: Belknap Press of Harvard University Press.

**Perez, C.C.** (2019) *Invisible Women: Exposing Data Bias in a World Designed for Men*. London: Random House.

**Rippon, G.** (2019) *The Gendered Brain: The New Neuroscience That Shatters the Myth of the Female Brain*. London: Random House.

# REFERENCES

Ajello, A.M., Caponera, E. and Palmerio, L. (2018) Italian students' results in the PISA mathematics test: does reading competence matter? *European Journal of Psychology of Education*, 33(3): 505–20.

Alan, S., Ertac, S. and Mumcu, I. (2018) Gender stereotypes in the classroom and effects on achievement. *Review of Economics and Statistics*, 100(5): 876–90.

Anders, J. (2012) *Using the Longitudinal Study of Young People in England for Research into Higher Education Access*. London: UCL IOE.

Anders, J. and Micklewright, J. (2015) Teenagers' expectations of applying to university: how do they change? *Education Sciences*, 5(4): 281–305.

Apps, P., Mendolia, S. and Walker, I. (2012) *The Impact of Pre-School on Adolescents' Outcomes: Evidence from a Recent English Cohort*. IZA discussion paper, no. 6971.

Atewologun, D., Cornish, T. and Tresh, F. (2018) *Unconscious Bias Training: An Assessment of the Evidence for Effectiveness*. Available at: www.equalityhumanrights.com/en/publication-download/unconscious-biastraining-assessment-evidence-effectiveness

Attanasio, O. and Kaufmann, K. (2009) *Educational Choices, Subjective Expectations, and Credit Constraints*. London: National Bureau of Economic Research.

Bettinger, E., Ludvigsen, S., Rege, M., Solli, I.F. and Yeager, D. (2018) Increasing perseverance in math: evidence from a field experiment in Norway. *Journal of Economic Behavior and Organization*, 146: 1–15.

Bian, L., Leslie, S.J. and Cimpian, A. (2017) Gender stereotypes about intellectual ability emerge early and influence children's interests. *Science*, 355(6323): 389–91.

Bisin, A. and Verdier, T. (2001) The economics of cultural transmission and the dynamics of preferences. *Journal of Economic Theory*, 97(2): 298–319.

Blank, A., Houkamau, C. and Kingi, H. (2016) *Unconscious Bias and Education: A Comparative Study of Māori and African American Students*. New Zealand: Oranui Diversity Leadership.

Blumberg, R.L. (2015) *Eliminating Gender Bias in Textbooks: Pushing for Policy Reforms That Promote Gender Equity in Education*. Background paper for EFA Global Monitoring Report.

Boaler, J. (2002) *Experiencing School Mathematics: Traditional and Reform Approaches to Teaching and Their Impact on Student Learning*. London: Routledge.

Boaler, J. and Greeno, J.G. (2000) Identity, agency, and knowing in mathematics worlds. *Multiple Perspectives on Mathematics Teaching and Learning*, 1: 171–200.

Campbell, T. (2015) Stereotyped at seven? Biases in teacher judgement of pupils' ability and attainment. *Journal of Social Policy*, 44(3): 517–47.

Carlana, M. (2018) *Implicit Stereotypes: Evidence from Teachers' Gender Bias*. HKS working paper, no. RWP18-034.

Carneiro, P. and Heckman, J. (2003) *Human Capital Policy*. NBER working paper, no. 9495.

Carrell, S.E. and West, J.E. (2010) Does professor quality matter? Evidence from random assignment of students to professors. *Journal of Political Economy*, 118(3): 409–32.

Carter, M.J. (2014) Gender socialization and identity theory. *Social Sciences*, 3(2): 242–63.

Ceci, S. and Williams, W.M. (2010) *The Mathematics of Sex: How Biology and Society Conspire to Limit Talented Women and Girls*. Oxford: Oxford University Press.

Centre for Longitudinal Studies (CLS) (n.d.) *1970 British Cohort Study*. Available at: https://cls.ucl.ac.uk/cls-studies/1970-british-cohort-study/

Chavatzia, T. (2017) *Cracking the Code: Girls' and Women's Education in Science, Technology, Engineering and Mathematics (STEM)*. Available at: http://unesdoc.unesco.org/images/0025/002534

Chowdry, H., Crawford, C. and Goodman, A. (2009) *Drivers and Barriers to Educational Success: Evidence from the Longitudinal Study of Young People in England*. Available at: https://dera.ioe.ac.uk//11332/

Chowdry, H., Crawford, C., Dearden, L., Goodman, A. and Vignoles, A. (2013) Widening participation in higher education: analysis using linked administrative data. *Journal of the Royal Statistical Society: Series A (Statistics in Society)*, 176(2): 431–57.

Cobb-Clark, D.A. and Schurer, S. (2012) The stability of big-five personality traits. *Economics Letters*, 115(1): 11–15.

Dee, T. (2005) A teacher like me: does race, ethnicity, or gender matter? *American Economic Review*, 95(2): 158–65.

Della Giusta, M., Hashimzade, N. and Myles, G.D. (2017) Schooling and the intergenerational transmission of values. *Journal of Public Economic Theory*, 19(1): 1–17.

Devine, A., Fawcett, K., Szűcs, D. and Dowker, A. (2012) Gender differences in mathematics anxiety and the relation to mathematics performance while controlling for test anxiety. *Behavioral and Brain Functions*, 8(33): 1–9.

Dweck, C.S. (2008) Mindsets: how praise is harming youth and what can be done about it. *School Library Media Activities Monthly*, 24(5): 55.

Eccles, J.S., Freedman-Doan, C., Frome, P., Jacobs, J. and Yoon, K.S. (2000) Gender-role socialization in the family: a longitudinal approach. In T. Eckes and H.M. Trautner (eds), *The Developmental Social Psychology of Gender*. London: Routledge.

Education Endowment Foundation (EEF) (n.d.) *Changing Mindsets*. Available at: https://educationendowmentfoundation.org.uk/projects-and-evaluation/projects/changing-mindsets/

Favara, M. (2012) *The Cost of Acting 'Girly': Gender Stereotypes and Educational Choices*. IZA discussion paper, no. 7037.

Figlio, D. (2005) *Names, Expectation and the Black-White Test Score Gap*. NBER working paper, no. 11195.

Gilliam, W.S., Maupin, A.N., Reyes, C.R., Accavitti, M. and Shic, F. (2016) *Do Early Educators' Implicit Biases Regarding Sex and Race Relate to Behavior Expectations and Recommendations of Preschool Expulsions and Suspensions?* New Haven, CT: Yale Child Study Center.

Gorard, S. (2013) What difference do teachers make? A consideration of the wider outcomes of schooling. *Irish Educational Studies*, 32(1): 69–82.

Guiso, L., Monte, F., Sapienza, P. and Zingales, L. (2008) Culture, gender, and math. *Science*, 320(5880): 1164–5.

Institute of Physics (IOP) (2013) *Closing Doors: Exploring Gender and Subject Choice in Schools*. Available at: http://tinyurl.com/IoP-girls

Jacob, B.A. and Wilder, T. (2010) *Educational Expectations and Attainment*. London: National Bureau of Economic Research.

Jerrim, J. (2011) *England's 'Plummeting' PISA Test Scores between 2000 and 2009: Is the Performance of Our Secondary School Pupils Really in Relative Decline?* London: UCL IOE.

Joensen, J.S. and Nielsen, H.S. (2009) Is there a causal effect of high school math on labor market outcomes? *Journal of Human Resources*, 44(1): 171–98.

Johns, M., Schmader, T. and Martens, A. (2005) Knowing is half the battle: teaching stereotype threat as a means of improving women's math performance. *Psychological Science*, 16(3): 175–9.

Johnston, D.W., Schurer, S. and Shields, M.A. (2014) Maternal gender role attitudes, human capital investment, and labour supply of sons and daughters. *Oxford Economic Papers*, 66(3): 631–59.

Jussim, L. and Harber, K.D. (2005) Teacher expectations and self-fulfilling prophecies: knowns and unknowns, resolved and unresolved controversies. *Personality and Social Psychology Review*, 9(2): 131–55.

Jussim, L., Crawford, J.T. and Rubinstein, R.S. (2015) Stereotype (in)accuracy in perceptions of groups and individuals. *Current Directions in Psychological Science*, 24(6): 490–7.

Kahneman, D. (2011) *Thinking, Fast and Slow*. New York: Allen Lane.

Karwowski, M., Lebuda, I., Wisniewska, E. and Gralewski, J. (2013) Big Five personality traits as the predictors of creative self-efficacy and creative personal identity: does gender matter? *Journal of Creative Behavior*, 47(3): 215–32.

Khoo, S.T. and Ainley, J. (2005) *Attitudes, Intentions and Participation*. Available at: https://pdfs.semantic scholar.org/05a4/6c933c8872f496ab18d83baf44fd185dec38.pdf

Lieberman, M.D. (2013) *Social: Why Our Brains Are Wired to Connect*. Oxford: Oxford University Press.

Looker, E.D. and Thiessen, V. (2004) *Aspirations of Canadian Youth for Higher Education*. Ottawa: Learning Policy Directorate, Strategic Policy and Planning, Human Resources and Skills Development Canada.

Mendolia, S. and Walker, I. (2014) The effect of noncognitive traits on health behaviours in adolescence. *Health Economics*, 23(9): 1146–1158.

Morris, E.W. and Perry, B.L. (2017) Girls behaving badly? Race, gender, and subjective evaluation in the discipline of African American girls. *Sociology of Education*, 90(2): 127–48.

NatCen Social Research (2019) *British Social Attitudes (BSA) Survey*. Available at: www.bsa.natcen.ac.uk/media/39248/bsa35_gender.pdf

Olivetti, C. and Petrongolo, B. (2008) Unequal pay or unequal employment? A cross-country analysis of gender gaps. *Journal of Labor Economics*, 26(4): 621–54.

Phelan, S.M., Puhl, R.M., Burke, S.E., Hardeman, R., Dovidio, J.F., Nelson, D.B., et al. (2015) The mixed impact of medical school on medical students' implicit and explicit weight bias. *Medical Education*, 49(10): 983–92.

Rampino, T. and Taylor, M.P. (2013) *Gender Differences in Educational Aspirations and Attitudes*. ISER working paper series, no. 2013-15.

Reuben, E., Sapienza, P. and Zingales, L. (2014) How stereotypes impair women's careers in science. *Proceedings of the National Academy of Sciences*, 111(12): 4403–8.

Rippon, G. (2019) Do women and men have different brains? *New Scientist*, 241(3219): 28–31.

Rosenthal, R. and Jacobson, L. (1968) *Pygmalion in the Classroom*. New York: Holt, Rinehart & Winston.

Sacerdote, B. (2014) Experimental and quasi-experimental analysis of peer effects: two steps forward? *Annual Review of Economics*, 6(1): 253–72.

Schmader, T. (2010) Stereotype threat deconstructed. *Current Directions in Psychological Science*, 19(1): 14–18.

Schneider, D.J. (2005) *The Psychology of Stereotyping*. New York: Guilford Press.

Shenouda, C.K. and Danovitch, J.H. (2014) Effects of gender stereotypes and stereotype threat on children's performance on a spatial task. *Revue Internationale de Psychologie Sociale*, 27(3): 53–77.

Smith, C. and Golding, J. (2015) *Gender and Participation in Mathematics and Further Mathematics: Interim Report for the Further Mathematics Support Programme*. London: UCL IOE.

Sprietsma, M. (2009) *Discrimination in Grading? Experimental Evidence from Primary School*. ZEW discussion paper, no. 09-074.

Strand, T. (2007) The discipline of education in a world of change. *Nordic Studies in Education*, 27(3): 265–76.

Tan, J.B. and Yates, S. (2011) Academic expectations as sources of stress in Asian students. *Social Psychology of Education*, 14(3): 389–407.

World Economic Forum (WEF) (2016) *The Global Gender Gap Report 2016*. Available at: http://reports. weforum.org/global-gender-gap-report-2016/

Zohar, A. and Sela, D. (2003) Her physics, his physics: gender issues in Israeli advanced placement physics classes. *International Journal of Science Education*, 25(2): 245–68.

Zumbuehl, M., Dohmen, T.J. and Pfann, G.A. (2013) *Parental Investment and the Intergenerational Transmission of Economic Preferences and Attitudes*. Available at: http://ftp.iza.org/dp7476.pdf

# 6

# GIRLS AND BOYS: THE ROLE OF PROFESSIONALS AND PLAY IN THE EARLY YEARS

## MARIA KAMBOURI-DANOS

## KEYWORDS

- **PLAY**
- **EARLY YEARS**
- **GENDER STEREOTYPES**
- **SEX**
- **GENDER IDENTITY**

### THIS CHAPTER

- explores the role of educators in relation to the construction of gender identity in the early years;
- focuses on how play and learning through play can encourage the development of gender stereotypes;
- explains some key principles that should inform planning of a more inclusive early years education pedagogy.

# INTRODUCTION

Play is a very distinct characteristic of childhood, and it is widely accepted and established that children learn through play. However, children's play choices differ, and gender has a significant role to play in relation to this. Even when children share the same play area, they often use it in different ways (e.g. boys choosing to play superheroes in the dress-up area, girls choosing to play princesses). What is important to note is that these choices can disadvantages both boys and girls in different ways; based on their play choices, they may end up missing opportunities in learning.

In addition, previous research has shown that it is more common for boys to play outside and present more risky behaviour in their play, whereas girls tend to stay inside. In female-dominant environments, such as education (especially early years), it might sometimes be challenging to ensure that children develop a gender identity that is free of gender stereotypes, as children have more women around them as role models and fewer men. In this chapter, we explore different ways to support educators in providing a gender stereotype-free environment for play. This chapter starts by looking at the importance of play in early years and the different definitions and types of play. It then moves on to explore how gender develops in the early years, as well as the role of play and educators in the way that children develop their ideas of gender and their own gender identity. The chapter concludes by emphasising the importance of professionals adopting a gender-inclusive pedagogy as an integral part of early years teaching.

---

## REFLECTION

'We've been really naughty today, we haven't done any work at all', said Amy, 5 years old, to her father when he was picking her up, after spending a whole day playing with water and different recyclable materials. The children had spent the whole day exploring different materials, their qualities, and how they behave when put into water. A lot of them had brought different recyclable materials from home, so parents were informed that children were going to be doing something with all those boxes and plastic bottles they brought in earlier in the day. The children worked in groups to make a robot, explored how much strength different materials need to be bended or crashed, and also put some of them in water to see which ones float and which ones sink.

What was it that made Amy say they hadn't done any work all day? What underlying values were apparent in her comment?

---

# UNDERSTANDING PLAY

When defining play, Scales et al. (1991) suggest that it is 'that absorbing activity in which healthy young children participate with enthusiasm and abandon' (p15). Csikszentmihalyi (1981) describes play as 'a subset of life ... an arrangement in which one can practice behaviour without dreading its consequences' (p14), whereas Garvey (1977) gives a useful description of play for teachers when she defines play as an activity that: (1) is positively valued by the player; (2) is self-motivated; (3) is freely chosen; (4) is engaging; and (5) 'has certain systematic relations to what is not play' (p5). Piaget (1962) defined play as children's efforts to make environmental stimuli match their own concepts, and he believed that children play for pleasure, while Vygotsky (1978) argued that play facilitates cognitive development, supporting the view that during play, children learn new things. In discussing Vygotsky's theory, Vandenberg (1986) remarks that play not only reflects thought (as Piaget suggests), but it also – and mostly – creates thought.

## EVIDENCE FROM PRACTICE

Observations of children at play yield examples to support both Piagetian and Vygotskian theories of play (Karia, 2014). For example, a child who pretends to be a police officer managing traffic, using a whistle and hand signals, is practising what they have previously learnt about police officers. This example supports Piaget's theory. On the other hand, a child who is playing with water and shouts, 'Look, when I put this rock in the water it sinks, but when I put this piece of wood in, it doesn't!' has constructed new knowledge in relation to sinking through their play. This example supports Vygotsky's theory. Either way, whether children are practising what they have learnt in other settings or are constructing new knowledge, it is clear that play has a valuable role in early years learning.

## REFLECTION

There are a lot of different theories of play. Some of these theories may resonate with you while others may not. Take a moment to reflect on your own view of play. You might want to write down your own definition and compare it with those outlined here.

Thinking about the example given above, you might also want to reflect on your own practice and list some examples of what you think children learn through different types of play.

Play is often regarded as one of the most distinctive features of childhood, something that all children have in common, which makes their world strikingly different from that of an adult (Miller and Almon, 2009). Some of the key characteristics of play are summarised in Table 6.1. Indeed, for many people, it is 'children's capacity for play, their enthusiasm for play and the importance attached to being allowed to play that defines what childhood is about' (Barnes and Kehily, 2003, p4).

Table 6.1   *Key characteristics of play, as noted in previous research*

| Source | Key characteristics |
|---|---|
| Rubin et al. (1983), cited in Hughes (2009, pp4-5) | 1.  intrinsically motivated;<br>2.  freely chosen;<br>3.  pleasurable;<br>4.  non-literal;<br>5.  actively engaged. |
| Gray (2015, pp139-53) | 1.  self-chosen and self-directed - players are always free to quit;<br>2.  an activity in which means are more valued than ends;<br>3.  guided by mental rules;<br>4.  non-literal, imaginative, marked off in some way from reality;<br>5.  as an active, alert but non-stressed frame of mind. |
| Mayesky (2014, p138) | 1.  a natural part of a child's life;<br>2.  self-directed;<br>3.  a creative activity, not a production;<br>4.  a total activity;<br>5.  a sensitive thing for children. |
| Kernan (2007, p9) | 1.  voluntary nature;<br>2.  meaningfulness to the players;<br>3.  low risk;<br>4.  spontaneity and openness to the surrounding world;<br>5.  symbolic;<br>6.  incorporates deep involvement and sustained concentration;<br>7.  active;<br>8.  sociability;<br>9.  joy, sense of humour and excitement. |
| De Holton et al. (2001, p404) | 1.  a solver-centred activity with the solver in charge of the process;<br>2.  using the solver's current knowledge;<br>3.  developing links between the solver's current schemata while the play is occurring;<br>4.  will, via (3), reinforce current knowledge;<br>5.  will, via (3), assist future problem-solving/mathematical activity as it enhances future access to knowledge;<br>6.  irrespective of age. |

Froebel (1885) was one of the first to highlight the importance of play as he recognised that play is not lazy behaviour, but a biological imperative to discover how things work. According to Froebel (1912), play is a pleasurable activity, but it is also biologically purposeful. Play opens the windows of learning in a child's life and acquaints them with movement, observation, relationships, emotions, and much more (Froebel, 1912). As Frobel said, play is the purest intellectual production of the child; it is the highest expression of human development in childhood, for it alone is the free expression of what is in the child's soul. Vygotsky (1978) agrees with this, and adds that during play, children always behave beyond their average age, above their daily behaviour. When looking at play closely, one can conclude that play can successfully support children's development and learning in many different areas, resulting in play being the main vehicle for learning (Vygotsky, 1978).

**REFLECTION**

Standardised testing and preparation for tests are now a daily activity in most kindergartens and early years settings, even though most uses of such tests with children under age 8 are of questionable validity and can lead to harmful labelling. This can curtail the time available for play, which is worrying since it has been proven that children who have opportunities to play in challenging natural environments score better in tests of balance, agility, strength and coordination (Fjortoft, cited in Tovey, 2007). For example, children who engage in complex forms of socio-dramatic play have greater language skills than non-players, better social skills, more empathy, more imagination, and more of the subtle capacity to know what others mean. They are also less aggressive and show more self-control and higher levels of thinking.

What does play mean for you and your practice, and how important is it? For example, how important do you think learning through play is in your practice setting? If you are working with older children, you may consider how much time and what sort of activities are intrinsically motivated, freely chosen and/or pleasurable.

No matter how we define play, it is important to remember that play is children's vehicle of learning to live; it helps them to learn through everyday experience rather than by direct instruction (Else, 2009). When pointing out the importance of play, Vygotsky (1978) stated:

*Play creates a zone of proximal development of the child [meaning that] ... in play the child always behaves beyond his average age, above his daily behaviour; in play it is as though he were a head taller than himself. As in the focus of magnifying glass, play contains all developmental tendencies in a condensed form and in itself is a major source of development.*

(p102)

Thus, during play, children can test their hypotheses, discover new things, and learn from their mistakes in their own ways and to the best of their knowledge and ability (Else, 2009). Play also gives children the opportunity to be 'in control' and encourages cooperation and perspective-taking, while providing unsuspected opportunities to symbolise and use objects in a way that is meaningful and thrilling to them (Samuelsson and Carlsson, 2008). This learning and exploration during play also applies to learning and exploring ideas around gender, as 'play encourages different forms of social interaction which enable the children to understand their place in the wider society' (Moyles, 1991, p14).

# PLAY AND GENDER DEVELOPMENT

Children's play is constructed by what they have observed in their environment; by watching adults and other children, through thinking and acting, and through playing, children create an understanding of how to behave according to their gender. As Browne (2004) highlights, play is a powerful medium for children's exploration of 'femininities' and 'masculinities', as well as understanding the gendered nature of society. However, although girls and boys do share the same play area, they sometimes use it differently (Nutbrown, 2011). Considering this, it is important to be aware that boys and girls sometimes show different kinds of behaviour and make different choices in their play, and the type of play they engage with can affect the behaviours and choices children make, as well as the experiences they are exposed to. As MacNaughton (1999, p81) notes, children's pretend play is rich in information about how they understand gender relations. As they play at 'having babies', 'being monsters' or 'making a hospital', they show others what they think girls and women can and should do, as well as what they think boys and men can and should do.

During playtime, it has been noted that children are more likely to show an interest towards gender-stereotyped toys, which can limit a child's learning and reinforce notions of activities and roles that are appropriate for their gender. For example, the home corner area is usually dominated by girls, where the girls, and maybe one or two boys, take on family roles (e.g. mum, dad, baby) and re-enact family situations. On the other hand, boys usually choose more risky outdoor play, during which they learn through trial and error and develop in different areas, such as confidence and risk-taking. What is important to remember is that both boys and girls can miss out on important experiences if their play is limited to only some of the opportunities available in their settings. The teacher's role is critical in ensuring that all children engage in gender stereotype-free play experiences, so that children's learning is not affected by gender stereotypes (Wolpert, 2005). For example, if girls never play at the construction area, they may lose important learning opportunities to explore scientific and mathematical concepts such as forces. Also, the organisation of sandboxes, home corners and imaginative learning experiences, familiar from many early years settings, are important, and yet not sufficient on their own.

So, it is important for professionals working with young children to think about how different areas can be set up and used to counter stereotypes. For example, the kind of materials provided at the home corner will affect the context that children will choose for their play, as well as the roles they will act out. When choosing materials, it is important to make gender-neutral choices (e.g. texture, colours, themes) and involve children in the process of selecting these materials to ensure that all children will be interested in playing in that area. The same principle would apply when designing and renewing other play areas, as well as when selecting books and stories for the book corner and for storytelling time.

## REFLECTION

How effective is the environment in engaging children to play and explore? For example, is there enough space both indoors and outdoors for children to play and explore? Are the indoors and outdoors equally inviting for both boys and girls?

How are resources or equipment used by children? Do boys and girls use the same resources, and do they use them in the same way? Do resources reflect children's interests? Are resources open-ended so that they can be used, moved and combined in a variety of ways?

**ACTIVITY**

- Observe the children in your practice setting and note the play choices they make.
- To what extent can children make choices and decisions about what they play?
- Are boys or girls missing out on any learning opportunities because of their play choices?

It is helpful to observe the children you work with to understand where they spend most of their time during free play time. Try to ensure that all children are encouraged and do engage in different types of play, such as creative play, role play, constructive play, quiet play and exploratory play.

What is important to remember is that a child's ideas of gender and their ideas of their own gender identity are not fixed; children are instead 'in a continuous process of constructing, revising and amending' their ideas of who they are, as well as their place in the world (Browne, 2004, p60). For this reason, Davies (1989) and MacNaughton (2000) proposed the term 'gender subjectivity' instead of 'gender identity' to emphasise the complexity of the process during which our multifaceted identity is created.

As Browne (2004) notes, our identity is composed of a variety of 'selves', meaning that we do not have one single identity, but instead many identities that we adopt and adapt depending on the situation and the context. Similarly, the gender identities that children adopt depend on the situations to which they are exposed. Therefore, it is of particular importance, as professionals working with children, to consider the breadth of experiences we offer to children, to allow them to practise and develop their own variety of 'selves'.

# GENDER DEVELOPMENT IN THE EARLY YEARS AND THE INFLUENCE OF PROFESSIONALS

Although many professionals agree that girls and boys should be treated equally within their practice, there is contrasting evidence indicating that professionals tend to categorise children according to their gender. The evidence demonstrates that usually, professionals demonstrate gender differences in their practice (Gray and Leith, 2004), such as in the use of activities, resources, and the grouping of children.

Challenging stereotypes seems to concern most professionals working with children, and many professionals admit that sometimes they may accidentally reinforce and emphasise stereotypes rather than counteracting them (Gray and Leith, 2004). Since gender is a social construct that involves and is dependent on information that children receive from others (Breneselovic and Krnjaja, 2016), encouraging professionals to question and challenge gender stereotypes becomes crucial. Professionals need to be confident enough to affirm unconventional choices, such as boys playing with dolls or dressing up in princesses' clothing, or girls' preference for traditional boys' toys or activities, as well as supporting children in becoming able to accept different behaviours, including those that might not follow traditional gender expectations (Blaise, 2005).

## REFLECTION

Have you ever noticed that children as young as 2 are aware of gender stereotyping, such as thinking that pink toys are for girls and blue toys are for boys, or that dolls are for girls and cars are for boys, as well as, similarly, that dressing up as a princess is for girls and dressing up as a superhero is for boys? Why is this, in your opinion?

## WHAT DO WE KNOW FROM RESEARCH?

Pinsent (1997) argues that by the age of 4, children have already developed their own views of what roles men and women have in society. Serbin et al. (2001) add that children's knowledge regarding gender roles begins to emerge between the ages of 2 and 3 years. Observing children during play is a very effective way to identify what ideas children have around gender, and one of the first signs of children following stereotypical traits is in their play with toys. Boys and girls sometimes show different kinds of behaviour and make different choices in their play. Where girls and boys do share the same play area, they sometimes use it differently (e.g. the home play area can be dominated by girls, with boys choosing more risky outdoor play).

By the age of 2–3, this is evident with girls favouring dolls over cars or trains, and vice versa. This has been demonstrated in research by children having greater recall of toys that are associated with their own gender (Bauer and Coyne, 1997). Moreover, children of this age also begin to demonstrate personality traits defined as male or female (Bauer and Coyne, 1997). Eagly (1997) suggests that it is these characteristics, such as females being compassionate, which encourages them to pursue stereotypical careers such as nursing. Blakemore, cited in Wilbourn and Kee (2010), suggests that at the age of 7, children's thinking becomes more complex and looks at the stereotypical norms in occupations. However, this study has shown that violating some stereotypical norms is more accepted than others. An example of this is a study with boys aged 7–10 that found they evaluated male nurses negatively in comparison with female doctors. Furthermore, children aged 8 and 9 are thought to have an established knowledge of occupational stereotypes and are able to understand that both genders can violate what are seen as gender-stereotypical norms.

## TRANSFORMING PRACTICE

The key principle to follow when organising play should be creativity, not gender. Within your setting, take a look at the space through a gender-neutral lens. Do you use a variety of colours, materials and textures? Do you have boys' sections and girls' sections? For example, are the kitchen, dolls, and dress-up container in one section while the blocks, cars and dinosaurs are in another? You should aim to use a variety of colours, materials and textures in all play areas, as well as in relation to the toys provided. It is important to avoid gender-stereotypical colours. Children respond visually to choosing where to go and in what play to engage. A vibrant, multicoloured space is more welcoming to all children. Check that the books, toys and resources provided are reinforcing gender-neutral activities. Let books be books and toys be toys by choosing resources that do not reinforce gender stereotypes.

What remains significant is the teacher's engagement with children and their play. A successful teacher will play with the children, observe their interests, and aim to see the world from their perspective. This requires constant movement and interchange between observation, participation, analysis and reflection. They will aim to enter children's own imaginary and exploratory play worlds as a respectful and sensitive participant, as well as guiding them further in trying out new ideas, approaches or resources (DfE, 2017).

Play situations tend to create meaningful and interesting contexts for children. It is the quality and timing of teacher interaction that has the potential to make a real difference for all children. Sylva et al. (2004) identified 'shared, sustained thinking' as an important aspect of practitioner–child interaction. In their influential, large-scale EPPE project, they noted that the quality of adult–child interactions varied between different types of settings. High-quality interaction, which they termed as 'shared, sustained thinking', was the defining characteristic that singled out successful teachers from others (Sylva et al., 2004).

# CHAPTER SUMMARY

- Play is the main vehicle of children's learning in the early years.

- Children may not get the same learning opportunities if their play choices are limited by gender stereotypes.

- Play can be a catalyst in the way that children develop their ideas around gender.

- Professionals working with children are key in influencing children's thinking around gender stereotypes.

# FURTHER READING

**Browne, N.** (2004) *Gender Equity in the Early Years*. Maidenhead: Open University Press.

**Else, P.** (2009) *The Value of Play*. London: Continuum.

**MacNaughton, G.** (2000) *Rethinking Gender in Early Childhood Education*. London: Paul Chapman.

**Wolpert, E.** (2005) *Start Seeing Diversity*. Boston, MA: Red Leaf Press.

# REFERENCES

Barnes, P. and Kehily, M.J. (2003) Play and the cultures of childhood. In M.J. Kehily and J. Swann (eds), *Children's Cultural Worlds*. Chichester: Wiley/Open University Press.

Bauer, P.J. and Coyne, M.J. (1997) When the name says it all: preschoolers' recognition and use of the gendered nature of common proper names. *Social Development*, 6(3): 271–91.

Blaise, M. (2005) *Playing It Straight: Uncovering Gender Discourses in the Early Childhood Classroom*. London: Routledge.

Breneselovic, D.P and Krnjaja, Ž. (2016) Discourses on gender in early childhood education and care (ECEC) setting: equally discriminated against. *Journal of Pedagogy*, 7(2): 51–77.

Browne, N. (2004) *Gender Equity in the Early Years*. Maidenhead: Open University Press.

Csikszentmihalyi, M. (1981) Some paradoxes in the definition of play. In A.T. Cheska (ed.), *Play as Context*. West Point, NY: Leisure Press.

Davies, B. (1989) *Frogs and Snails and Feminist Tales: Pre-School Children and Gender*. Sydney: Allen & Unwin.

De Holton, D., Ahmed, A., Williams, H. and Hill, C. (2001) On the importance of mathematical play. *International Journal of Mathematical Education in Science and Technology*, 32(3): 401–15.

Department for Education (DfE) (2017) *Statutory Framework for the Early Years Foundation Stage*. London: DfE.

Eagly, A.H. (1997) *Sex Differences in Social Behavior: A Social-Role Interpretation*. Mahwah, NJ: Lawrence Erlbaum.

Else, P. (2009) *The Value of Play*. London: Continuum.

Froebel, F. (1885) *The Education of Man*, trans. J. Jarvis. New York: A. Lovell & Co.

Froebel, F. (1912) *Froebel's Chief Writings on Education (Rendered into English)*, trans. S.S.F. Fletcher and J. Welton. London: Edward Arnold.

Garvey, C. (1977) *Play*. Cambridge, MA: Harvard University Press.

Gray, C. and Leith, H. (2004) Perpetuating gender stereotypes in the classroom: a teacher perspective. *Educational Studies*, 30(1): 3–17.

Gray, P. (2015) *Free to Learn*. New York: Basic Books.

Hughes, F.P. (2009) *Children, Play, and Development*, 4th edn. Los Angeles, CA: SAGE.

Karia, E. (2014) *The Full-Day Kindergarten Classroom in Ontario: Exploring Play-Based Learning Approach and Its Implications for Child Development*. Doctoral dissertation, University of Toronto.

Kernan, M. (2007) *Play as a Context for Early Learning and Development*. Dublin: National Council for Curriculum and Assessment.

Mayesky, M. (2014) *Creative Activities and Curriculum for Young Children*. Boston, MA: Wadsworth.

MacNaughton, G. (1999) Even pink tents have glass ceilings: crossing the gender boundaries in pretend play. In E. Dau (ed.), *Child's Play: Revisiting Play in Early Childhood Settings*. Sydney: MacLennan & Petty.

MacNaughton, G. (2000) *Rethinking Gender in Early Childhood Education*. London: Paul Chapman.

Miller, E. and Almon, J. (2009) *Crisis in the Kindergarten: Why Children Need Play in School*. New York: Alliance for Childhood.

Moyles, J.R. (1991) *Play as a Learning Process in Your Classroom*. Kent: Mary Glasgow.

Nutbrown, K. (2011) *Key Concepts in Early Childhood Education and Care*, 2nd edn. London: SAGE.

Piaget, J. (1962) *Play, Dreams, and Imitation in Childhood*. New York: W.W. Norton & Co.

Pinsent, P. (1997) *Children's Literature and the Policy of Equality*. London: David Fulton.

Rubin, K.H., Fein, G. and Vandenberg, B. (1983) Play. In E.M. Hetherington (ed.), *Handbook of Child Psychology, Vol. 4: Socialization, Personality, and Social Development*. New York: Wiley.

Samuelsson, I.P. and Carlsson, A.M. (2008) The playing learning child: towards a pedagogy of early childhood. *Scandinavian Journal of Educational Research*, 52(6): 623–41.

Scales, B., Almy, M., Nicolopulou, A. and Ervin-Tripp, S. (1991) Defending play in the lives of children. In B. Scales, M. Almy, A. Nicolopulou and S. Ervin-Tripp (eds), *Play and the Social Context of Development in Early Care and Education*. New York: Teachers College, Columbia University.

Serbin, L.A., Poulin-Dubois, D., Colburne, K.A., Sen, M.G. and Eichstedt, J.A. (2001) Gender stereotyping in infancy: visual preferences for and knowledge of gender-stereotyped toys in the second year. *International Journal of Behavioral Development*, 25(1): 7–15.

Sylva, K., Melhuish, E., Sammons, P., Siraj-Blatchford, I. and Taggart, B. (2004) *The Effective Provision of Pre-School Education (EPPE) Project: Final Report*. London: Sure Start.

Tovey, H. (2007) *Playing Outdoors: Spaces and Places, Risk and Challenge*. Maidenhead: Open University Press/McGraw-Hill.

Vandenberg, B. (1986) Play theory. In G. Fein and M. Rivkin (eds), *The Young Child at Play*. Washington, DC: NAEYC.

Vygotsky, L.S. (1978) *Mind in Society: The Development of Higher Psychological Processes*. Cambridge, MA: Harvard University Press.

Wilbourn, M. and Kee, D. (2010) Henry the nurse is a doctor too: implicitly examining children's gender stereotypes for male and female occupational roles. *Sex Roles*, 62(9): 670–83.

Wolpert, E. (2005) *Start Seeing Diversity*. Boston, MA: Red Leaf Press.

# 7

# GENDER STEREOTYPES IN MATHEMATICS EDUCATION

## CATHERINE FOLEY

## KEYWORDS

- MATHEMATICS
- MATHEMATICIAN
- IDENTITY

- SELF-EFFICACY
- RESILIENCE
- PLAY

- DISPOSITION
- MYTHS

## THIS CHAPTER

- explores issues relating to perceived and actual gender differences in mathematics attainment and ability;
- focuses on the key role of educators in understanding stereotypes held by families and wider society, as well as their own mathematical identity;
- provides evidence-based examples of ways in which schools and teachers can build a resilient mathematical identity among all young people regardless of gender.

# INTRODUCTION

In this chapter, we explore the world of mathematics education from a gender stereotyping perspective. We begin by establishing what we know about the current and historical context, as well as challenging a deficit model of female 'performance' in terms of mathematics outcomes. We go on to examine what mathematics is in order to challenge assumptions on which stereotypes are based. Key issues, such as the role of parents, teachers and society in forming mathematical stereotypes, will be discussed, and we will go on to explore your own identity as a mathematician, as well as how this might influence you as a practitioner. The chapter ends with examples of tackling gender stereotyping in practice.

# CURRENT AND HISTORICAL CONTEXT: MYTHS AND REALITIES

You may be surprised at the reality around gender differences and mathematics. In the UK, gender differences in attainment during the years of compulsory study are small and have diminished over time. For example, in 2019, at the end of primary schooling, the proportion of boys and girls reaching the expected standard followed the pattern of previous years in being very similar (DfE, 2019). In previous decades, when gender gaps were greater, research often focused on biological differences in mathematical aptitude as the reason for lower female attainment (McCormack, 2014). Thankfully, we are now in more enlightened times – not only have attainment gaps themselves narrowed, but, as recognised by the OECD (2014), the fact that gender differences are greater within than between genders means it is logical to assume that these differences relate to social, cultural and educational pressures rather than being inherent to gender itself.

## ACTIVITY

Consider the data that you have available in your context. This might relate to assessment at the end of the Foundation Stage, end-of-year or stage assessments within primary schools, progress data within secondary schools, or formal examination results. Look over two to three years, and find out:

- What, if any, gender differences are there in attainment? Is there anything that surprises you?
- Have any strategies been put in place in relation to any differences? If so, has there been any review of their impact?

While carrying out this activity, don't forget to retain a healthy scepticism – even if there are differences, these may relate to the nature of assessment or testing rather than inherent characteristics of schooling or those being assessed!

Alongside the relative parity in attainment outcomes, there are, however, two stubbornly persistent and interrelated differences (Foley et al., 2019), as shown in Table 7.1.

*Table 7.1    Differences*

| Under-representation of females in post-compulsory study of mathematics and 'STEM' careers historically more associated with males (Sheldrake et al., 2015). | Tendency of females in the UK to rate themselves as less able or display lower rates of self-efficacy than their male peers (OECD, 2014). |
|---|---|

Gender-related differences in careers are explored within Chapter 5 and will not be repeated here, other than to note that these differences take root in early childhood and reveal themselves within A-level and degree choices; instead, we will focus on factors such as perceptions of mathematics and mathematicians, how these can lead to stereotypes and knock-on impacts on identity and self-efficacy, and how these can be avoided or overcome.

## REFLECTION

Read the following extract from the OECD's Programme for International Student Assessment (PISA) 2012 report:

*Even when girls perform as well as boys in mathematics, they tend to report less perseverance, less openness to problem solving, less intrinsic and instrumental motivation to learn mathematics, less self-belief in their ability to learn mathematics and more anxiety about mathematics than boys, on average; they are also more likely than boys to attribute failure in mathematics to themselves rather than to external factors.*

(OECD, 2014, p18)

Consider the following questions:

1.  How does this relate to your experience of boys' and girls' learning and playing with mathematics?

2.  Is the language of 'even when' and the repeated emphasis on 'less than' helpful? What messages does this convey?

You might feel that phrases such as 'even when' and 'less than' contribute to a deficit model of girls as mathematicians. Writing over a decade ago, Leder (2007) asserted that there was a shift towards focusing upon approaches to mathematics teaching that empower all students to meet their potential, and away from a deficit model focused upon how females' attainment might be raised to that of males. The language of the above quote might suggest that there is still some way to go! This is a concern because we know that stereotypes become self-perpetuating: in the case of mathematics, girls simply being aware that boys are seen as better at mathematics can lower their performance (Martinot and Désert, 2007).

# WHAT IS MATHEMATICS?

This may sound like an odd question in a book about gender stereotyping rather than a mathematics textbook. However, the argument of this chapter is that it is necessary to challenge views about mathematics itself and what it means to be a mathematician before addressing stereotypes.

The word cloud shown in Figure 7.1 represents some adjectives that might be used to describe mathematics. As you can see, there are some contrasting characterisations! Without spending too long, consider which words resonate with you.

*Figure 7.1    Adjectives to describe mathematics*

One way of conceptualising views of mathematics is as a two-way split between absolutism and constructivism, with the first of these positioning mathematics as 'certain, permanent, and independent of human activity' (Stemhagen, 2011, p2). This can lead to thinking of mathematics as somehow being 'other' – in the domain of those who can recall number facts or calculate at will, readily create formulae to bridge the concrete and abstract, or magically 'see' a mathematical route to solving a problem. Alternatively, mathematics can be thought of as living and active, socially constructed, with a cultural history and dependent upon time, culture and context (Bishop, 1988). More recently, Allen (2011) proposed a democratic model of mathematics education with an emphasis on collaboration and collective endeavour. This is echoed in the words of Maryam Mirzakhani, described in the pen portraits later in the chapter:

> I got involved in Math Olympiads that made me think about harder problems. As a teenager, I enjoyed the challenge. But most importantly, I met many inspiring mathematicians and friends at Sharif University. The more I spent time on mathematics, the more excited I became.

> (*The Guardian*, 2014)

Positioning mathematics as a subject of connection-making and collaborative exploration has the potential to attract a wider range of converts, including girls (Boaler et al., 2011).

# A WORD ON SELF-EFFICACY AND IDENTITY

Self-efficacy, or 'the conviction that one can successfully execute the behaviour required to produce the outcomes' (Bandura, 1977, p191), is vital to any discussion about gender stereotypes, mathematics and the notion of building a mathematical identity. This is because the two are so closely intertwined – stereotypes can threaten self-efficacy, and lack of self-efficacy creates the conditions in which stereotypes can thrive. Self-efficacy is also domain-specific (Chmielewski et al., 2013), so that a child may struggle to view themselves as capable in mathematics when they are perfectly confident elsewhere in the curriculum. Part of this picture of self-efficacy is the notion of a 'productive disposition', developed in the US: 'the tendency to see sense in mathematics, to perceive it as both useful and worthwhile, to believe that steady effort in learning mathematics pays off, and to see oneself as an effective learner and doer of mathematics' (Kilpatrick et al., 2001, p131). Keep this in mind as we examine how ideas about mathematics are formed and how pre-existing stereotypes can be challenged.

# HOW DO CHILDREN FORM THEIR IDEAS ABOUT MATHEMATICS?

We have already established that children do not carry out mathematics in a vacuum. It was Fiona Walls, attempting to model the mathematical lives of children, who coined the phrase 'sociomathematical world'. This incorporates the 'complex and dynamic social environments within which children experience, internalise and reflect socially constructed meanings about mathematics, about learning and knowing mathematics, and about their mathematical "selves"' (Walls, 2003, p7). Children develop their ideas about mathematics from a complex mix of media and culture, toys and television, interactions with family and friends, experience of lessons and homework, and the throwaway remarks and subconscious messages of their teachers.

## The role of families and mathematics in the home

Families are highly influential in the impressions that children form about mathematics. Parents themselves may have had less than positive experiences when they were at school, and transfer their own experiences: Maloney et al. (2015) report a link between higher mathematical anxiety among parents and higher levels of anxiety among children. Parents can underestimate the mathematical ability of girls while overestimating that of boys, and we know that parents' judgements can be strong predictors of children's own perceptions of their ability (Herbert and Stipek, 2005). This can begin all too easily: the pattern of boys spending more time playing with construction materials, for example, leads to greater spatial awareness, underpinning complex problem-solving later in life (Boaler, 2009; Klein et al., 2010). There is also some evidence that mothers' perceptions of their daughters' mathematical ability are particularly important for girls (Gladstone et al., 2018), leading to a concern of an ever-repeating cycle if we do not successfully challenge these patterns and assumptions.

## TRANSFORMING PRACTICE

Here are just three starting points you might consider to help children and their families become resilient against gender stereotypes in mathematics education:

1.   Make the most of activities that lend themselves to developing mathematics within the home. For example, you could promote games that are set in a wide range of

(Continued)

(Continued)

contexts: Zeus on the Loose (Gamewright), for example, links number bonds and rounding with Greek mythology; Labyrinth (Ravensburger) provides opportunities to explore topology and spatial awareness; Shut the Box (various) provides endless opportunities to develop number confidence; and Dominoes develops pattern recognition and knowledge of doubles, and can be played collaboratively with the aim of using the whole set in one network.

2.  Think carefully about the setting and carrying out of homework. This can be a real cause of trauma, with children having to mediate home and school mathematics and the danger of stereotypes being reinforced. Providing workshops or drop-in sessions, or changing the 'direction' of activity (for example, rather than carrying out a sheet of questions on telling the time to consolidate learning, children and parents work together to photograph the different clocks and watches they have in the house for the child to bring into school) can help to broaden perspectives on mathematics and support the whole family to engage.

3.  Consider how you report on and praise mathematical success. If the only feedback provided to a parent is how their child is performing on online times tables packages or tests, this can reinforce the tendency to view mathematical talent solely in terms of 'computation ability' (Mann, 2008, p51). Praising and sharing success in joint problem-solving activities linking mathematics and art or music and geometry all widen perceptions and avoid pressure to conform to stereotypes of what it means to be mathematical.

## The role of teachers

Teachers and the environments they create have a powerful role to play in introducing, perpetuating, challenging and negating gender stereotypes. Children do not just learn mathematics itself within their mathematics lessons (Grootenboer et al., 2002); they are forming ideas about themselves and others as mathematicians, picking up on a wide range of cues. Some of these are represented in Table 7.2, which provides a range of questions to consider in reflecting on the messages that children may be taking away from their classroom experiences and interactions.

*Table 7.2  Messaging about mathematics*

| How are children grouped? Are there lower- or higher-attaining groups, and are these male- or female-dominated? | How are questions targeted? | Do response styles (e.g. first hand up) reward those who are more confident or quicker to compute answers? | Is there a gender balance in whose work is selected to be shared or praised? |
| --- | --- | --- | --- |
| Does feedback praise effort, outcome or resilience equally for boys and girls, or is there a bias? | Whose work is on display in the classroom? | Who is invited into the classroom or setting to talk about mathematics? | Are the contexts for 'real-life problems' balanced, realistic and engaging for all? |

| Are there opportunities for cooperation and collaboration as well as competition? | Are mathematics textbooks balanced in terms of roles and imagery? | Do assessment methods involve observation and discussion as well as test performance? | Are a range of real-world role models incorporated into mathematics provision? |
| --- | --- | --- | --- |

The message here is to be mindful of the impression created by the environment around mathematics in the classroom and how this might disenfranchise some children, rather than necessarily to make different provision for girls. As McCormack (2014) observes, planning teaching based on an observation that girls may perform better when understanding and connections are emphasised, rather than abstract rule-following, risks perpetuating a false binary of boys versus girls. It might even risk achieving the opposite aim to that intended: ultimately, the power of mathematics lies in its ability to explore, manipulate and model ideas in the abstract – our job, as educators, is to build all children's confidence to do this, not to deny that it is important.

There is some evidence that teachers can overrate boys' proficiency above that of girls even when they perform to the same level, and also conflate compliance with proficiency (Lubienski et al., 2013), so girls are seen as doing well because they follow the instructions and set out tasks as instructed rather than because they show mathematical insight, for example. This attribution is key. For example, girls can attribute success to luck or hard work rather than insight, thus undermining their confidence to continue with mathematics beyond compulsory study, so the teacher has a vital role in supporting girls to recognise their own self-efficacy.

# BEYOND THE IMMEDIATE: BROADENING CHILDREN'S PERSPECTIVES

We know that there are mixed images of mathematicians within media. The few mathematicians seen tend to follow certain stereotypes – male, white, obsessed with equations or quick-fire calculation, and lacking in communication skills – leaving young people without alternative images to draw upon (Epstein et al., 2010). These authors put out a plea for children to have access to role models of a wide range of mathematicians, including those for whom mathematics is a hobby, those who use it in their day-to-day lives, and leading mathematicians in research or industry.

## Influential mathematicians

Consider the following contrasting pen portraits. How might you use these to broaden the perspectives of children?

### Maryam Mirzakhani (1977–2017)

- Born in Tehran and became the first female Iranian student to win the International Mathematical Olympiad in Hong Kong in 1994.

- Taught at Princeton University before becoming a Professor at Stanford University.

- Became the first woman and first Iranian to win the prestigious Fields Medal (a kind of mathematicians' Nobel Prize) in 2014 for her work on dynamics and geometry.

## Katherine Johnson (1918–2020)

- Fell in love with mathematics at a young age.

- Joined NASA in 1953, although she was rejected the first time she applied.

- Became a pioneering example and role model as an African American woman in STEM.

- Key role in calculating the trajectory for Project Mercury and the Apollo 11 flight to the moon, as well as the rescue trajectory for the Apollo 13 flight.

## Helaman Ferguson (1940–)

- Graduated from arts school in New York, then received a PhD in mathematics from the University of Washington in 1971.

- An American sculptor combining his love of mathematics and art.

- His most famous piece of work is his 8.5-metre-high sculpture of an umbilic torus, a single-edged three-dimensional shape.

- 'I celebrate mathematics with sculpture and sculpture with mathematics. Eons-old stone strikes me as a perfect medium through which to celebrate timeless mathematics' (Ferguson, n.d.).

These are just three examples with the potential to engage young people in a wider view of mathematics. Returning to the end-of-primary schooling data that we noted above, a gender gap opens up in the higher attainment band with the proportion of girls attaining the higher-level 5 percentage points below that of boys (DfE, 2019). It remains vital to ensure that girls hear about high-performing women who carry out mathematics with pride and enjoyment.

So far, we have considered family, teachers and wider cultural role models as influencing factors in forming ideas about mathematics and mathematicians. Before going any further, let's stop to consider your own perceptions of mathematics and how they have formed.

## REFLECTION

How has your own mathematical identity evolved? To what extent do you see yourself as a mathematician, or might you be positioning yourself as someone who sees mathematics as done by somebody else? Consider one or more of the following:

- Who do you think of when you think of a mathematician? Try to jot down three people without thinking for too long.
- Think back to 'doing maths' when you were at primary school. Where were you and what were you doing?
- What do you think of when visualising people carrying out mathematics in their everyday lives? Try to list two or three examples.
- What do you believe are the characteristics of a 'good mathematician' in your class or setting? Try to have someone in mind.

These questions are not designed with specific answers in mind. Instead, they may prompt you to reflect on your own formative mathematical experiences, as well as the impact they have on your practice and the messages you convey. When Picker and Berry (2000) asked children to draw a mathematician, for example, they found that images were male-dominated and chiefly comprised their own mathematics teachers, rather than anyone from family, friends or wider society. Did you find the same when reflecting on those who influenced you? The importance we established above of providing positive and inclusive role models for children means that it is vital you have a wide range of mathematical contexts and characteristics to draw upon. In addition to the pen portraits above, the STEMettes website (**https://stemettes.org/**) and Twitter page (**https://twitter.com/Stemettes**) provide a source of contemporary mathematicians in action.

## WHAT DO WE KNOW FROM RESEARCH?

### Self-concept and the case of mathematical picture books

Let's return to the premise established previously, that social and cultural stereotypes are highly influential in forming our ideas about our potential to be successful in the world of mathematics. Cvencek et al. (2011) used self-reporting measures to explore mathematics gender stereotypes, finding that the identification of girls with mathematics was weaker than for their male counterparts. They acknowledged the possibility of the developmental sequence 'me = girl, me ≠ math, therefore girls ≠ math', suggesting instead that the evidence pointed towards 'me = girl, girls ≠ math, therefore me ≠ math' (p775). In other words, the stereotype that mathematics is not for girls can be sufficiently strong to lead girls to the conclusion that they and mathematics do not go together, even where their level of mathematics attainment is high.

This is where we will turn to the work of Dr Natthapoj Trakulphadetkrai, founder of the Maths Through Stories initiative. Trakulphadetkrai (2017) carried out a pilot study exploring mathematical picture books and analysing the gender representations in titles, on front covers and in terms of the amount of dialogue they contained. His results were striking. For example, where titles contained names, these were over seven times more likely to be male than female; for books featuring images of one gender,

*(Continued)*

(Continued)

this was more than three times more likely to be male; and even where female characters were present, the proportion of dialogue they were assigned was significantly lower than that of males. This led him to question, 'if young girls are growing up subconsciously observing that mathematics is less associated with females, how might they see themselves in relation to mathematics?' (Trakulphadetkrai, 2017, p25). This then becomes a call to action, to ensure a wide range of representation not only in providing the kind of direct role models discussed above, but in ensuring that mathematics encountered by children through literature also includes 'people like me'.

## TRANSFORMING PRACTICE

Drawing on picture books provides a great way to help children associate with mathematics. Try titles such as *It's a Firefly Night* by Dianne Ochiltree, *The Dragon's Scales* by Sarah Albee or *The Lion's Share* by Matthew McElliggott as texts with a good gender balance or strong female leads. Think carefully before drawing upon series that are male-dominated, or in which females overcome a long-standing fear or hatred of mathematics (well-meaning, but not entirely helpful in terms of dispelling stereotypes).

# DEVELOPING PRACTICE

Before being able to transform practice, a good starting point is to establish children's beliefs about and attitudes towards mathematics. There are various strategies to do this; those picked out here avoid testing strategies in favour of more inclusive pupil voice approaches.

## Drawing

Asking children or young people to draw a mathematician can provide fascinating results and allow children to communicate in a fun and non-threatening way. Compare the drawings of children, asking them to explain their drawings, and compare any patterns in gender differences that emerge.

Alternatively, ask children to draw themselves doing mathematics and add a thought bubble to explain what they are thinking or feeling. Again, this provides a fascinating insight into patterns that may exist within your own class.

## Metaphor

Although you may not naturally associate metaphor with mathematics, it provides a great opportunity to really unpick the stereotypes that children may hold about the subject (see Özgün-Koca, 2010).

Use prompts such as 'If mathematics were a colour/animal/vehicle/type of weather/food/person, it would be ... because ...', and enjoy analysing the results!

## Photography

With the appropriate permissions and safeguards in place, ask children to take photographs of mathematics in action or people 'doing mathematics'. This technology allows researchers and educators to gain an insight into children's perspectives in new ways (Morgan, 2007), as well as providing an engaging opportunity for children to reveal their assumptions and beliefs. You can invite children to explain their photographs and get them talking about why they associate particular objects, places, activities or people with mathematics, both within school and their life beyond the classroom.

## Sharing impressions of mathematics

Earlier in the chapter, we saw a word cloud (Figure 7.1) providing insight into different impressions of mathematics. This is a straightforward yet powerful activity to carry out with children. Ask them to each write down up to three words that come to mind when they think of mathematics. Use these to create a word cloud using an online tool, which you can then use to prompt discussions to expose and challenge stereotypes around mathematics.

### ACTIVITY

Identify one of these strategies that is age-appropriate for the children you work with, or alternatively try it out with a group of colleagues. Involve your participants in looking at the results and see what patterns you can spot. What does it tell you about their assumptions about the nature of mathematics?

### EVIDENCE FROM PRACTICE

As we come towards the end of this chapter, let's use two brief case studies to consolidate what we have considered so far.

#### Choices and opportunities in the early years

Everyone working with children will know that every now and then, one of them says or does something that makes us stop and think. So it was when a four-and-a-half-year-old girl declared to her teacher, 'But I can't do that, I'm no good at maths'. How did such a young child come to that conclusion? Where were

*(Continued)*

(Continued)

the messages coming from? With the support of his leadership team, the teacher decided he needed to really look at what was happening under his nose. He embarked on a small-scale, low-key investigation: observing children during free play and the choices they made, talking to them and their parents, and asking teaching assistants to note what he said to children and how he spent his time. Table 7.3 summarises some of his observations, the conclusions he drew and the changes he made.

*Table 7.3    Investigating early gender differences*

| What was happening | Comments and analysis | Adjustments to practice |
| --- | --- | --- |
| Boys tended to receive praise for intelligence in maths – 'Well done, you counted all the numbers to 10 – clever boy' – whereas girls were praised for effort – 'You tried hard, better luck next time'. | The teacher realised that it would help all the children in the class to focus praise on progress and understanding, rather than intelligence or luck. | The teacher and teaching assistants supported each other to review their use of language in praise, as well as capturing moments for the children's learning journey that showed resilience and progress. |
| Both boys and girls engaged in maths-related creative activities (e.g. using geometric shapes to create rockets or butterflies), but boys were more likely to engage in construction play. | Children seemed to be sticking with what they knew well and responding to social norms developed out of the classroom. | The teacher reviewed the variety of contexts used for construction and small world play. Each time a new context was introduced, it was accompanied with photographs (e.g. male and female vets, doctors, engineers) or visitors from the profession who could bring the tools and applications to life. |
| Both boys and girls used mathematical ideas in their free play, but girls tended not to recognise this when asked to draw a picture or take a photograph of some maths. | This can lay the foundations for girls being less likely to believe in themselves as mathematicians, despite being perfectly capable. | The teacher put in place a 'We love maths' display featuring photographs of all children engaged in a wide range of activities. This was used once a day for a 'five-minute chat', when children were encouraged to talk about what they were doing and be proud of their mathematical achievements. |

## An intervention group

Analysis of end-of-year assessments and classroom observations revealed that something strange was happening in a mixed class of 10-year-olds. In previous assessments, the performance of girls and boys was fairly equal across all levels. However, in the last two years, the performance of the highest-attaining boys had overtaken that of girls. The girls were not speaking up in lessons, and often a misunderstanding was only revealed when their work was reviewed after the lesson. The teacher decided to get this group together and talk through with them what they felt was going on. From this, the following emerged:

- the girls felt intimidated in volunteering answers within whole-class discussions;
- some of the boys in their class always seemed to get to an answer faster than they could, so they had lost confidence in trying;
- they accepted mistakes as an indication that they weren't really very good at maths after all.

Working together, the teacher and group put together an action plan. They agreed:

- practice in the classroom would shift away from hands-up responses towards talk partners, so that children always had the opportunity to rehearse their responses;
- for some lessons, children would be regrouped to allow girls to sit together and receive targeted support and challenge;
- occasionally, the group would come together for pre-teaching so that they felt confident in the vocabulary of the lesson and their knowledge and skill base was strong.

These two contrasting case studies illustrate that in terms of challenging gender stereotypes in mathematics, there are no quick fixes. You will need to reflect on the steps these practitioners took. For example, does the approach of providing gender-specific support groups risk perpetuating the very stereotypes we are trying to avoid? Or is it an appropriate, pragmatic step taken to meet a need and support these girls to thrive in their mathematics lessons?

# CHAPTER SUMMARY

In this chapter, we have explored a variety of perspectives on gender stereotypes in mathematics education, including their origins and the roles of different people in challenging them. We need to:

- avoid perpetuating a misplaced assumption that one gender group is better at mathematics than another;
- provide positive role models, from real life and within literature or problem-solving contexts, that challenge stereotypes about mathematics and mathematicians;
- take time, as practitioners, to examine our own and children's beliefs about mathematics and themselves as mathematicians as a foundation for challenging assumptions;
- build all children's positive mathematics identity through inclusive approaches that foster self-efficacy.

# FURTHER READING

**McCormack, M.** (2014) Mathematics and gender. In D. Leslie and H. Mendick (eds), *Debates in Mathematics Education*. London: Routledge.

**Mendick, H., Moreau, M.-P. and Hollingworth, S.** (2008) *Mathematical Images and Gender Identities: A Report on the Gendering of Representation on Mathematics and Mathematicians in Popular Culture and Their Influences on Learners*. Bradford: UK Resource Centre for Women in Science, Engineering and Technology.

# REFERENCES

Albee, S. (1998) *The Dragon's Scales*. New York: Random House.

Allen, K. (2011) Mathematics as thinking: a response to 'democracy and school math'. *Democracy and Education*, 19(2). Available at: http://democracyeducationjournal.org/home/vol19/iss2/

Bandura, A. (1977) Self-efficacy: toward a unifying theory of behavioral change. *Psychological Review*, 84(2): 191–215.

Bishop, A. (1988) Mathematics education in its cultural context. *Educational Studies in Mathematics*, 19(2): 179–91.

Boaler, J. (2009) *The Elephant in the Classroom: Helping Children Learn and Love Maths*. London: Souvenir Press.

Boaler, J., Altendorff, L. and Kent, G. (2011) Mathematics and science inequalities in the United Kingdom: when elitism, sexism and culture collide. *Oxford Review of Education*, 37(4): 457–84.

Chmielewski, A., Dumont, H. and Trautwein, U. (2013) Tracking effects depend on tracking type: an international comparison of students' mathematics self-concept. *American Educational Research Journal*, 50(5): 925–57.

Cvencek, D., Mentzoff, A. and Greenwald, A. (2011) Math-gender stereotypes in elementary school children. *Child Development*, 82(3): 766–79.

Department for Education (DfE) (2019) *National Curriculum Assessments at KS2 in England, 2019 (Provisional)*. Available at: https://assets.publishing.service.gov.uk/government/uploads/system/uploads/attachment_data/file/830285/KS2_Provisional_publication_text_2019.pdf

Epstein, D., Mendick, H. and Moreau, M.-P. (2010) Imagining the mathematician: young people talking about popular representations of maths. *Discourse: Studies in the Cultural Politics of Education*, 31(1): 45–60.

Ferguson, H. (n.d.) *Celebrating Mathematics in Stone and Bronze*. Available at: https://helasculpt.com/?v=ba43077c0ac9

Foley, C., McNeill, J. and Suter, S. (2019) *Leading Primary Mathematics*. London: SAGE.

Gladstone, R., Häfner, I., Turci, L., Kneißler, H. and Muenks, K. (2018) Associations between parents and students' motivational beliefs in mathematics and mathematical performance: the role of gender. *Contemporary Educational Psychology*, 54: 221–34.

Grootenboer, P., Roley, J., Stewart, B. and Thorpe, P. (2002) Kids talking about their learning in mathematics. *Australian Primary Mathematics Classroom*, 7(4): 16–21.

Herbert, J. and Stipek, D. (2005) The emergence of gender differences in children's perceptions of their academic competence. *Applied Developmental Psychology*, 26: 276–95.

Kilpatrick, J., Swafford, J. and Findell, B. (eds) (2001) *Adding It Up: Helping Children Learn Mathematics*. Washington, DC: National Academy Press.

Klein, P.S., Adi-Japha, E. and Hakak-Benizri, S. (2010) Mathematical thinking of kindergarten boys and girls: similar achievement, different contributing processes. *Educational Studies in Mathematics*, 73: 233–45.

Leder, G. (2007) Mathematics performance. In B. Bank (ed.), *Gender and Education: An Encyclopedia*. Available at: http://search.credoreference.com.idpproxy.reading.ac.uk/content/entry/abcge/mathematics_performance/0

Lubienski, S., Robinson, J., Crane, C. and Ganley, C. (2013) Girls' and boys' mathematics achievement, affect, and experiences: findings from ECLS-K. *Journal for Research in Mathematics Education*, 44(4): 634–45.

Maloney, E., Ramirez, G., Gunderson, E., Levine, S. and Beilock, S. (2015) Intergenerational effects of parents' math anxiety on children's math achievement and anxiety. *Psychological Science*, 26(9): 1480–8.

Mann, E. (2008) Parental perceptions of mathematical talent. *Social Psychology of Education*, 11(1): 43–57.

Martinot, D. and Désert, M. (2007) Awareness of a gender stereotype, personal beliefs and self-perceptions regarding math ability: when boys do not surpass girls. *Social Psychology of Education*, 10(4): 455–71.

McCormack, M. (2014) Mathematics and gender. In D. Leslie and H. Mendick (eds), *Debates in Mathematics Education*. London: Routledge.

McElligott, M. (2009). *The Lion's Share: A Tale of Halving Cake and Eating It, Too*. New York: Walker & Company.

Morgan, A. (2007) Using video-stimulated recall to understand young children's perceptions of learning in classroom settings. *European Early Childhood Education Research Journal*, 15(2): 213–26.

Ochiltree, D. (2018) *It's a Firefly Night*. Maplewood, NJ: Blue Apple Books.

Organisation for Economic Co-operation and Development (OECD) (2014) *PISA 2012 Results in Focus: What 15-Year-Olds Know and What They Can Do with What They Know*. Available at: www.oecd.org/pisa/keyfindings/pisa-2012-results-overview.pdf

Özgün-Koca, S. (2010) If mathematics were a color. *Ohio Journal of School Mathematics*, 62: 5–10.

Picker, S. and Berry, J. (2000) Investigating pupils' images of mathematicians. *Educational Studies in Mathematics*, 43(1): 65–94.

Sheldrake, R., Mujaba, T. and Reiss, M. (2015) Students' intentions to study non-compulsory mathematics: the importance of how good you think you are. *British Educational Research Journal*, 41(3): 462–88.

Stemhagen, K. (2011) Democracy and school math: teacher belief–practice tensions and the problem of empirical research on educational aims. *Democracy and Education*, 19(2). Available at: http://democracyeducationjournal.org/home/vol19/iss2/4/

*The Guardian* (2014) *Maryam Mirzakhani: 'The More I Spent Time on Maths, the More Excited I Got'*. Available at: www.theguardian.com/science/2014/aug/13/interview-maryam-mirzakhani-fields-medal-winner-mathematician

Trakulphadetkrai, N. (2017) Where are the girls and women in mathematical picture books? *Mathematics Teaching*, 258: 23–5.

Walls, F. (2003) *Sociomathematical Worlds: Investigating Children's Developing Relationships with Mathematics*. Available at: www.merga.net.au/documents/RR_walls.pdf

# 8

# THE HISTORY CURRICULUM IN PRIMARY AND SECONDARY SCHOOLS AND THE REPRESENTATION OF GENDER

## REBECCA HARRIS

## KEYWORDS

- **HISTORY EDUCATION**
- **WOMEN**
- **GENDER**

- **CURRICULUM**
- **CURRICULUM PLANNING**
- **STEREOTYPES**

- **DIVERSITY**

## THIS CHAPTER

- explores issues around the construction of history curricula, particularly what is taught;

*(Continued)*

> (Continued)
>
> • focuses on how existing curricula and school planning inadequately addresses the role, status and experience of women in the past;
> • explains some key principles that should inform planning of a more diverse curriculum which examines the range of experiences of women in the past.

# INTRODUCTION

This chapter starts by looking at curriculum planning in history, particularly what should be taught, and highlights some key issues that we need to consider in this process. We will discuss the impact that curriculum content choices can have on how young people view the past and the world in which they live, and therefore why it is important for us to ensure that the history curriculum engages with a diversity of people's experiences. By looking at government curriculum documents and school schemes of work, we will see the extent to which gender diversity in history is taught in schools. This chapter will look at examples of approaches to making gender diversity an integral part of what we cover about the past, as well as some of the challenges that we need to consider.

# THE CHALLENGES OF CURRICULUM PLANNING: WHAT TO INCLUDE?

Converting any subject into a curriculum suitable for schools is an intriguing and challenging task. This requires us to think about 'what to teach', 'how we teach it' and 'why we teach it'. Each question reveals a layer of complexity, and many of the issues to consider are interlinked; however, for the sake of this chapter, we will focus largely on the question of 'what to teach'.

'What to teach' is a deceptively simple question. In some subject areas, this is dictated by how knowledge structures work (e.g. in mathematics, knowledge is 'hierarchical'). This means that some things need to be studied before other things; thus, young children have to learn to count before they can tackle addition and subtraction – this can make it easier in some respects to plan a curriculum that supports children's and young people's progression. However, in other subject areas, knowledge structures are 'cumulative', which means there is no particular order in which things should be studied. History is an example of this, as children and young people can start anywhere and move backwards and forwards through time, learning about different periods and topics, ideally building up a more sophisticated 'map' of the past as they learn more.

Consequently, subjects such as mathematics have relatively stable areas of curricula content to be covered – looking at curricula in different educational contexts shows a general consensus about what ought to be taught in maths. Where maths curricula tend to differ is in approaches to teaching, as educators try to find the most effective and appropriate ways to teach mathematical concepts. However, decisions about what to teach in subjects such as history are more complex. This is not only because historical knowledge is cumulative, but because there is a vast amount of history to choose from, and the work of historians keeps refreshing how we understand the past! It would be impossible to teach children and young people about the entirety of history in any feasible breadth, let alone depth. Consequently, the choices we make are often dictated by a combination of our prior experiences, areas of content with which we feel confident and familiar, and what we perceive to be considered important (either in government documents or our personal perspectives).

## REFLECTION

- What historical topics do you teach?
- Why do you teach these topics?
- What 'cumulative' picture of the past will your pupils build by studying these topics?
- To what extent are your pupils aware of the 'cumulative' picture you want them to construct?

To an extent, this is where the question 'why we teach it' can inform what we choose to teach. If, as some argue, history is about developing a sense of identity, then that can dictate what should be studied; however, this can become controversial if it is decided that history should promote some form of national identity or favour some specific group, so particular events are embraced while others are overlooked. It is for reasons such as this that deciding what to teach in a subject like history can become incredibly politicised.

Essentially, a history curriculum is something that we construct, so decisions about what we include and (perhaps more importantly) what we exclude are highly significant. Excluding certain events and experiences can serve to marginalise and silence particular groups and present a message that their place in the past is less worthy of study, thereby implying that their presence and contribution in the present are also deemed less worthy. This is one issue that we need to keep in mind as we look at how we might piece together a history curriculum.

Alongside this is the complex question of what constitutes an acceptable level of simplification in history. We cannot teach highly complex concepts to younger children, nor can we teach all topics in depth to develop more sophisticated insights to older children. This means that at some point, we have to teach a simplified view of the past. Also, if history is purely taught chronologically, students are most likely to encounter a topic or event only once; therefore, if our students only study the Norman conquest when aged 11, they are likely to have an 11-year-old's understanding of the topic. The question of simplifying history and whether pupils revisit any topics means there is a concern that we unwittingly create or reinforce stereotypes about people and events in the past in young people's minds. This is the second issue we should consider when planning a history curriculum.

## WHAT DO WE KNOW FROM RESEARCH?

### How women are represented in the history curriculum

There is surprisingly little research into the way women are portrayed and included in the history curriculum in the UK, as well as what impact this has on how children and young people understand women's role and status in the past.

However, studies in the US (e.g. Chick, 2006; Engebretson, 2014; Williams and Bennett, 2016) all present a similar picture, namely a disproportionate over-representation of men in history textbooks. Although these authors acknowledge that history textbooks in the US are increasingly including more females in their materials, women are still less likely to appear, and where they do, they are overwhelmingly involved in stereotypical female activities. The reason for this appears to be a strong focus on teaching political and military history, which largely involved male actors in the past, so this means that women are by default marginalised within textbook representations of the past. The consequence of this is that 'students can then read the absence of women as an element of the null curriculum that is not relevant or valued in the formal space of school' (Engebretson, 2014, p30).

These studies, however, do not give us any insight into how this affects children's views of women. The closest research that offers us a way to understand the impact on children of a curriculum that excludes elements of society is research into how minority ethnic students engage with history. Various studies in the US and UK (e.g. Epstein, 2009; Harris and Reynolds, 2014; Wilkinson, 2014) show similar outcomes – where students are unable to see themselves represented in the past or are only represented as victims of events, they fail to engage with the subject and can develop a sense of hostility and hurt. This is because the curriculum is overwhelmingly 'white'. As one girl interviewed in the study by Harris and Reynolds (2014) said, 'you talk about British history and British history and British history, they don't talk about like us ... it's like there's no black people in the history, they're always talking about ... what the white people did in history' (p481).

This is largely because the majority group in the UK is 'white', and this provides the dominant default perspective for looking at events in the past. It takes extra effort for someone from the majority group to step outside of their world view and adopt a different perspective. It means that we all have to consciously consider the diversity of the past. In some ways, this should not be surprising – current society is inherently diverse and the past was inherently diverse, so this ought to be reflected in the content we choose to teach in history (more of this later).

If we examine the history curriculum in the UK from a gendered perspective, we start to see that there are similar issues to those experienced by minority ethnic groups. Generally speaking, the role and place of women in the past is marginalised.

An examination of the content of the history national curriculum in England helps us to see this. A glance at Table 8.1 shows that there have been more named historical male figures in all iterations of the history national curriculum since 1991, although those in italics are only mentioned as possible examples for study. The list highlights how little prescription there is regarding content; only the 1991 and 1995 versions had named individuals that had to be studied. The large degree of repetition in the names included also indicates how little the history curriculum has actually changed over the years. However, the preponderance of males (who are overwhelmingly political and military leaders), explorers and inventors gives a clear flavour as to the focus of much of the content contained within the curriculum. The choice of so many political and military leaders suggests a curriculum that focuses more on studying individual events, rather than following the flow of specific themes through time.

Table 8.1 *Named historical females and males in the history national curriculum, 1991–2014 (names in italics are suggestions for study rather than requirements)*

| 1991 | Named women | Named men | |
|---|---|---|---|
| Key Stage 1 | Boudicca | Alfred the Great<br>Isaac Newton<br>Francis Drake<br>Walter Raleigh<br>William Shakespeare | |
| Key Stage 2 | | Christopher Columbus<br>Montezuma<br>Cortes<br>Emperor Augustus<br>Emperor Constantine | |
| Key Stage 3 | | Hitler<br>Churchill<br>Stalin<br>Roosevelt | |
| **1995** | **Named women** | **Named men** | |
| Key Stage 1 | *Boudicca* | *Alfred the Great* | |
| Key Stage 2 | *Elizabeth I*<br>*Florence Nightingale*<br>*Victoria* | *Henry VIII*<br>*Sebastian and John Cabot*<br>*Francis Drake*<br>*Walter Raleigh*<br>*Thomas More*<br>*Earl of Essex* | *William Shakespeare*<br>*Robert Stephenson*<br>*Isambard Kingdom Brunel*<br>*Lord Shaftesbury*<br>*Alexander the Great* |
| Key Stage 3 | | *Thomas Becket*<br>*Henry II*<br>*Richard I*<br>*King John*<br>*Edward I*<br>*Edward III*<br>*Henry V*<br>*Henry VI*<br>*Oliver Cromwell*<br>*Nelson* | *Wellington*<br>*Peel*<br>*Gladstone*<br>*Disraeli*<br>*Churchill*<br>*Hitler*<br>*Stalin*<br>*Mussolini*<br>*Roosevelt*<br>*Gandhi* |

*(Continued)*

*Table 8.1  (Continued)*

| 2000 | Named women | Named men | |
|---|---|---|---|
| Key Stage 1 | *Boudicca* <br> *Hilda* | *Caratacus* <br> *Bede* <br> *Alfred the Great* <br> *King Cnut* | |
| Key Stage 2 | *Elizabeth I* <br> *Mary, Queen of Scots* <br> *Elizabeth Fry* <br> *Victoria* <br> *Florence Nightingale* <br> *Mary Seacole* <br> *Mary Kingsley* <br> *Amy Johnson* | *Henry VIII* <br> *Thomas More* <br> *Francis Drake* <br> *Sebastian and John Cabot* <br> *Walter Raleigh* <br> *Thomas More* <br> *Earl of Essex* <br> *William Shakespeare* <br> *Lord Shaftesbury* <br> *Robert Owen* <br> *Prince Albert* | *Robert Stephenson* <br> *Isambard Kingdom Brunel* <br> *David Livingstone* <br> *Alexander Graham Bell* <br> *John Logie Baird* <br> *Alec Issigonis* <br> *Frank Whittle* <br> *Pheidippides* <br> *Pericles* <br> *Philip of Macedon* <br> *Alexander the Great* |
| Key Stage 3 | *Matilda* <br> *Joan of Arc* <br> *Mary II* <br> *Queen Anne* <br> *Mary Somerville* <br> *Jane Austen* <br> *George Eliot* <br> *Victoria* <br> *Elizabeth Garret* <br> *Christabel and Emmeline Pankhurst* <br> *Rosalind Franklin* | *King Stephen* <br> *Henry II* <br> *Thomas Becket* <br> *Richard I* <br> *Salah-ad-Din* <br> *King John* <br> *Edward I* <br> *Edward III* <br> *Henry V* <br> *Henry VI* <br> *Geoffrey Chaucer* <br> *Charles I* <br> *Oliver Cromwell* <br> *Charles II* <br> *William III* <br> *William Harvey* <br> *Isaac Newton* <br> *Robert Boyle* <br> *Edmund Halley* <br> *Nelson* <br> *Wellington* | *Charles Darwin* <br> *William Hogarth* <br> *JMW Turner* <br> *Charles Dickens* <br> *Gustav Holst* <br> *Henry Wood* <br> *William Gilbert and Arthur Sullivan* <br> *William Wilberforce* <br> *Olaudah Equiano* <br> *Robert Peel* <br> *William Gladstone* <br> *Benjamin Disraeli* <br> *John Howard* <br> *Churchill* <br> *Hitler* <br> *Stalin* <br> *Mussolini* <br> *Roosevelt* <br> *Gandhi* <br> *Mao Zedong* |

| | Named women | Named men | |
|---|---|---|---|
| | | Edward Jenner | Martin Luther King |
| | | Humphrey Davy | Albert Einstein |
| | | James Watt | James Watson |
| | | Michael Faraday | Francis Crick |
| | | | Maurice Wilkins |
| **2008 (Note: This only affected Key Stage 3)** | **Named women** | **Named men** | |
| Key Stage 3 | | Olaudah Equiano | |
| | | William Wilberforce | |
| **2014** | **Named women** | **Named men** | |
| Key Stage 1 | Elizabeth I | Christopher Columbus | |
| | Victoria | Neil Armstrong | |
| | Rosa Parks | William Caxton | |
| | Emily Davison | Tim Berners-Lee | |
| | Mary Seacole | Pieter Bruegel the Elder | |
| | Florence Nightingale | LS Lowry | |
| | Edith Cavell | | |
| Key Stage 2 | Boudicca | Julius Caesar | |
| | Queen Anne | Claudius | |
| | Victoria | Alfred the Great | |
| | | Edward the Confessor | |
| | | King John | |
| Key Stage 3 | Mary I | Henry VIII | |
| | | Oliver Cromwell | |
| | | Charles Darwin | |
| | | Churchill | |

Table 8.2 looks at the various versions of the history national curriculum in another way. It lists all the core study units, which reflect the topics and periods expected to be covered, and alongside this are some of the specific content strands that should be studied as part of the unit. These strands have been identified because they either explicitly mention women or the area of study could conceivably include the lives of women quite readily. The content highlighted in this table is generally linked to domestic and working lives; the content is essentially descriptive, looking at what lives were like and how they changed. This tends to position women as essentially passive participants in the past, who are not active agents in shaping what has happened. Interestingly, this is a particular characteristic of the primary school curriculum (Key Stages 1 and 2), while the two most recent versions of the national curriculum in 2008 and 2014 appear to offer less obvious requirements to include women as part of history.

*Table 8.2   Named periods/topics that could include the role of women in the past in the history national curriculum, 1991–2014*

| | 1991 history national curriculum | |
|---|---|---|
| | **Core study units** | **Reference to general content that explicitly or implicitly includes the lives of women** |
| Key Stage 1 | | Changes in their own lives and those of their family or adults around them |
| | | Changes in the way of life of British people since the Second World War |
| | | The way of life in a period of the past beyond living memory |
| | | Pupils should be taught about the lives of different kinds of famous men and women |
| Key Stage 2 | Invaders and settlers: Romans, Anglo-Saxons and Vikings in Britain | Way of life of the settlers: everyday life in town and country; houses and home life |
| | Tudor and Stuart times | Rulers and court life: Tudor and Stuart rulers |
| | | People in town and country: the way of life of different groups in town and country |
| | Victorian Britain | Domestic life: Victorian families; houses and home life; leisure and pastimes |
| | Britain since 1930 | Social changes: changes in the role of men and women in family life |
| | | Cultural changes: popular culture, including fashion, music and sport |
| | Ancient Greece | Everyday life: the lives of men, women and children |
| | Explorations and encounters 1450-1550 | Aztec civilisation: the Aztec way of life |
| Key Stage 3 | The Roman Empire | Roman society: ways of life in Rome and the provinces; family and society |
| | Medieval realms: Britain 1066-1500 | Medieval society: how material needs were met - farming, crafts, trade; health and disease, including the Black Death and its impact |
| | The Making of the UK: crowns, Parliaments and peoples 1500-1750 | The diversity of British society: social classes in early modern Britain; regional differences in wealth, lifestyle, religion and culture |

| | Expansion, trade and industry: Britain 1750-1900 | Social and economic change in Britain: the impact of economic change on families and communities, working and living conditions, and the size and distribution of Britain's population |
|---|---|---|
| | | Britain's world-wide expansion: the expansion of the Empire and its impact on the economy and way of life of British people |
| | | The political development of Britain: popular protest movements |
| | The era of the Second World War | The experience of war: the home front in Britain |
| **1995 history national curriculum** | | |
| | **Core study units** | **Reference to general content that explicitly or implicitly includes the lives of women** |
| Key Stage 1 | | Changes in their own lives and those of their family or adults around them |
| | | Aspects of the way of life of people in Britain in the past beyond living memory |
| | | Pupils should be taught about the lives of different kinds of famous men and women, including personalities drawn from British history |
| Key Stage 2 | Romans, Anglo-Saxons and Vikings in Britain | Everyday life, *e.g. houses and home life, work, religion* |
| | Life in Tudor times | Ways of life in town and country, *e.g. home life, work and leisure, health and trade* |
| | Victorian Britain OR Britain since 1930 | Steam power, factories and mass production, *e.g. economic growth and the provision of jobs for men and women, the impact of mass production on living and working conditions* |
| | | At work, *e.g. factory life, domestic service, workhouses*; at home, *e.g. family life at different levels of society*; at leisure; at school |
| | | OR |
| | | The impact of the Second World War on the people of Britain |
| | | At home, *e.g. family life at different levels of society, housing conditions, changes in the roles of men and women*; at work, *e.g. men and women at work*; at leisure |

*(Continued)*

Table 8.2   (Continued)

| | 1995 history national curriculum | |
|---|---|---|
| | **Core study units** | **Reference to general content that explicitly or implicitly includes the lives of women** |
| | Ancient Greece | Athens and Sparta, *e.g. everyday life* |
| | | Myths and legends of Greek gods and goddesses, heroes and heroines |
| | Local history | |
| | A past non-European society | Key features, including the everyday lives of men and women |
| Key Stage 3 | Medieval realms: Britain 1066–1500 | The structure of medieval society, including the role of the Church, *e.g. farming, crafts, towns and trade* |
| | | Health and disease, including the Black Death |
| | The making of the United Kingdom: crowns, parliaments and peoples 1500–1750 | Changes in town and countryside, and differences in wealth, lifestyle and culture, *e.g. different groups in society, the changing role of women, trade and the impact of overseas expansion, poverty and Poor Laws, Restoration London* |
| | Britain 1750–*c.*1900 | Industrial change and its impact on the way of life of people at different levels of society |
| | | The extension of the franchise; popular protest and reform |
| | The twentieth-century world | *The changing role and status of women* |
| | | *The extension of the franchise in Britain* |
| | 2000 history national curriculum | |
| | **Core study units** | **Reference to general content that explicitly or implicitly includes the lives of women** |
| Key Stage 1 | | Changes in their own lives and the way of life of their family or others around them |
| | | The way of life of people in the more distant past who lived in the local area or elsewhere in Britain |
| | | The lives of significant men, women and children drawn from the history of Britain and the wider world |
| Key Stage 2 | Local history study | |

| | Romans, Anglo-Saxons and Vikings on Britain | |
|---|---|---|
| | Britain and the wider world in Tudor times | A study of some significant events and individuals, including Tudor monarchs, who shaped this period and of the everyday lives of men, women and children from different sections of society |
| | Victorian Britain OR Britain since 1930 | A study of the impact of significant individuals, events and changes in work and transport on the lives of men, women and children from different sections of society<br><br>OR<br><br>A study of the impact of the Second World War or social and technological changes that have taken place since 1930, on the lives of men, women and children from different sections of society |
| | A European history study: Ancient Greece | A study of the way of life, beliefs and achievements of the people living in Ancient Greece |
| | A world history study | |
| Key Stage 3 | Britain 1066-1500 | Characteristic features of the lives of people living throughout the British Isles |
| | Britain 1500-1750 | The major political, religious and social changes affecting people throughout the British Isles<br><br>*The changing role of women* |
| | Britain 1750-1900 | |
| | A European study before 1914 | |
| | A world study before 1900 | |
| | A world study after 1900 | |
| | **2008 history national curriculum (*Note:* This only affected Key Stage 3)** | |
| | **Core study units** | **Reference to general content that explicitly or implicitly includes the lives of women** |
| | The development of political power from the Middle Ages to the twentieth century ... | |

*(Continued)*

*Table 8.2* (*Continued*)

| | 2008 history national curriculum (*Note*: This only affected Key Stage 3) | |
|---|---|---|
| | **Core study units** | **Reference to general content that explicitly or implicitly includes the lives of women** |
| | The different histories and changing relationships through time of the peoples of England, Ireland, Scotland and Wales | |
| | The impact through time of the movement and settlement of diverse peoples to, from and within the British Isles | |
| | The way in which the lives, beliefs, ideas and attitudes of people in Britain have changed over time and the factors ... that have driven these changes | *This includes studying the lives, beliefs, ideas and attitudes of ordinary people at various points in the past, how these have changed over time ...* |
| | The development of trade, colonisation, industrialisation and technology, the British Empire and its impact on different people in Britain ... | |
| | The impact of significant political, social, cultural, religious, technological and/ or economic developments and events on past European and world societies | |
| | The changing nature of conflict and cooperation between countries and peoples and its lasting impact ... | |
| | **2014 history national curriculum** | |
| | **Core study units** | **Reference to general content that explicitly or implicitly includes the lives of women** |
| Key Stage 1 | Changes within living memory | |
| | Events beyond living memory that are significant nationally or globally | |

| | | |
|---|---|---|
| | The lives of significant individuals in the past who have contributed to national and international achievements | |
| | Significant historical events, people and places in their own locality | |
| Kay Stage 2 | Changes in Britain from the Stone Age to the Iron Age | |
| | The Roman Empire and its impact on Britain | |
| | Britain's settlement by Anglo-Saxons and Scots | |
| | The Viking and Anglo-Saxon struggle for the Kingdom of England to the time of Edward the Confessor | Village life |
| | A local history study | |
| | A study of an aspect or theme in British history that extends pupils' chronological knowledge beyond 1066 | |
| | The achievements of the earliest civilisations | |
| | Ancient Greece | A study of Greek life and achievements |
| | A non-European society that provides contrasts | |
| Key Stage 3 | The development of Church, state and society in medieval Britain 1066-1509 | *Society, economy and culture: for example, feudalism, religion in daily life (parishes, monasteries, abbeys), farming, trade and towns (especially the wool trade), art, architecture and literature* |
| | The development of Church, state and society in Britain 1509-1745 | *Society, economy and culture across the period: for example, work and leisure in town and country, religion and superstition in daily life, theatre, art, music and literature* |

*(Continued)*

*Table 8.2   (Continued)*

| | 2014 history national curriculum | |
|---|---|---|
| | **Core study units** | **Reference to general content that explicitly or implicitly includes the lives of women** |
| | Ideas, political power, industry and empire: Britain, 1745-1901 | *Britain as the first industrial nation - the impact on society* |
| | Challenges for Britain, Europe and the wider world 1901 to the present day | *Social, cultural and technological change in post-war British society* |
| | A local history study | |
| | The study of an aspect or theme in British history that consolidates and extends pupils' chronological knowledge from before 1066 | |
| | At least one study of a significant society or issue in world history and its interconnections with other world developments | |

Note: The names in italics were suggested individuals; those in non-italicised font were expected to be taught.

In some ways, the material presented here offers a different way of conceptualising the curriculum compared to that in Table 8.1. As mentioned, the material in Table 8.1 would lend itself to an 'event-based' curriculum that would focus on a series of seemingly significant episodes in the past. For example, in the Key Stage 3 topic about medieval Britain, this might typically consist of the Battle of Hastings in 1066, the murder of Thomas Becket in 1170, the Magna Carta in 1215, the outbreak of the Black Death in 1348, and the Peasants' Revolt of 1381. The material in Table 8.2 would suggest a more thematic approach to studying the past. From this, we can see that the way we piece together the curriculum, as either a series of largely political/military events or a range of themes through time that focus more on change and continuity in people's lives, will affect how we understand the history of women.

## EVIDENCE FROM PRACTICE

It is up to schools how they interpret the history national curriculum, but yet again there is little research into the decisions that schools make. However, drawing on some history schemes of work I had analysed for another project, I was able to explore how ten secondary schools had included women's history into their teaching. One school, which happened to be a girls' school, had two lessons on women in Roman times, nothing for the Saxon and Norman periods, four lessons within the Tudor era (all focused on queens in the period), two lessons on suffragettes, mentions of the role of women in the

First World War and Nazi Germany, and a lesson on Rosa Parks. So, over a three-year period, this school explicitly included a focus on women in the past in 11 lessons. Only one other school in this sample actually had more lessons about women in history, but this was mainly because they set aside six lessons to look at changes in women's rights from 1750 to 1928. Looking at all the schools for which I had schemes of work, it was possible to distinguish some common areas. They all studied Mary I and Elizabeth I as well as the suffrage movement. Otherwise, women seem largely absent from history. If women appear elsewhere in lessons, it is often as victims (e.g. witches, victims of Jack the Ripper) or passive agents (e.g. women with few rights in Roman times, nuns, objects of Nazi family policy). Men are generally presented as active agents in the past, shaping what happens. What is clear is that these schools largely approach the construction of their history curriculum chronologically and focus more on particular political, religious and military events; this leads to a more episodic approach to teaching history, with little attention paid to the range of experiences of people in the past.

Reflecting on general issues to do with curriculum planning in history, what is included in national curriculum guidance and what we know from what is taught in schools, we can deduce that:

- the history of women is largely marginalised within national curriculum guidance and in what schools teach;

- schools generally construct their history curriculum around major events taught chronologically, rather than thematically;

- where women are represented, they appear in generally simplified, stereotypical roles.

## REFLECTION

- Where in your curriculum do you examine gender roles, status and experiences as part of the history you teach?
- To what extent do you feel your approach to teaching about the past might create or reinforce gender stereotypes of women and men?
- To what extent does your choice of content focus on major events as opposed to themes that run through history?
- To what extent does your choice of content focus on major political and/or military events as opposed to social issues?

One way to address several of the issues raised, namely the marginalisation of women's roles and experiences, the oversimplification of the past (with the creation of stereotypes), and a disconnected, episodic view of the past is to construct a history curriculum around the idea of diversity. This would conceivably create a curriculum that:

- is based on providing opportunities to explore the diversity of experience of a range of individuals and groups;

- is focused on a more thematic approach or one that emphasises change and continuity in the past;

- avoids creating or reinforcing stereotypes by showing the complexity of experiences in the past.

## TRANSFORMING PRACTICE

Christine Counsell (2004) provides an interesting example of how to bring women's history effectively into a unit of work on medieval history. Although originally presented as a means of engaging pupils with the work of historians and getting those pupils to read and understand how historians construct and present arguments, there is a whole range of interesting issues being addressed in this example.

The text used is from Eileen Power's *Medieval Women* (Power, 1997, pp73-4). Counsell gets pupils to explore the language used to understand how Power makes us understand her perspective - by initially reading the text aloud to the class, students can come to appreciate the puzzled, cautious tone being adopted about a seemingly insignificant issue (whether French and Latin were taught by nuns), which then turns into a mocking tone about how later historians have embellished what is taught:

*Students of human nature cannot but smile to see music creep into the list and become both instrumental and vocal. Confectionery extends itself to include perfumes, balsams, simples and sweetmeats; arithmetic appears out of nowhere, and even dancing trips in on light fantastic toe. In Sir Thomas Malory's stories about King Arthur there is a passage where it is said of Arthur's fairy sister, who bewitched Merlin, that 'she was put to school in a nunnery and there she learned so much that she was a great clerk of necromancy'. This would add black magic to the curriculum of nunnery schools!*

Finally, the text returns to the evidential record and what can be meaningfully inferred from the source material:

*The sober fact is we have no evidence about what was taught except inferences from what we know of the education of nuns themselves. Latin could not have been taught in the fourteenth century or French in the fifteenth century since nuns themselves did not know these languages in those times. Children were doubtless taught the Credo, the Ave and the Paternoster by rote, and must have been taught to read, although it is more doubtful whether they learned to write. Probably, they learned songs with the nuns, and spinning and needlework. Beyond these accomplishments, nuns doubtless taught piety and good breeding; and the standard of these, though good in some houses, could not have been very high in others, judging from the visitation reports.*

This exercise introduces students to the work of a female historian, looking at women in the medieval period, examines how language is used, and looks at how sources are used as the basis for making informed inferences about the past.

A subsequent activity requires pupils to create their own piece of writing, drawing on the stylistic features of Power. The activity is focused on the working lives of medieval peasant women - the pupils are given a range of sources and pieces of information, and have to construct an account of these women's lives based on the evidential base. Pupils are then able to compare what they have written to Eileen Power's own version.

One of the issues in studying women's history is a perceived lack of source material in comparison to other areas of historical study. The example above, drawing on Eileen Power's work, provides a good way in which the lives of women could be drawn naturally into the history curriculum – using the work of a historian and making a virtue of the relative absence of source material as a means to determine what it is possible to say about women's lived experiences.

We can also see how this example could be placed within a wider study of people's experiences in the medieval period, as well as drawing on examples of lives from different points and/or places in the medieval period and experiences of those from different social classes. Equally, it could be part of a longer-term study on change and continuity in the lives of women. These approaches would allow children and young people to appreciate a greater diversity of past experiences.

## TRANSFORMING PRACTICE

Another way to explore diversity within the curriculum and address concerns about oversimplification of the past is to start with identifying pupils' preconceptions or stereotypes. For example, pupils could be asked to create a spider diagram of what they believe women's roles and experiences of a particular period to be (e.g. the First World War). Drawing together all these ideas can then be the basis for an enquiry question. I find that using the word 'typical' is a good way to explore diversity. For example, 'To what extent is it possible to say there was a typical experience for women in the First World War?' or, 'How typical was the experience of ... in the First World War?'

Pupils could then be given information relating to, or asked to research, particular individuals, or a range of sources relating to women's wartime experiences. Examples could include Helen Johns Kirtland, an American wartime photojournalist, Vera Brittain, whose work as a nurse during the war led to her active role in pacifism following the war, or other intriguing characters, such as Flora Sandes and Maria Bochkareva. Sandes was initially a British volunteer nurse in Serbia, but eventually joined the ranks of the Serbian army as a private soldier in 1915, and was subsequently promoted to officer rank. She therefore served in the Serbian army and led male soldiers into action. Bochkareva joined the Russian army in 1915, and like Sandes was promoted and led male troops into battle. In 1917, she was in part responsible for the creation of the 1st Russian Battalion of Death, an all-female army unit.

This approach has the benefit of starting with children and young people's existing views of the past. The degree of knowledge or sophistication they possess does not really matter as the activity allows new knowledge and insights to be provided for everyone. We also know that many pupils find stories engaging and easier to relate to. The activity also means we are allowing the pupils to work things out for themselves, initially through engaging with the material (as either information sheets or as a research activity), followed up by good-quality discussion. Students will most probably recognise that the individuals are not 'typical', but will be more aware of issues about what might be construed as 'typical' and 'stereotypical'.

---

## REFLECTION

- How well do you think these examples address the issues highlighted previously about incorporating gender into your history curriculum?
- What other approaches are you aware of and/or are able to devise that you feel would also address the issues highlighted?
- What do you see as the benefits and challenges of adopting such approaches in your curriculum planning and teaching?

---

Constructing a more diverse curriculum requires us to be knowledgeable about different aspects of the past. This is challenging as none of us are experts in all areas of the past.

However, it is clearly absurd that the role of women in the past is neglected as much as it is in the school curriculum, and it is really a reflection of the overwhelmingly paternalistic nature of society. Yet incorporating women's history into the curriculum does require a conscious effort on the part of many of us.

## CHAPTER SUMMARY

We need to be:

- aware of the need to ensure the curriculum is reflective of the diversity of society and the range of experiences of people in the past – content choices matter (excluding experiences of groups can lead to them being marginalised);

- aware of how to plan a curriculum to reflect this diversity that also allows children and young people to see the complexity of the past and become aware of what might be considered 'typical' and/or 'stereotypical';

- knowledgeable about the roles, status and experiences of women in the past – a curriculum can only be as diverse as the knowledge of the person who creates it.

## FURTHER READING

**Boyd, S.** (2019) From 'great women' to an inclusive curriculum: how should women's history be included at Key Stage 3? *Teaching History*, 175: 16–23.

**Wilson, F.** (2012) Warrior queens, regal trade unionists and warring nurses: how my interest in what I don't teach has informed my teaching and enriched my students' learning. *Teaching History*, 146: 52–9.

# REFERENCES

Chick, K.A. (2006) Gender balance in K–12 American history textbooks. *Social Studies Research and Practice*, 1(3): 284–90.

Counsell, C. (2004) *History and Literacy in Y7*. London: Hodder & Stoughton.

Engebretson, K.E. (2014) Another missed opportunity: gender in the national curriculum standards for social studies. *Social Studies Research and Practice*, 9(3): 21–34.

Epstein, T. (2009) *Interpreting National History*. New York: Routledge.

Harris, R. and Reynolds, R. (2014) The history curriculum and its personal connection to students from minority ethnic backgrounds. *Journal of Curriculum Studies*, 46(4): 464–86.

Power, E. (1997) *Medieval Women*. Cambridge: Cambridge University Press.

Wilkinson, M. (2014) The concept of the absent curriculum: the case of the Muslim contribution and the English national curriculum for history. *Journal of Curriculum Studies*, 46(4): 419–40.

Williams, F.J. and Bennett, L.B. (2016) The progressive era: how American textbooks' visuals represent women. *Social Studies Research and Practice*, 11(1): 124–35.

# 9

# WOMEN IN COMPUTING

## YOTA DIMITRIADI

## KEYWORDS

- **COMPUTING**
- **COMPUTER SCIENCE**
- **IT**
- **TECHNOLOGY**

- **GENDERED LANGUAGE**
- **LEAKY PIPELINE**
- **ROLE MODELS**
- **STEREOTYPES**

- **MENTORING**
- **INTERSECTIONALITY**

## THIS CHAPTER

- discusses the complexity of factors that influence female participation in computing;
- explores inclusive strategies proposed for female engagement in computing education;
- provides a suggested set of activities to support inclusive computing education.

## INTRODUCTION

As a starting point, I would like to invite you to name ten well-known female computer scientists and engineers, including a few contemporary ones beyond the great names of the past. You can do it? Brilliant! Now let's try to name at least five famous ethnic minority pioneer women in IT. Great! How about five famous women in IT who represent other protected characteristics such as disability or LGBT+? The last part of this warm-up task is to think of ten women in computing that you personally know.

If you found it easy to list those women and their significant contributions to IT, great! You may have worked in the IT field or focused on the topic of female engagement in IT before. If naming all these women was a challenging task, you are not alone. We can reflect together whether this task was just a memory exercise, or whether it offers a starting point for contextualising some of the issues around female representation in the fields of IT, computer science and engineering, as well as considering approaches to address that imbalance.

It may seem paradoxical that despite research and focused interventions around female engagement in IT, participation of women in the technology sector, either as students or employees, remains a challenge, especially in the Western world. It is widely acknowledged that this is a multifaceted issue. While diversity and inclusion are acknowledged as important attributes in the prosperity of the global workforce, conversations around the inclusion of women in computing sometimes start as a number exercise rather than as recognition of the value that such contributions make.

In this chapter, we will explore some of the frameworks by which female disengagement in computing is understood. To do so, we will begin by reflecting on the dominant metaphor of the 'leaky pipeline' used in research around women in STEM. We will use the discussion to introduce some of the factors that affect gender parity in technology before moving on to interventions highlighted in the literature. A case study is shared with you to reinforce reflections on the ways that female engagement in computing can be promoted. The chapter will end with a list of suggested activities to explore in your practice.

I will be using the terms 'IT', 'computing' and 'computer science' interchangeably as I feel that the points explored relate to the role of women in technology and more widely in STEM. The organisation Computing at School 'recognises that Computer Science (CS) and Information Technology (IT) are disciplines within Computing' (CAS, 2012, p1). IT and CS are complementary in terms of scoping, analysing problems, and finding efficient and purposeful solutions through the use of technology, but differ in their technical or knowledge-based focus. There are also some misconceptions of CS being more of an isolating, solitary profession in comparison to the collaborative and socially skilled nature of IT, which at times have shaped current perceptions of computing as a pathway for female students.

## WHOSE VOICE?

Engaging more female students in STEM subjects and the career pathways that accompany them has been the focus of research and practice for the last two decades, especially around the Western world. UK curriculum reforms have seen the repositioning of the subject of ICT to computing in 2014, and as a result a further focus on the history of technology as well as the contributions that women have made in that field, which at times had gone unseen or was shadowed by gendered technology agendas.

While we are reflecting on our curricula considering how to support further female engagement in computing, we can think of how the lens that we are using to address the unbalanced ratio of male versus female students in computing conveys a balanced agenda itself. Let's start with language. The metaphor of a 'leaky pipeline' has been used widely in the literature to describe a progressive and diminishing flow of women from academia and industry as they advance their education and careers in STEM. The model was originally used to describe women's representation in quantitatively based disciplines and the gender gap through progression from MA to PhD degrees (Berryman, 1983; Alper, 1993). It served well the purpose of identifying issues around the under-representation of women in science as a structural deficit model based on societal stereotypes about lifestyle choices and alleged gender learning abilities and aptitudes. As a result, it identified discriminatory practices in the participation of women in science and promoted equal rights legislation for women. There is a question now whether the use of this metaphor carries an unfavourable gendered focus for women for the following reasons. It does not necessarily acknowledge how women utilise their training and skills in transgressing more traditional boundaries of the STEM field. As a result, it does not always capture the breadth of career pathways that their training can serve or the breadth of subjects that can lead to careers in STEM. It also alludes to a deficit model around women's rights to make career and lifestyle choices that centre around family priorities (e.g. combining career with family). When such choices include leaving the field, the dropping out is considered a failure.

The metaphor may also present the decline of women in computing as a constant phenomenon, and in this way disregard the significant presence and contributions that women have made in the history of computing. It may pose a Western bias on gender representation in the field without acknowledging the variability of women participation in computing across the globe and reflecting on the reverse gender gap in non-Western countries such as India and Malaysia.

This perspective on the 'leaky pipeline' aimed to highlight some of the complexities in addressing gender imbalance in computing, as well as the importance of seeing the whole person, rather than education, career and lifestyle as separate, when we consider interventions around female engagement in computing. As such, it raises the opportunity to reflect further on interventions geared towards female students, such as the importance of exposing them to female role models. When we promote the potential of success in computing at schools, we need to consider a wide range of role models, including contemporary and accessible ones that can be within young students' reach, role models who can also show that career intentions do not always follow a linear progression – they can be shaped and reshaped, and that is OK. They can also promote the idea of flexible working arrangements and caring responsibilities not as a hindrance in women's careers.

Media depiction of exaggerated stereotypical characters in IT and computer science have exploited sexuality and gender fluidity and may have also contributed to female students distancing themselves from computing pathways. In order to promote equality for all, we need to adopt an intersectional lens to our interventions around gender imbalance. Role models can also demonstrate that gender expression and sexuality should not be a starting point in considering a future or acceptance in computing. Such practices can unravel other terms, such as 'geeks' or 'nerds', that have been reported as male-domineered, empower all young people to reflect on the notion of being a minority, and question practices in areas of life relevant to them, such as perceived legitimacy of participation, hierarchy in fandoms and the idea of the 'fake geek girl' (Reagle, 2015), or the gendered notion of care that is associated with the female personas (e.g. voices, names, responses) of digital assistants such as Siri, Alexa and Cortana (West et al., 2019).

Access to role models coupled with mentoring should be used beyond being a 'blanket' for women to navigate through the potential 'chilly climate', another metaphor related to unequal treatment of women in the workplace. This ecological metaphor was coined by Hall et al. (1982) to describe the cumulative effect that discrimination – both subtle and overt – has on women's self-confidence and performance in the classroom and beyond. Mentoring should be used for women to recognise existing gendered practices in organisational structures, policies and practices, as well as informing 'climate' changes towards gender-neutral and equitable opportunities for expectations and recognition.

# CONTRIBUTING FACTORS IN THE DECLINE OF WOMEN IN COMPUTING

The publication of this chapter is timely and coincides with the launch of the Gender Balance in Computing research project. Funded by the Department for Education (DfE), it will be the largest national study to date focusing on improving female students' participation in computing education. It will employ a range of tailored interventions and address factors around female disengagement of computing identified in the literature, such as challenging stereotypes, celebrating role models, addressing perceived lack of relevance of the subject, nurturing the sense of belonging, and perceived self-efficacy for computing.

This initiative comes as a result of recommendations by the *After the Reboot* report (Royal Society, 2017), that 'research projects on pedagogy and curriculum development in Computing should investigate how to improve female participation' (p44) and 'government and industry-funded interventions must prioritise and evaluate their impact on improving the gender balance of Computing' (p45). Data from *The Roehampton Annual Computing Education Report* (Kemp et al., 2018) describing the continued gender gap in computer science back up these recommendations. Even if girls outperform boys at GCSE, they remain a minority in the subject of computer science, with less than one in five (20 per cent) GCSE and less than one in ten (10 per cent) A-level computing students being girls in 2017.

While the visibility of women's contributions in IT has been obscured, there is also acknowledgement that the declining number of women in computing is a recent phenomenon in the UK and US (Abbate et al., 2012). Emerging in the 1980s, it coincided with personal computers becoming more widely available at home and a market focusing on computer games for boys, which had – possibly unintentional – gendered educational consequences. This frequent exposure to computers led to higher levels of confidence in programming by boys and higher education 'entry requirements that favored candidates with precollege computer experience' (Abbate et al., 2012, p150). The results of such uneven starting points in terms of computing experiences are explored in *Unlocking the Clubhouse*, now considered a classic study by Margolis and Fischer (2002). They researched the high attrition of female computer science students from Carnegie Mellon University, who started their course confident in their skills, but as they felt that they did not fit within the 'geek mythology' of 'dreaming in code' of their male peers, were discouraged, failed or left their course with their self-confidence shattered. While studies on gender differences in self-evaluation of abilities or 'self-efficacy' (Bandura, 1977) in CS have reached contradictory results (Friend, 2015), it has been acknowledged that if female students feel less confident in their CS skills, they are less likely to pursue a career in technology (Won Hur et al., 2017).

Other contributing factors of women under-represented in the digital industry in the 1980s included the growing integration of computers in businesses. It resulted in reconsideration of the significance of computers, as well as re-evaluation of what was perceived as skilled labour in building, maintaining and operating computers. Consequently, women were either pushed out of jobs or were excluded from career development opportunities (Hicks, 2017). Combined with unfriendly working conditions for family-oriented female professionals, unequal pay and disregard towards women's labour (Abbate et al., 2012), the masculinisation of the computing profession in the Western world was shaped. However, studies from the non-Western world show a different picture. Stoet and Geary (2018) report on the paradox of this largest STEM gap in countries with high levels of gender equality. The appreciation for social status and prestige associated with the role of IT in shaping 'the knowledge society' (Raghuram, 2007) seem to remain constant across the world, but the wide range of career opportunities that computing offers, as well as the safety of working indoors (Varma, 2010), make it a woman-friendly profession in non-Western countries. Even fewer studies have commented on minority ethnic female students' positive attitudes towards computing studies and careers in the Western world (Varma, 2010). Such reports are important in order 'to problematise the mantra of "there are no women in Computing"' (Vitores and Gil-Juárez, 2016, p673) and highlight the importance of intersectionality in exploring the gender imbalance. More importantly, for us, as educators, such reports offer the opportunity to consider computing in inclusive ways beyond binary gender distinctions: from curriculum planning that fosters collaboration and relatedness, to observation of whether our classroom artefacts, such as posters or displays, promote stereotypical views of the field (Cheryan et al., 2009) or whether they reflect the diversity of our student profiles.

There are numerous studies offering practical suggestions for engaging more female students in computing. The proposed solutions are suggested from different standpoints (e.g. feminist ideologies, psychological viewpoints, child development perspectives). For instance, Dasgupta and Stout (2014) identify that interventions should target different stages of development, with parental encouragement being important from childhood to the adolescence stage, particularly maternal influence being important to girls. Parental support, accompanied by teachers' support, can include encouragement for engagement in IT activities but also express 'positive values about the importance, usefulness and appropriateness of computing, and by modelling ICT use' (Vekiri, 2010, p17). Especially for parents who work in the field, making links with the social contributions that their jobs offer can relate to female students' perceived interest for real-life contexts and supporting social change. Stone's research also identifies the socio-economic background as a differential in shaping perceptions about computing. His work reinforces the importance of involving parents in interventions to address the gender gap in computing but also the need for thoughtful widening participation approaches. Educators continue to be a strong influence, though, especially for girls (Stone, 2019). Approachable and encouraging teachers are important to female students and can influence their self-confidence (Cohoon, 2003).

## REFLECTION

- What is your gender lens in exploring CS? For instance, to what extent do your units of work celebrate women's achievements in computing?

- For the relatively new curriculum subject of computing, students' experiences and attitudes may also be formed as a result of their perceptions of other STEM subjects such as mathematics and science. For instance, at GCSE level, computer science is included in the English Baccalaureate (EBacc) under the sciences, alongside physics, chemistry and biology. How can we build links with these other STEM subjects and how can we promote the difference of the subject of computing?

*(Continued)*

(Continued)

- The 2021 Programme for International Student Assessment (PISA) mathematics assessment will incorporate aspects of computational thinking (CT) for the first time under mathematical reasoning. If you want to find out more about CT, start with Wing's (2006) influential CT manifesto, which revolves around problem-solving processes. How can we plan for creative cross-curricular problem-solving tasks that promote CT skills and love for technology? For instance, schools may be participating in national competitions that support CT, such as the UK Bebras Challenges (primary and secondary) or the CyberFirst Girls Competition (Year 8 girls in England and Wales, Year 9 in Northern Ireland and second year in Scotland).

- The STEAM movement aims to incorporate the arts into the STEM curriculum. How do you think merging the two can support more female engagement in computing?

## EVIDENCE FROM PRACTICE

As an example of an inclusive approach towards female engagement in computing, I am sharing the case study of a non-selective mixed secondary school, which at the time of the study in 2016 had a high ratio of girls to boys studying CS for two consecutive years. This resulted in an almost equal number of girls and boys taking GCSEs in CS. During the year of the study, that translated to 26 girls and 34 boys. The school was involved in the pilot for the GCSE computer science pathway and had provided this academic option for students over the previous three years. At the start of Year 10, the first year for GCSE preparations for the school, the cohort were asked about their self-confidence in their CS abilities, and a higher number of girls (62 per cent) over 47 per cent of the boys were positive about their abilities. By the end of the year, and while progress was very good for the whole cohort, their self-reported self-efficacy score changed to 73 per cent and 74 per cent respectively, which indicated a much higher increase for boys over the girls. These results made the school reflect further on their Key Stage 3 curriculum and the ways they introduced the Key Stage 4 curriculum, which has a heavy emphasis on programming, and plan the following year to ensure that female students continue to consider computing an option and feel confident throughout the GCSE course.

The female students reported positively on the contributions of outside-school experiences, such as participation in TeenTech and DigiGirlz. These contributions accompanied a carefully considered Key Stage 3 curriculum that emphasised the social aspects of CS across all topics and made links with real-life activities. The department was placing emphasis on teaching the why, not only the what, and used unplugged activities and problem-solving as the norm to introduce computing topics. As a result, those field trips provided further opportunities to revisit classroom work and reinforce the wide range of professions that IT offers. The majority of these trips and the school computing club were offered to all students. Targeted interventions for girls always involved sharing and follow-up work for all when they returned to the classroom. The computing department were working on an inclusive CS approach and had placed emphasis on developing Key Stage 3 female students' confidence in technology. Their approaches were embedded in a wider school ethos of community engagement. They were ensuring that the school digital ambassadors included boys and girls and that these young people were involved in several school-wide initiatives, such as representing the school at national technology events, leading assemblies and offering peer mentoring. The department outreach activities focused on both leading lessons at local primary schools as well as organising computing days at the school and inviting primary schools from across the region. Digital ambassadors played a key role in supporting those initiatives.

Located in an area of high socio-economic status, parental encouragement was evident. However, there was also acknowledgement of the strong working relationship with the teachers, as well as the teachers' approachable style, but also healthy scepticism from those Year 10 young women acknowledging that they would study the subject even if they did not like the teachers. The girls were aware of the existing gender gap nationally but did not see their classroom as a male-dominant environment. The ones who identified a CS pathway for their future career also said that they felt strong enough to resist such a male-dominated culture if it existed.

## TRANSFORMING PRACTICE

### Activity 1: Your classroom environment is an inclusive environment

What opportunities to reflect on equality in computing does the physical environment of your classroom give your students? For instance, review your current wall displays and consider how they can act as ways to celebrate achievements and stimulate points for discussion around role models and current technologies. There is an argument about wall displays acting more as a distraction rather than support for learning in the younger years (Hanley et al., 2017). However, carefully considered displays co-constructed with students will reflect the school values of equality, inclusion and respect for all. Review other artefacts in your classroom. To what extent are they gendered and may alienate female students, or how do they present an inclusive computing environment for all?

### Activity 2: Inclusive pedagogical approaches are good for all

Working beyond classroom layout restrictions is hard, but, where possible, incorporate unplugged activities and always foster opportunities for collaboration. The idea of working together will reinforce the collaborative nature of computing and help towards demystifying the computer-based problem-solving process as a set of learnt skills, not luck. Carefully structured partnerships are important, and decisions between mixed-ability pairings and grouping arrangements with shared social drives, such as friendship groups, need to be considered. Pair programming (Werner and Denning, 2009) is one of those approaches where students can work together to solve a problem. You can also consider, as the class develop their problem-solving skills and more resilience to deal with the unexpected challenges of a task, how the pairing arrangements can vary for students to work with different partners. Such an approach, challenging though it may be, can reinforce a culture of tolerance, mutual respect and shared responsibility, as expected in collaborative tasks, and more generally in the workplace.

*(Continued)*

(Continued)

### Activity 3: Consider interventions inclusively rather than in isolation

The importance of focused campaigns to attract female students to computer science education has been recognised in the literature. Field trips, guest speakers and extracurricular computing clubs can contribute to raising the profile of computing for all. Together, boys and girls can learn to reflect on technological advances and problem-solve. Consider how such interventions can be embedded as part of systemic approaches that can foster long-term impact. Decide on the learning focus of such interventions and build them into your long-term planning for the subject. How can campaigns around stereotypes and celebrating women in IT support identity development? How does your gender focus fit within the wider celebrations around diversity and inclusion at your school? How can we move the discussions from considering students' self-efficacy to questioning social structures and recognising social inequalities? How do these interventions link with the school responsibility to promote spiritual, moral, social and cultural (SMSC) development?

### Activity 4: Take an inclusive curriculum approach that fosters citizenship

The focus on digital citizenship, part of our e-safety curriculum, can provide opportunities to explore topics that relate to the technical and social scope of digital technologies, as well as viewing technology as socially constructed, a focus that can appeal to all students. Developing technical fluency becomes a cross-curricular prospect, part of wider discussions around rights and responsibilities in online and offline communities. Our activities become a playground to discuss ethics, empathy and emotionality, not because of a gendered lens, but because they will inform decisions around technology use. Part of digital citizenship will support our students' community activism. While 'this term has become politicized, in a context of citizenship it simply means taking an active role in the affairs of one's state or community' (Johnson, 2015, p343). Consider opportunities to link online activities with community engagement; think of ways to involve local resources and companies that will allow your students to make links with real-world contexts and reinforce that building professional networks can act as support opportunities and professional recognition. Plan for peer mentoring across Key Stages as part of the citizenship focus. You can also explore how to involve your students in international programmes and awards, as well as online micro-accreditation courses that focus on digital enterprise, citizenship and employability, such as iDEA.

# CHAPTER SUMMARY

The term 'computer' is linked to performing mathematical calculations, 'to compute'. Before computers were mechanical devices, being a computer was a job classification, and many of these positions were occupied by women, as the article 'When Computers Were Women' highlights (Light, 1999). Social reasons have perhaps hidden these contributions, but the point remains that women have always been involved in computing.

In this chapter, we offered another voice in exploring *why* and *how* the gender gap in computing has occurred, as well as discussing attempts to support more gender parity in computing education. It is important that we continue to:

- explore how gendered practices, representations and language can affect female engagement in computing education;

- provide opportunities to celebrate diversity and inclusion in our curricula for which gender is an aspect, through celebrating role models, reflecting on the history of computing, and engaging with community stakeholders and parents/carers;

- offer opportunities for collaborative problem-solving tasks and make links with technologies in real life in order to promote active citizenship and social responsibility.

## FURTHER READING

**Cheryan, S., Master, A. and Meltzoff, A.N.** (2015) Cultural stereotypes as gatekeepers: increasing girls' interest in computer science and engineering by diversifying stereotypes. *Frontiers in Psychology*, 6: 1–8.

**Sentance, S., Barendsen, E. and Schulte, C.** (2018) *Computer Science Education*. London: Bloomsbury Academic.

**Vitores, A. and Gil-Juárez, A.** (2016) The trouble with 'women in computing': a critical examination of the deployment of research on the gender gap in computer science. *Journal of Gender Studies*, 25(6): 666–80.

## REFERENCES

Abbate, J., Aspray, W. and Misa, T.J. (2012) *Recoding Gender: Women's Changing Participation in Computing*. Cambridge, MA: MIT Press.

Alper, J. (1993) The pipeline is leaking women all the way along. *Science*, 260(5106): 409–11.

Bandura, A. (1977) Self-efficacy: toward a unifying theory of behavioural change. *Psychological Review*, 84(2): 191–215.

Berryman, S. (1983) *Who Will Do Science? Minority and Female Attainment of Science and Mathematics Degrees: Trends and Causes*. New York: Rockefeller Foundation.

Cheryan, S., Plaut, V.C., Davies, P.G. and Steele, C.M. (2009) Ambient belonging. *Journal of Personality and Social Psychology*, 97(6): 1045–60.

Cohoon, J.M. (2003) Must there be so few? Including women in CS. In *Proceedings of the 25th International Conference on Software Engineering*. Portland, OR: IEEE.

Computing at School (CAS) (2012) *Computer Science: A Curriculum for Schools*. Available at: www.computing atschool.org.uk/data/uploads/ComputingCurric.pdf

Dasgupta, N. and Stout, J.G. (2014) Girls and women in science, technology, engineering, and mathematics: STEMing the tide and broadening participation in STEM careers. *Policy Insights from the Behavioural and Brain Sciences*, 1(1): 21–9.

Friend, M. (2015) Middle school girls' envisioned future in computing. *Computer Science Education*, 25(2): 152–73.

Hall, R.M., Bernice, R. and Sandler, B.R. (1982) *The Classroom Climate: A Chilly One for Women?* Washington, DC: Project on the Status and Education of Women, Association of American Colleges.

Hanley, M., Khairat, M., Taylor, K., Wilson, R., Cole-Fletcher, R. and Riby, D.M. (2017) Classroom displays: attraction or distraction? Evidence of impact on attention and learning from children with and without autism. *Developmental Psychology*, 53(7): 1265–75.

Hicks, M. (2017) *Programmed Inequality*. Cambridge, MA: MIT Press.

Johnson, M. (2015) Digital literacy and digital citizenship: approaches to girls' online experiences. In J. Bailey and V. Steeves (eds), *eGirls, eCitizens*. Ottawa: University of Ottawa Press.

Kemp, P.E.J., Berry, M.G. and Wong, B. (2018) *The Roehampton Annual Computing Education Report: Data from 2017*. London: University of Roehampton.

Light, J.S. (1999) When computers were women. *Technology and Culture*, 40(3): 455–83.

Margolis, J. and Fisher, A. (2002) *Unlocking the Clubhouse: Women in Computing*. Cambridge, MA: MIT Press.

Raghuram, P. (2007) Migrant women in male-dominated sectors of the labour market: a research agenda. *Population, Space and Place*, 14(1): 43–57.

Reagle, J. (2015) Geek policing: fake geek girls and contested attention. *International Journal of Communication*, 9: 2862–80.

Royal Society (2017) *After the Reboot: Computing Education in UK Schools*. Available at: www.royalsociety.org/computing-education

Stoet, G. and Geary, D.C. (2018) The gender-equality paradox in science, technology, engineering, and mathematics education. *Psychological Science*, 29(4): 581–93.

Stone, J. (2019) Student perceptions of computing and computing majors. *Journal of Computing Sciences in Colleges*, 34(3): 22–30.

Varma, R. (2010) Why so few women enroll in computing? Gender and ethnic differences in students' perception. *Computer Science Education*, 20(4): 301–16.

Vekiri, I. (2010) Boys' and girls' ICT beliefs: do teachers matter? *Computers & Education*, 55(1): 16–23.

Vitores, A. and Gil-Juárez, A. (2016) The trouble with 'women in computing': a critical examination of the deployment of research on the gender gap in computer science. *Journal of Gender Studies*, 25(6): 666–80.

Werner, L. and Denning, J. (2009) Pair programming in middle school: what does it look like? *Journal of Research on Technology in Education*, 42(1): 29–49.

West, M., Kraut, R. and Chew, H.E. (2019) *'I'd Blush if I Could': Closing Gender Divides in Digital Skills through Education*. Available at: http://creativecommons.org/licenses/by-sa/3.0/igo/

Wing, J. (2006) Computational thinking. *Communications of the ACM*, 49(3): 33–5.

Won Hur, J., Andrzejewski, C.E. and Marghitu, D. (2017) Girls and computer science: experiences, perceptions, and career aspirations. *Computer Science Education*, 27(2): 100–20.

# 10

# GENDER AND DYSLEXIA

## ANNA TSAKALAKI

## KEYWORDS

- **DYSLEXIA**
- **READING DIFFICULTIES**
- **ACADEMIC ACHIEVEMENT**
- **SUPPORT**
- **INCLUSION**
- **DIAGNOSIS**

## THIS CHAPTER

- explores the prevalence of reading difficulties in girls and boys from their early years in education through to adolescence;
- discusses innate and social factors that may affect diagnosis of dyslexia, including expectations of teachers, parents and learners themselves;
- proposes ways to identify signs of dyslexia in boys and girls, as well as supporting reading and writing development for all.

## INTRODUCTION

*I have visions of first grade reading groups. And just, I never could figure out what – why those kids could understand – or could get from the written page what I couldn't. Well, I mean, they could look at the page and say, 'This says this,' and I'm going, 'Where? How does it say that?' And, you know, eventually, you know, figured out enough pieces so I could struggle through.*

(Hurst, 2010, p70)

This quote is an excerpt from the doctoral thesis of Ellen Burns Hurst, who explored the memories of schooling of three female adults with dyslexia in the US. Although referring to an educational system set in another country between 20 and 30 years ago, the thoughts, impressions, feelings and challenges expressed by the interviewees do not sound completely alien to a contemporary educator in the UK.

In this chapter, we are going to explore the specific learning difficulty (SpLD) broadly known as 'dyslexia', as well as looking at its impact on how students perceive themselves as learners in primary and secondary education. We will draw from research on internal and external factors that may lead to identifiable signs of dyslexia in boys and girls. We will discuss the role of the child, the parents and the school in identifying and supporting learners with dyslexia of both genders in the classroom. Ways to challenge potentially stereotypical practices in contemporary literacy classes will also be explored. Finally, ways to promote best practice to foster confidence and promote literacy skills in all learners, irrespective of their gender, will be suggested.

# DYSLEXIA: DEFINITION AND TERMINOLOGY

The term 'dyslexia' etymologically comes from Greek; the first component of the word, *dys*, means 'difficulty', and the second, *lexis*, means 'word'. Put together, the condition means 'difficulty with words', but unlike other compound terms with the second component (e.g. alexia), dyslexia is thought to affect access to written language only. This is why the first signs to suggest that a young child may have dyslexia are significant difficulties with reading and spelling when understanding of oral language may be comparable to that of other children of the same age.

Developmental dyslexia has been widely researched in the last 30 years in an effort to identify its behavioural manifestation (i.e. signs on a behavioural level when reading and writing), its prevalence, its causes and ways to address learners' needs. Despite the plethora of research, there is still no consensus on its definition. It is referred to as a deficit, a disability, a specific learning difficulty (SpLD) and a disorder, among others. In this chapter, we adopt the term 'condition' to avoid medicalisation and potential collocations with deviation from 'normality'. Research in different languages has shown that dyslexia manifests differently depending on the writing system (e.g. alphabetical versus pictographic systems). Nevertheless, there seem to be commonalities in the pattern of difficulties that learners across the globe show (Smythe and Everatt, 2004; Smythe et al., 2008).

Investigation of the underlying neuropsychological mechanisms has associated developmental dyslexia with a range of factors, including a phonological deficit, a double deficit in phonological awareness and rapid automatised naming (RAN), subtle difficulties in sensory perception (e.g. visual, auditory), and impaired attention, working memory and motor difficulties (Goswami, 2002; Ramus et al., 2003; Ziegler and Goswami, 2005; Pennington, 2006). Lately, researchers seem to have found a common ground on embracing the phonological deficit and 'double deficit' hypothesis to explain developmental dyslexia. In addition, it is widely recognised that developmental dyslexia may co-occur with other developmental conditions, such as language disorder (Snowling, 2000), attention deficit hyperactivity disorder (ADHD) (Peterson and Pennington, 2012) and mathematical disability (Landerl and Moll, 2010).

For the purposes of this chapter, we are going to use the definition of the International Dyslexia Association:

*Dyslexia is a specific learning disability that is neurological in origin. It is characterized by difficulties with accurate and/or fluent word recognition and by poor spelling and decoding abilities. These difficulties typically result from a deficit in the phonological component of language that is often unexpected in relation to other cognitive abilities and the provision of effective classroom instruction. Secondary consequences may include problems in reading comprehension and reduced reading experience that can impede growth of vocabulary and background knowledge.*

(IDA, 2002)

By adopting the IDA definition, we acknowledge recent evidence on the causality of dyslexia, its neurological origins, and the deliberate exclusion from the definition of factors such as instructional practices, race, class or gender as reasons that could cause or contribute to developing the condition. The interest of this chapter is in literacy difficulties caused by developmental dyslexia as opposed to acquired dyslexia, which may be a result of brain damage due to neuropathological diseases, or other non-neurological causes (e.g. class, poor instruction). Therefore, from now on, we will use the terms 'dyslexia' or 'literacy difficulties' to refer to the condition.

## EVIDENCE FROM PRACTICE

### Are there gender differences in dyslexia?

Despite extensive research in the causality of dyslexia, as well as the general confidence of practitioners in diagnosing its signs, it is very interesting that the above question may not seem relevant or even valid for a number of professions that work in the field as researchers, educational psychologists, educators, and so on. In preparation for this chapter, I used a reflective activity with a group of postgraduate students, all experienced teachers in primary and secondary education with an overview of their schools' practices in supporting learners with dyslexia. In groups, I asked them to talk about the questions in the following reflection box. I got very interesting answers that helped me get a feel for what my students believed, as well as how practice was shaped in their schools. I will refer to their answers in corresponding sections throughout this chapter. You may want to try them to reflect on your own views and practices as an both individual and a school.

## REFLECTION

1.  Select one of the following options. Dyslexia is seen:

    - mainly in boys;
    - mainly in girls;
    - no difference between sexes.

*(Continued)*

(Continued)

Think about your experience of teaching learners with dyslexia or your peers when you were at school or university, or any general picture that you may get from what you see in your day-to-day life.

2.  In my school, we find that boys with dyslexia respond differently than girls.

    Think about reaction to difficulties, response to intervention, confidence in their abilities, behaviour, and so on.

3.  In my school, we often find that it is easier to gear girls towards reading/writing than boys.

    Discuss your practice, especially in relation to reading difficulties and specific tricks that you use with pupils to motivate them to read/write or support them in their writing.

4.  Has the question of gender differences in dyslexia and literacy difficulties occurred as a subject of discussion to you or your environment (e.g. peers, school)?

    If so, why? If not, why not? What factors may have led or not led you to ask the question?

In the next sections, we are going to discuss how dyslexia and literacy difficulties may be identified and addressed in boys and girls, as well as how their identity as learners may be affected by gender stereotypes towards reading and writing during their school life. In order to do this, we will draw from research evidence on the prevalence of dyslexia in boys and girls, as well as approaches to developing literacy skills in mainstream education.

## WHAT DO WE KNOW FROM RESEARCH?

### Prevalence of dyslexia

Dyslexia is found to affect between 5 and 12 per cent of school-aged children across different countries (Peterson and Pennington, 2015; Krafnick and Evans, 2019), and educators nowadays would expect to have at least one child with dyslexia in a class of 25-30 children. Twin studies show that it is heritable just like other developmental conditions (Paracchini et al., 2007) at an estimated level between 40 and 70 per cent. Higher concordance rates in monozygotic (identical) (84-100 per cent) than dizygotic (non-identical) (20-35 per cent) twins further support the notion of heritability of the condition (Pennington and Olson, 2007).

## EVIDENCE FROM PRACTICE

In the learning activity with my postgraduate students, there were a good number of teachers that thought there are no differences between boys and girls. Some of them pointed out that there must be more girls than boys that go through school undiagnosed because girls are better at disguising the signs of dyslexia. In the discussion that followed, teachers associated their views with the rise of visibility of females with autism and felt more alert to signs of masking social difficulties that girls with autism may adopt by copying social norms (Mandy et al., 2012).

The above example shows that in a sample of 30 teachers, there was awareness of the possibility that some girls with autism may be able to hide their difficulties by copying the behaviour expected from them, which suggests that they were alert to observe and identify such signs in their schools. However, only a small number of teachers were confident to answer the question about dyslexia. In order to answer this question, we need to look at evidence coming from research.

There are very few behavioural studies on the ratio of boys versus girls with dyslexia, which perhaps explains the unified procedures used to diagnose it, as well as the identical support programmes for learners across genders (Krafnick and Evans, 2019). Just as not many practitioners seem to have asked the question of whether there are gender differences in literacy difficulties, equally researchers have not yet fully responded to the call for more research into the field. However, there is a large-scale study by Rutter et al. (2004), which examined 10,000 children aged 7–15 years in Britain and New Zealand using standardised reading tests. It was found that between 18 and 22 per cent of the boys and between 8 and 13 per cent of the girls were identified with reading difficulties. Pennington and Gilger (1996) estimated up to a 40 per cent risk of dyslexia for sons of fathers with dyslexia, showing that boys are more vulnerable than girls in inheriting the genes associated with the condition.

## SEX DIFFERENCES IN READING AND WRITING

Neuropsychological research in the field of dyslexia looks into differences in how the brain is activated when reading and writing for boys and girls. Behavioural research examines the academic performance of boys and girls using reading and writing tests. Both types of research use the biological characteristics assigned at birth to identify their samples (i.e. male or female). The term 'sex' is commonly used in brain studies rather than 'gender', which is often associated with identity and is thought to be socially constructed (see Chapter 2). Behavioural studies use 'sex' and 'gender' interchangeably regardless of the fact that samples were identified using sex assigned at birth. In this chapter, we will use 'sex' to discuss research that used biological characteristics to sample, and 'gender' for studies that used self-identified gender for sampling. In order to understand potential sex differences in brain functions and literacy performance in individuals with dyslexia, we first need to ask the essential question of whether there are any such differences in the way typical learners approach reading and writing.

One of the richest databases with results in reading achievement for 15-year-olds across 90 countries is the Programme for International Student Assessment (PISA) conducted by the Organisation for Economic Co-operation and Development (OECD). Lynn and Mikk (2009) and Reilly (2012) found significantly lower scores for boys in comparison with girls in the 2000, 2003, 2006 and 2009 data sets across all participating countries. Reilly et al. (2019) replicated these results with data drawn from the

National Assessment of Educational Progress (NAEP) in the US. An examination of reading and writing data from 3.035 million students in grades 4, 8 and 12 between 1988 and 2015 showed that boys performed consistently lower than girls in all three grades. What is interesting in the findings is the gradual widening of the gender gap in both reading and writing from grades 4 to 12. Especially for reading, it was found that the ratio of girls versus boys achieving an advanced standard of reading proficiency was almost 2:1. Looking at poor readers, the ratio of girls versus boys was 1:1.5. For writing, advanced proficiency standards were achieved by 2.5 girls for every 1 boy. As with reading, the ratio for poor writing was 2 boys for every 1 girl. If the distribution of data is depicted as a bell-shaped curve, these findings show that gender difference is smaller in the middle and much larger in the two tails representing either poor (left tail) or advanced (right tail) reading and writing. Gender differences were consistent across grades, which suggests that early foundations in literacy seem to determine performance until later in education.

Research that looks specifically into poor reading replicates the above findings (Hawke et al., 2009). Girls with dyslexia have been found to show a relative advantage as compared with boys in other cognitive skills related to language, reading and writing, such as orthographic coding skills (i.e. the ability to recognise or use conventions used for writing, such as spelling) and phonological skills (i.e. the ability to manipulate sounds in language, including phonemes, syllables and whole words) (Berninger et al., 2008). Researchers suggest that there is greater variability in the cognitive performance of males compared to females (Feingold, 1992). This greater variability may partly account for the over-representation of boys at the extreme left tail of the distribution for literacy and related skills (Hawke et al., 2009). Even though there is no consensus in research cycles about the effect size of differences between boys and girls in reading and writing, there is evidence of a small to medium advantage of girls versus boys in specific skills related to literacy achievement (for the gender similarities hypothesis, see Hyde, 2005; for a discussion on literacy skills being an exception to this hypothesis, see Reilly et al., 2019).

## WHAT DO WE KNOW FROM RESEARCH?

### Evidence from brain and genetic studies

In a comprehensive account of brain studies published between 2008 and 2018, Krafnick and Evans (2019) present evidence of differences in brain structure of males and females, which may account for the differences observed in their literacy performance. They discuss recent studies which suggest that the traditional reading network in the brain seems to be impacted to a greater extent in males with dyslexia than in females. In addition, as shown in Table 10.1, different regions and structures have been found to be affected in males with dyslexia as compared with males without dyslexia than when comparing females with dyslexia and females without dyslexia. For example, the extent of difference in the volume of grey matter between females with dyslexia and control females was greater than that found for males with dyslexia as compared to control males (Sandu et al., 2008). In another study, the opposite effect was observed in relation to Heschl's gyrus, a region often associated with dyslexia. Altarelli et al. (2014) found a higher incidence of right hemisphere Heschl's gyrus duplication in male brains with dyslexia as compared with their controls, while no such difference was obvious in females.

Table 10.1    *Sex differences in magnetic resonance imaging (MRI) studies of dyslexia (adapted from Krafnick and Evans, 2019, p5)*

| Article | Subject demographics | | Description of dyslexia sex differences |
|---|---|---|---|
| | **Sex** | **Age (years)** | |
| Sandu et al. (2008) | Control: 8M, 10F<br>Dyslexia: 8M, 5F | Control: 13.5<br>Dyslexia: 13.2 | Control females had greater RH GMV, greater WB/LH/RH WMV, and lower GMV/WMV ratio than females with dyslexia, but no significant differences in male comparisons. |
| Altarelli et al. (2013) – study 1 | Control: 11M, 8F<br>Dyslexia: 10M, 8F | Control: 11.58<br>Dyslexia: 11.75 | Thicker functionally relevant occipitotemporal cortex in female controls compared to females with dyslexia, but no difference in male comparisons. |
| Altarelli et al. (2013) – study 2 | Control (age-matched): 7M, 6F<br>Control (reading-matched): 7M, 6F<br>Dyslexia: 7M, 6F | Control (age-matched): 9.75<br>Control (reading-matched): 6.67<br>Dyslexia: 9.83 | Thicker functionally relevant occipitotemporal cortex in female controls compared to females with dyslexia, but no difference in male comparisons. |
| Clark et al. (2014)* | Control: 8M, 5F<br>Dyslexia: 5M, 6F | Control: 11.7<br>Dyslexia: 11.9 | Thicker cortex in several regions throughout LH in male controls compared to males with dyslexia, but no difference in female comparisons. |
| Evans et al. (2014)** | Adult control: 14M, 13F<br>Child control: 15M, 17F<br>Adult dyslexia: 14M, 13F<br>Child dyslexia: 15M, 17F | Adult female control: 27.9<br>Adult female dyslexia: 34.0<br>Child female control: 9.1<br>Child female dyslexia: 10.1<br>Adult male control: 41.1<br>Adult male dyslexia: 42.9<br>Child male control: 8.3<br>Child male dyslexia: 9.6 | Greater GMV in male controls compared to males with dyslexia, mostly in regions within the traditional reading network, while female controls show greater GMV compared to females with dyslexia in sensorimotor regions. |

*(Continued)*

Table 10.1 (Continued)

| Article | Subject demographics | | Description of dyslexia sex differences |
|---------|----------------------|----|-------------------------------------|
| | Sex | Age (years) | |
| Altarelli et al. (2014) | Control: 20M, 15F<br>Dyslexia: 25M, 21F | Control: 11.0<br>Dyslexia: 11.0 | Greater rightward asymmetry of planum temporale surface area in males with dyslexia, but not in females with dyslexia. |
| Su et al. (2018) | Control: 11M, 11F<br>Dyslexia: 11M, 7F | Control: 11.1<br>Dyslexia: 11.1 | Greater axial diffusivity of left interior longitudinal fasciculus in control females compared to females with dyslexia, but no difference between male groups. |

*Subject demographics given only for the portion of study relevant to sex differences.

**Evans et al. (2014) separately examined males and females (and adults and children), resulting in eight different groups.

M: male; F: female; WB: whole brain; LH: left hemisphere: left half of the brain linked to language production and perception; RH: right hemisphere: right half of the brain linked to understanding discourse; GMV: grey matter volume: grey matter is composed of nerve cells (neurons) of the brain; WMV: white matter volume: white matter connects grey matter areas and caries nerve impulses between neurons.

Krafnick and Evans (2019) also review studies exploring genetic factors associated with dyslexia. They discuss the lack of consensus on whether there are sex differences in the heritability of literacy difficulties, providing controversial evidence from recent studies. They conclude, however, that even in the absence of sex difference inheritability, there still is a possibility that genetic risk factors may impact males and females differently. Examples are drawn from the oestrogen-specific DYX1C1 effect, which is also discussed by Guidi et al. (2018) in their review of genetic studies from the last 30 years, among five more genes that have been associated with reading difficulties. Both Guidi et al. (2018) and Krafnick and Evans (2019) seem to agree that we don't yet know enough about the full range of genes that might be associated with dyslexia, and more research is needed to identify potential sex differences in the way genetic factors affect literacy performance. The takeaway message is that it is important not to assume that male-dominated brain models of dyslexia fit and can explain the behaviour of female or mixed-sex samples.

# GENDER AS A FACTOR SHAPING IDENTITY AND PERFORMANCE EXPECTATIONS

In the previous section, we discussed innate factors that might influence literacy performance of boys and girls. We are now going to look at factors external to the learner with dyslexia that may shape their identity and performance expectations.

## EVIDENCE FROM PRACTICE

At this point, you can go back to the second and third questions for reflection that we posed at the beginning of this chapter. Think about your responses. My students gave mixed answers. Some found that their male pupils with dyslexia showed more frustration than females, while others reported that boys, on average, become more disruptive and aggressive as a result of their struggles with reading and writing. In the class discussion that followed, teachers offered different justifications for this perceived difference in behaviour. Some examples included girls being quieter by nature, having more ways to seek support by (other female) peers or teachers, and boys being more competitive and reluctant to seek help. Teachers couldn't give a definite answer on whether they felt girls are easier to gear towards reading. They felt that this is done on a case-by-case basis, irrespective of the gender of the pupil. They also thought that linking reading and writing to subjects that seem relevant to or interesting for the child is one of the essential strategies they would use for a struggling reader. When following up their answers, we had an interesting conversation about girls not being particularly motivated by books with monsters and the quest of teachers to enrich the school's library with more 'girly' topics.

What we can see from teachers' views is that although there does not seem to be an explicit differentiation by gender in the way literacy habits or difficulties are identified and addressed in schools, there might be general trends in teachers' perception of how different genders react to literacy struggles, as well as how motivation for reading may be fostered by gender-specific themes. This is not new in the literature on gendered attitudes impacting on referrals and diagnosis of dyslexia. The main argument made by the supporters of this view is that boys and girls differ in the way they react to their literacy difficulties, with boys often acting up to express their frustration and girls internalising their feelings and withdrawing. This results in adults acting quicker in the case of disruptive or aggressive behaviour of boys, which leads to a disproportionate rate of referral and diagnosis of boys versus girls. In this line of thought, the girls who finally get referred and diagnosed are the ones that show a similarly disruptive behaviour to boys (Shaywitz et al., 1990).

# THE ROLE OF SOCIETY IN FORMING GENDERED ATTITUDES IN READING

In the previous section, we discussed evidence from behavioural, brain and genetic studies, suggesting that reading and writing may be an exception to the hypothesis that males and females function in identical ways. However, we have also seen that teachers, as well as some schools of thought in research, continue to attribute specific behaviours to students based on their gender. The results of a longitudinal study by Smart et al. (2001) seem to confirm a stronger link between externalised behaviour and reading difficulties in boys rather than girls. However, they argue that this relationship is not necessarily causal (i.e. acting up is not necessarily a result of struggling with literacy). By attributing causality to the relationship between dyslexia and boys' externalised behaviour, we add, perhaps inadvertently, to gender stereotypes, wanting boys to act up to show frustration, to lose focus easily and to be interested in other activities than reading, and girls to enjoy reading, to be quieter and to know how to seek help from peers. The formation of such subconscious views is not the sole responsibility of teachers, parents or researchers.

## REFLECTION

I welcomed a reflective moment during preparation of this chapter when I stumbled upon a £10 note in my purse. Looking at the picture of Jane Austen on the back of the note, I realised the content of the celebratory quote accompanying the portrait, taken from her book *Pride and Prejudice*: 'I declare after all there is no enjoyment like reading!' Could it be the case that society portrays reading and writing for pleasure as an activity predominantly for girls (see Elsesser, 2019)?

You may want to think about the following:

- Have you ever reflected on the messages conveyed about literacy and enjoyment of reading and writing in daily situations?
- How much information is conveyed directly (e.g. through words) or indirectly (e.g. through pictures)?
- Have you thought about the ratio of famous female versus famous male figures associated with literature nationally and internationally?

The role of teachers has drawn the attention of recent research. There is no consensus about the direction of the relationship between teachers' stance, teachers' expectations, and reading-related skills and stances for boys and girls. Boys' motivation for reading at preschool has been found to be affected by the more traditional gendered attitudes of their teachers (Wolter et al., 2015). Conversely, Boerma et al. (2016) found that girls' reading self-concept and value of reading at the end of primary education was influenced by their teachers' expectations for their students' reading level (i.e. poor, average, good). This relationship between teachers' expectations and their own reading achievement was found for secondary school students of both genders in a study by Muntoni and Retelsdorf (2018). In addition, higher expectations for girls explained the differences in the reading achievement of girls and boys. Lastly, teachers with a more traditional gendered attitude (i.e. girls are better than boys in reading) expected their female students to perform higher than their male students in reading. Although these studies don't agree on the degree of influence of teachers' stances on reading and performance in boys and girls, they demonstrate a clear relationship between teachers' gendered attitudes and what they expect of their students.

A range of studies have shown how cultural beliefs about gender roles influence children's classification of certain social behaviours and tasks as masculine and feminine in nature (see Chapters 2 and 5). Language and literacy skills are seen as predominantly feminine talents by both males and females

(Halpern et al., 2011). Martin and Ruble (2010) show how sex-typing – attribution of specific charac-teristics to a specific gender – influences behaviour and self-concept consistent with traditional gender roles. Along similar lines, children's achievement in reading and writing, as well as their attitudes towards such skills, may be influenced by cultural beliefs regarding reading.

---

**REFLECTION**

You may want to reflect on the following:

- Could our high expectations of girls' abilities in literacy result in differentiated sup-port for students of different genders?
- If so, what is the impact of our practice on our students' self-concept as readers/writers, as well as on our ability to identify a struggling reader regardless of their gender?

---

For an interesting case study of a female with dyslexia that settled for many years in the profile of 'poor Lucy', see the story of Lucy (Hurst, 2010, p59). In her thesis, Hurst discusses the case of Lucy, who adopted a profile of academic inability as a response to her family's failure to identify the signs of her literacy difficulties. Lucy got diagnosed in adulthood, which led to her change of stance towards her cognitive abilities and self-concept.

# WHY UNDERSTANDING GENDER DIFFERENCES IN DYSLEXIA MATTERS

Understanding that boys and girls with dyslexia may have differences due to biological factors, but also due to common beliefs attributing specific talents to a specific gender, is essential so that both teachers and learners form expectations in relation to academic achievement. Research shows that early poor reading can predict reading ability and academic achievement throughout primary and sec-ondary education (Gabrieli, 2009). Stanovich (1986) talked about the Matthew effect, whereby poor reading often correlates with less exposure to print, which results in low improvement in reading and a negative cycle of achievement. It is, therefore, important to be aware of the behavioural signs of dys-lexia (i.e. reading and writing difficulties, phonological deficit, difficulties with memory, co-morbidity with other conditions), but also of the risk factors associated with it, such as heritability, so that we can identify potential signs early.

Understanding what dyslexia is and which factors affect it may help in supporting children to understand it themselves, to learn how to seek support and how to support themselves, to construct identities that move away from wanting to conform to a unified profile of reader/writer, and to accept individual differences in learning. It is also essential to understand our stances in relation to the role of education in empowering individuals. In most contemporary societies, attitudes towards literacy place individuals in particular social groups with hierarchical positions (Compton-Lilly, 2007). Literacy skills are often associated with high social status and empowerment. Early diagnosis and intervention can result in better support for learners of all genders. Future research should help move away from a male-dominated model of dyslexia based on predominantly male samples, with the aim of understanding any gender-related differences and supporting literacy skills for all.

## TRANSFORMING PRACTICE

We can use strategies that foster love of reading/writing without stereotypical expectations of what learners can or cannot do, or like or do not like, based on their gender. Some ideas are:

- Being alert to compensation strategies, such as 'passing' (Hurst, 2010). This includes pretending that they do silent reading, memorising and repeating information previously learnt or relying on peers'/teacher's transmission of information instead of extracting new information from the given text, and guessing from initial or ending sounds of words.

- Being alert to avoidance strategies, such as distracting attention to other tasks, finding excuses to avoid tasks (e.g. becoming sick to go to nurse, asking to go to toilet), the 'shutdown' phenomenon (i.e. becoming silent, not responding to prompts), and asking 'good questions' to appear engaged.

- Avoiding negative labelling (i.e. the label associating dyslexia with low cognitive ability) and promoting positive labelling (i.e. giving a name to the condition and explaining what it means, as well as how the learner can work towards individual progress, as opposed to comparing with the 'normal' or 'typical' learner).

- Avoiding ability grouping, which can widen achievement gap through lack of motivation or settling in a specific ability profile that cannot be overcome.

- Promoting interaction for learning with peers as a means to receive support but also contribute to the learning of others, as a way to boost self-esteem and feel part of a learning community with equal roles.

- Using assistive technology, such as electronic readers, to tailor learning to their specific needs and make it interactive.

# CHAPTER SUMMARY

- Understanding innate and external factors that may explain gender differences in dyslexia and the development of literacy skills is important because it relates to the role of education and educators in empowering their students.

- Knowing that there may be biological differences in the way dyslexia is inherited or in the way the traditional reading network functions in the brain of boys and girls helps us appreciate that there is no one-rule-fits-all in diagnosing and supporting learners with dyslexia.

- Realisation of how subconscious views on literacy abilities of boys and girls may influence our expectations of them, which may impact on their expectations of themselves and their academic achievement, can help us identify struggling readers, regardless of what society would commonly expect of learners of their gender.

# FURTHER READING

**Berninger, V.W., Nielsen, K.H., Abbott, R.D., Wijsman, E. and Raskind, W.** (2008) Gender differences in severity of writing and reading disabilities. *Journal of School Psychology*, 46(2): 151–72.

**Duff, F.J. and Clarke, P.J.** (2010) Practitioner review: reading disorders – what are the effective interventions and how should they be implemented and evaluated? *Journal of Child Psychology and Psychiatry*, 52(1): 3–12.

**Krafnick, A.J. and Evans, T.M.** (2019) Neurobiological sex differences in developmental dyslexia. *Frontiers in Psychology*, 9: 1–14.

**Vellutino, F.R., Fletcher, J.M., Snowling, M.J. and Scanlon, D.M.** (2004) Specific reading disability (dyslexia): what have we learned in the past four decades? *Journal of Child Psychology and Psychiatry*, 45(1): 2–40.

# REFERENCES

Altarelli, I., Leroy, F., Monzalvo, K., Fluss, J., Billard, C., Dehaene-Lambertz, G., et al. (2014) Planum temporale asymmetry in developmental dyslexia: revisiting an old question. *Human Brain Mapping*, 35(12): 5717–35.

Berninger, V.W., Nielsen, K.H., Abbott, R.D., Wijsman, E. and Raskind, W. (2008) Gender differences in severity of writing and reading disabilities. *Journal of School Psychology*, 46(2): 151–72.

Boerma, I.E., Mol, S.E. and Jolles, J. (2016) Teacher perceptions affect boys' and girls' reading motivation differently. *Reading Psychology*, 37(4): 547–69.

Compton-Lilly, C. (2007) The complexities of reading capital in two Puerto Rican families. *Reading Research Quarterly*, 42(1): 72–98.

Elsesser, K. (2019) *Is Reading Just for Girls? 3 Reasons We're Failing Boys 8–11*. Available at: www.forbes.com/sites/kimelsesser/2018/10/29/is-reading-just-for-girls-3-reasons-were-failing-boys/#58318ed94f47

Feingold, A. (1992) Sex differences in variability in intellectual abilities: a new look at an old controversy. *Review of Educational Research*, 62(1): 61–84.

Gabrieli, J.D.E. (2009) Dyslexia: a new synergy between education and cognitive neuroscience. *Science*, 325(5938): 280–3.

Goswami, U. (2002) Phonology, reading development, and dyslexia: a cross-linguistic perspective. *Annals of Dyslexia*, 52: 139–63.

Guidi, L.G., Velayos-Baeza, A., Martinez-Garay, I., Monaco, A.P., Paracchini, S., Bishop, D.V.M., et al. (2018) The neuronal migration hypothesis of dyslexia: a critical evaluation 30 years on. *European Journal of Neuroscience*, 48(10): 3212–33.

Halpern, D.F., Straight, C.A. and Stephenson, C.L. (2011) Beliefs about cognitive gender differences: accurate for direction, underestimated for size. *Sex Roles*, 64(5–6): 336–47.

Hawke, J.L., Olson, R.K., Willcut, E.G., Wadsworth, S.J. and DeFries, J.C. (2009) Gender ratios for reading difficulties. *Dyslexia*, 15(3): 239–42.

Hurst, E. (2010) *Passing as Literate: Gender, Dyslexia, and the Shaping of Identities*. Available at: https://scholarworks.gsu.edu/msit_diss/71

Hyde, J.S. (2005) The gender similarities hypothesis. *American Psychologist*, 60(6): 581–92.

International Dyslexia Association (IDA) (2002) *Definition of Dyslexia*. Available at: http://ma.dyslexiaida.org/wp-content/uploads/sites/7/2016/03/Definition_of_Dyslexia.pdf

Krafnick, A.J. and Evans, T.M. (2019) Neurobiological sex differences in developmental dyslexia. *Frontiers in Psychology*, 9: 1–14.

Landerl, K. and Moll, K. (2010) Comorbidity of learning disorders: prevalence and familial transmission. *Journal of Child Psychology and Psychiatry and Allied Disciplines*, 51(3): 287–94.

Lynn, R. and Mikk, J. (2009) Sex differences in reading achievement. *Trames*, 13: 3–13.

Mandy, W., Chilvers, R., Chowdhury, U., Salter, G., Seigal, A. and Skuse, D. (2012) Sex differences in autism spectrum disorder: evidence from a large sample of children and adolescents. *Journal of Autism and Developmental Disorders*, 42(7): 1304–13.

Martin, C.L. and Ruble, D.N. (2010) Patterns of gender development. *Annual Review of Psychology*, 61(1): 353–81.

Muntoni, F. and Retelsdorf, J. (2018) Gender-specific teacher expectations in reading: the role of teachers' gender stereotypes. *Contemporary Educational Psychology*, 54: 212–20.

Paracchini, S., Scerri, T. and Monaco, A.P. (2007) The genetic lexicon of dyslexia. *Annual Review of Genomics and Human Genetics*, 8(1): 57–79.

Pennington, B.F. (2006) From single to multiple deficit models of developmental disorders. *Cognition*, 101(2): 385–413.

Pennington, B.F. and Gilger, J.W. (1996) How is dyslexia transmitted? In G.F. Chase, C.H. Rosen and G.D. Sherman (eds), *Developmental Dyslexia: Neural, Cognitive, and Genetic Mechanisms*. Baltimore, MD: York Press.

Pennington, B.F. and Olson, R.K. (2007) Genetics of dyslexia. In M.J. Snowling and C. Hulme (eds), *The Science of Reading: A Handbook*. Oxford: Blackwell.

Peterson, R.L. and Pennington, B.F. (2012) Developmental dyslexia. *The Lancet*, 379(9830): 1997–2007.

Peterson, R.L. and Pennington, B.F. (2015) Developmental dyslexia. *Annual Review of Clinical Psychology*, 11: 283–307.

Ramus, F., Rosen, S., Dakin, S., Day, B., Castellote, J., White, S., et al. (2003) Theories of developmental dyslexia: insights from a multiple case study of dyslexic adults. *Brain*, 126(4): 841–65.

Reilly, D. (2012) Gender, culture, and sex-typed cognitive abilities. *PLOS One*, 7(7): e39904.

Reilly, D., Neumann, D.L. and Andrews, G. (2019) Gender differences in reading and writing achievement: evidence from the National Assessment of Educational Progress (NAEP). *American Psychologist*, 74(4): 445–58.

Rutter, M., Caspi, A., Fergusson, D., Horwood, L.J., Goodman, R., Maughan, B., et al. (2004) Sex differences in developmental reading disability: new findings from 4 epidemiological studies. *JAMA*, 291(16): 2007–12.

Sandu, A.L., Specht, K., Beneventi, H., Lundervold, A. and Hugdahl, K. (2008) Sex-differences in grey-white matter structure in normal-reading and dyslexic adolescents. *Neuroscience Letters*, 438(1): 80–4.

Shaywitz, S.E., Shaywitz, B.A. and Fletcher, J.M. (1990) Prevalence of reading disability in boys and girls: results of the Connecticut longitudinal study. *JAMA*, 264(8): 998–1002.

Smart, D., Prior, M., Sanson, A. and Oberklaid, F. (2001) Early primary school to secondary school. *Australian Journal of Psychology*, 53(1): 45–53.

Smythe, I. and Everatt, J. (2004) Dyslexia: a cross-linguistic framework. In I. Smythe, J. Everatt and R. Salter (eds), *International Book of Dyslexia: A Cross-Language Comparison and Practice Guide*. Chichester: Wiley & Sons.

Smythe, I., Everatt, J., Al-Menaye, N., He, X., Capellini, S., Gyarmathy, E., et al. (2008) Predictors of word-level literacy amongst grade 3 children in five diverse languages. *Dyslexia*, 14(3): 170–87.

Snowling, M.J. (2000) *Dyslexia*, 2nd edn. Oxford: Blackwell.

Stanovich, K.E. (1986) Matthew effects in reading: some consequences of individual differences in the acquisition of literacy. *Reading Research Quarterly*, 21(4): 360–407.

Wolter, I., Braun, E. and Hannover, B. (2015) Reading is for girls!? The negative impact of preschool teachers' traditional gender role attitudes on boys' reading related motivation and skills. *Frontiers in Psychology*, 6: 1–11.

Ziegler, J.C. and Goswami, U. (2005) Reading acquisition, developmental dyslexia, and skilled reading across languages: a psycholinguistic grain size theory. *Psychological Bulletin*, 131(1): 3–29.

# 11

# SEXISM, SEXUAL HARASSMENT AND SEXUAL VIOLENCE IN SCHOOLS

## KAREN JONES

## KEYWORDS

- **MISOGYNY**
- **SEXISM**
- **AMBIVALENT SEXISM**
- **BENEVOLENT SEXISM**
- **BLATANT SEX DISCRIMINATION**

- **COVERT SEXISM**
- **SUBTLE SEXISM**
- **HOSTILE SEXISM**
- **SEXUAL HARASSMENT**
- **SEXUAL VIOLENCE**

- **SEXIST LANGUAGE**
- **RAPE**
- **SAFEGUARDING**

## THIS CHAPTER

- defines key terms, such as 'sexism', 'sexual harassment' and 'sexual violence', as well as terms related to these issues;
- explores evidence of sexism, sexist language and sexist bullying in schools, and provides examples of how to deal with this;
- examines evidence of sexual harassment and sexual violence in research and government reports, and looks at evidence of what should be done to tackle this.

# INTRODUCTION

We will begin this chapter by exploring the terms 'sexism', 'sexual harassment' and 'sexual violence'. Following that, we will examine evidence from a UK government inquiry, conducted in 2015, into the scale and impact of sexual harassment and sexual violence against girls and boys in schools (WEC, 2016). Focusing on the findings of a large-scale survey with girls aged 11–16, we will look at specific pressures facing girls in school today, as well as the impact of everyday sexism and sexual harassment on girls' happiness, wellbeing and opportunities in life (NEU and UK Feminista, 2017). The chapter then turns to examine the experiences and implications for boys. We will look at recommendations from the UK government and the National Education Union (NEU and UK Feminista, 2017). Some of this content might be disturbing for you to read and think about, so at the end of this chapter we have included links to additional sources of advice and support.

# WHAT IS SEXISM?

Over the past few decades, psychologists and experts on sex discrimination have studied sexism to understand its underlying causes, how it is exhibited, the behaviour it encompasses, and its impact on people, whether they are victims, bystanders or perpetrators. From the work of these experts, we know that sexism can be exhibited in different ways. Sometimes sexism is very obvious because it is blatant and involves hostile behaviour, such as verbal abuse or sexual harassment, but it can also be more subtle, or even covert, making it less easy to identify and challenge. We will look at some of the terms used to describe these different forms of sexism in Table 11.1.

*Table 11.1   Understanding sexism*

| Term | Definition and scope | Author |
|---|---|---|
| Sexism | Obvious unequal treatment of women and the questioning of women's intelligence. | Swim et al. (1995) |
| Blatant sex discrimination | 'Unequal and harmful treatment of women that is intentional, quite visible and can easily be documented'. This includes sexual harassment, sexist language and jokes, and physical violence, as well as other forms of obviously unequal treatment. | Benokraitis (1997, p7) |
| Hostile sexism | Harassment, sexual violence and behaviour, discrimination in employment, being perceived less favourably than men when enacting roles typically enacted by men, and restricting women to social roles with less status. | Glick and Fiske (1996, p492) |
| Covert sexism | Unequal and harmful treatment of women in a hidden or clandestine manner. | Swim and Cohen (1997) |
| Subtle sexism | 'Openly unequal and harmful treatment of women that goes unnoticed because it is perceived to be customary or normal behavior'. | Swim and Cohen (1997, p104) |

| Benevolent sexism | 'A set of interrelated attitudes toward women that are sexist in terms of viewing women stereotypically and in restricted roles but that are subjectively positive in feeling tone (for the perceiver) and also tend to elicit behaviors typically categorized as pro-social (e.g., helping) or intimacy seeking (e.g., self-disclosure)'. | Glick and Fiske (1996, p491) |
| Misogyny | A hatred of women. The word is formed from the Greek roots *misein* ('to hate') and *gyn* ('woman'). | Merriam-Webster (2019) |

Glick and Fiske (2001) argue that sexism is a multidimensional construct which encompasses both hostile and benevolent sexism. They call this 'ambivalent sexism'. Both hostile and benevolent forms of sexism are rooted in paternalism, gender differentiation and heterosexuality. Hostile sexism is rooted in prejudice as antipathy (or deep dislike) of females (usually), whereas benevolent sexism involves prosocial or intimacy-seeking behaviour. It encompasses attitudes towards females that are sexist (e.g. viewing females as the weaker sex). This means that people may revere females for being gentle, kind and considerate to the needs of others, but at the same time view them as incompetent in other ways, such as in tasks that involve problem-solving or mathematics.

You may have noticed that most of the definitions and descriptions of sexism view females as the victims and males as the perpetrators. Although women are more often the targets of sexism, anyone can be a victim and anyone, regardless of sex, can exhibit sexist attitudes.

You may also notice that most of the definitions and descriptions we have looked at so far refer to adults and the workplace. This is because until recently, very little research existed on sexism targeted at children or young people in education settings.

This has changed in light of growing evidence (e.g. DCSF, 2009; WEC, 2016; NEU and UK Feminista, 2017; Girlguiding, 2018) of *sexist language* and *sexist bullying*, both in education and outside of it (e.g. online). This includes, but is not limited to:

- comments to reinforce gender stereotypes that typically stem from beliefs about the inferiority of a sex;

- comments that seek to demean, ridicule, intimidate, isolate or harm others, innuendo, lewd comments, sexual remarks about clothing, spreading rumours about a person's sexual reputation, sexualised name-calling or sexually abusive terms, and sexual jokes or taunting;

- comments or sexual remarks on a person's bodily appearance, and sexual objectification – treating a person or parts of their body just as an object of sexual desire or a commodity without concern for their personality or dignity;

- transphobic bullying, often stemming from a hatred or fear of people who are transgender.

We will look at this evidence in more detail next.

## WHAT DO WE KNOW FROM RESEARCH?

### Pupils' and teachers' experiences of sexism in schools

In 2017, the National Education Union (NEU) and UK Feminista commissioned research into pupils' and teachers' experiences and views of sexism in schools. Anonymous surveys were distributed to pupils and staff. In addition, three discussion groups were conducted with pupils who were of secondary school age. The surveys were completed by 1,508 secondary school pupils and 1,634 teachers at secondary and primary schools in England and Wales. The findings revealed that gender stereotyping is a typical feature of school culture and use of misogynist language is commonplace in schools:

- 34 per cent of primary school teachers witnessed gender stereotyping on a weekly basis in schools and 54 per cent on a termly basis;

- 36 per cent of females, compared to 15 per cent of males, in mixed-sex secondary schools felt that they had been treated differently because of their gender;

- 45 per cent of primary school teachers experienced or witnessed sexist language at least on a termly basis and 15 per cent on at least a weekly basis – the majority (77 per cent) said that it involved boys making inappropriate comments to girls;

- 64 per cent of teachers in mixed-sex secondary schools heard sexist language on at least a weekly basis and 29 per cent on a daily basis;

- 66 per cent of female pupils and 37 per cent of male pupils in mixed-sex sixth forms had experienced or witnessed sexist language in school;

- only 6 per cent of pupils reported sexist language to a teacher;

- only 27 per cent of secondary school teachers said they would feel confident tackling a sexist incident if they experienced or witnessed it in school.

(NEU and UK Feminista, 2017, pp2-3)

These findings are supported by evidence from a poll of 16-18-year-olds, which found that 71 per cent of boys and girls said they heard sexual name-calling, such as 'slut' or 'slag', used towards girls at school daily or a few times a week (End Violence Against Women, 2010).

It is worrying that teachers and pupils had poor knowledge of how to tackle this damaging behaviour. Only 22 per cent of female pupils in mixed-sex secondary schools thought their school took sexism seriously enough, and 78 per cent of secondary pupils didn't know if their school had a policy to tackle the problem. Similarly, 64 per cent of secondary teachers were unaware or unsure of policies or practices. Only 20 per cent had received training on how to recognise and tackle sexism in their initial teacher training, and 20 per cent through continuing professional development (CPD) (NEU and UK Feminista, 2017).

## REFLECTION

- Do you feel confident that you know how to recognise and deal with sexism in your practice setting?
- Are you aware of any policy that is applicable?
- Have you received training or CPD?
- If not, what can you do to address this?

The answers to these questions may prompt you to find out more by reading the recommendations from the studies we have looked at in further reading at the end of this chapter, as well as perhaps the full list in the References. You could also speak to colleagues you work with, your line manager and the senior leadership team to bring this to their attention.

## EVIDENCE FROM PRACTICE

One teacher at a secondary school in England was so concerned about the prevalence of sexist language to which pupils were exposed that they decided to teach pupils about the impact of verbally abusive language. Much of the offensive language was directed at girls but was used by girls and boys. The lesson included an activity where pupils were asked to write down on sticky notes examples of language they'd heard or experienced that might be misogynistic or prejudiced against women. This produced a large and depressing number of sexist words, such as 'slag', 'bitch', 'whore', 'sket' and 'feminazi', and offensive phrases, such as 'get back in the kitchen', 'runs like a girl' and other more sexually offensive comments. The sticky notes covered a board in the classroom.

Next the teacher discussed with the pupils the impact that such words and phrases can have on other people. Girls talked about how sexist language belittled them and made them feel self-conscious and anxious, to the extent that some did not want to leave the house or talk to people. Girls also talked about how sexist language made them feel angry, low and small compared to boys. Boys commented that they had not really thought about the consequences of sexist language. They said that the lesson made them think about the language they use and the impact it has on others.

The teacher who created this lesson spoke about her experience to 5 Live Breakfast, and the story featured in BBC News (2018). You can read more about this case study by following the link in the References.

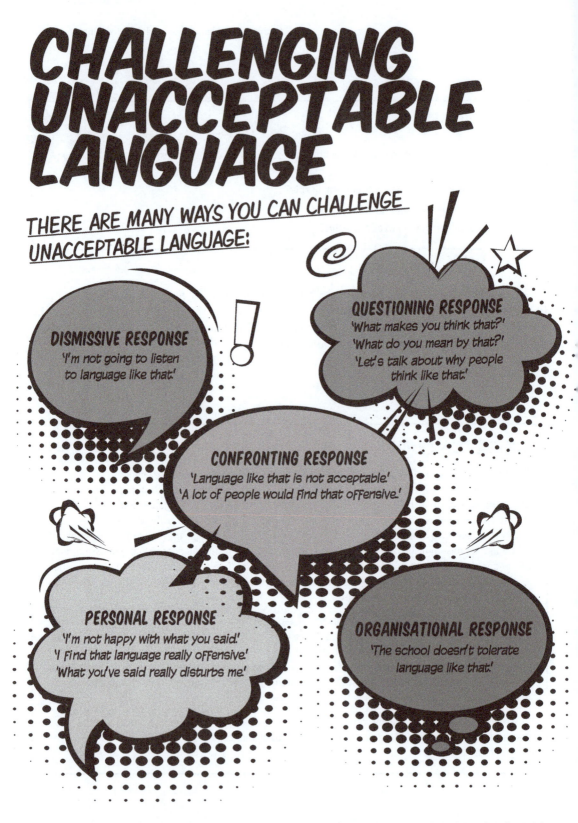

These examples have been recommended by the Department for Children, Schools and Families (DCSF) (2009, p. 28) *Guidance for schools on preventing and responding to sexist, sexual and transphobic bullying. Safe to Learn: Embedding anti-bullying work in schools.* **Nottingham: DCSF Publications.**

## ACTIVITY

Following the example in the case study, this activity will help you think about how to respond to sexist language. You might want to do this activity with colleagues or adapt it in an age-appropriate way for use with pupils, if you work in a school. You could use the examples of sexist comments in Table 11.2 or generate a list of words or comments with colleagues/pupils that they have experienced in education.

Table 11.2  Sexist comments

| Don't be a pussy | Man up | Slut, slag, whore |
| --- | --- | --- |
| You throw like a girl | That's not a boys'/girls' subject | Haha, you run like a girl! |
| Not bad work for a girl/boy | That's so gay | Act like a lady |

For each comment, consider the following questions:

- What gender stereotype is the comment based on?
- How might it make someone feel if they were the target of the offensive word/phrase?
- How would you respond if you witnessed a pupil making this comment? What would you say to the pupil? Jot down some possible responses.
- What action would you take following the incident?
- How confident would you be in your chosen response and actions?

It can be difficult to know how to respond to sexist language, and sometimes people dismiss it as 'banter'. By downgrading the problem or ignoring it, we inadvertently reinforce the view that sexist language is acceptable. Ignoring the problem normalises it.

## EVIDENCE FROM PRACTICE

There are many ways you can challenge unacceptable language. The following examples have been recommended by the Department for Children, Schools and Families:

- *Dismissive response*: 'I'm not going to listen to language like that.'
- *Questioning response*: 'What makes you think that?' 'What do you mean by that?' 'Let's talk about why people think like that.'
- *Confronting response*: 'Language like that is not acceptable.' 'A lot of people would find that offensive.'

*(Continued)*

(Continued)

- *Personal response*: 'I'm not happy with what you said.' 'I find that language really offensive.' 'What you've said really disturbs me.'
- *Organisational response*: 'The school doesn't tolerate language like that.'

(DCSF, 2009, p28)

Compare the possible responses you thought of in the activity to those in the list above. Try to classify your responses according to the categories listed (e.g. dismissive, questioning, confronting, personal, organisational). Then reflect on how well you communicate that sexist language is unacceptable, as well as if you can do this more effectively.

The child who is the target of sexist language will need reassurance that the incident has been taken seriously and steps are being taken to protect them from further harm. Follow the policy on reporting incidents and seek help from your leadership team if you are unsure of what action to take.

# WATCH YOUR LANGUAGE!

Findings from research by the NEU and UK Feminista (2017) also show that in interactions with pupils, teachers sometimes inadvertently reinforced gender stereotypes in the comments they made to students. For example, a female student was told it was OK to fail mathematics because girls are better at expressive lessons. Boys in one school were regularly told to 'man up'. Boys were often allocated class tasks such as lifting tables or boxes, while girls were told to leave those jobs for the boys and sort out books instead.

## EVIDENCE FROM PRACTICE

At the first sixth form parents' evening, Becky and her mum met with teachers. One, the geography teacher, complained at length that Becky's (naturally) frizzy hair was distracting boys in class. Next, glancing at a stack of school reports on his desk, the head of chemistry gave his report on Becky's progress. Becky's mum asked if he had read the correct report because Becky was top of chemistry across the entire year group the previous year, whereas the pupil he had described was clearly struggling. He checked through the pile of reports and, without apologising, read the correct one, which showed that Becky was making excellent progress. By way of explanation for his mistake, he said, 'You wouldn't think she'd be good at chemistry to look at her, would you?' Astounded, Becky's mum asked him to explain his comment, but he simply repeated the comment.

## REFLECTION

- What assumptions do you make about the abilities, behaviour and preferences of boys and girls?
- Do you offer encouragement and praise equally to boys and girls in all subjects and activities, such as mathematics, science, sport, English and reading?
- Do you express surprise when a boy or girl behaves in a counter-stereotypical way for their gender (e.g. a boy who enjoys cookery, a girl who enjoys mathematics)?
- How might the language you use shape children's perceptions of gender stereotypes?
- How might this impact on children and young people?

The school environment is a good place to communicate messages about gender equality to counter sexism and sexist language. Unfortunately, sometimes we can inadvertently perpetuate the problem. By reflecting on your own deep-rooted beliefs, values and practice, you can identify and act on your own gender stereotypes. Let's look at some examples of evidence of best practice next.

## TRANSFORMING PRACTICE

- Treat sexist language in the learning environment as unacceptable at all times. Use codes of conduct to communicate norms and expected behaviour. Involve children in this activity. For example, involve pupils in the design of equality posters on specific issues, such as the use of sexist language and challenging gender stereotypes in science, maths, sport, and so on.
- Refrain from using sexist language yourself.
- Present curricular subjects equally to pupils in terms of their relative difficulty and refrain from making remarks about how easy or difficult a subject is or whether a child is suited to it because of their gender.
- This also applies when offering praise or encouragement.
- Expose pupils to counter-stereotypical role models. For example, diversify wall displays with a gender balance of portraits of people, such as male and female alumni, famous scientists, mathematicians, historical figures and sportspeople. Include positive examples of counter-stereotypical role models in lesson planning. Involve pupils in sourcing and producing this material.
- Create an inclusive learning environment by encouraging pupils to listen to and respect each other. Encourage diverse perspectives to be heard and give then equal airtime.
- Listen to pupils who raise issues. Be sensitive to their circumstances. If you don't know how to deal with their issue, seek help from someone who can help or advise you.
- Avoid tokenism when constructing teams or group work. Don't use pupils to manage behaviour in class (e.g. sitting girls next to boys to prevent boys from misbehaving).

# SEXUAL HARASSMENT AND SEXUAL VIOLENCE

This is a very difficult topic to discuss, and you might find some parts of this section upsetting. However, people working with children and young people increasingly have a role in preventing and dealing with sexual harassment and sexual violence, so it is important that you are aware of the nature of these issues and your responsibilities. We will begin by looking at definitions for key terms used in this section:

- *Sexual harassment*: 'Unwanted conduct of a sexual nature' (WEC, 2016, para 4).

- *Sexual violence*: 'Any physical, visual, verbal or sexual act that is experienced by the woman or girl, at the time or later, as a threat, invasion or assault, that has the effect of hurting her or degrading her and/or takes away her ability to control intimate contact' (Kelly, 1988, cited in WEC, 2016, para 4). 'It should be noted that men and boys also experience sexual harassment and sexual violence' (WEC, 2016, para 4). 'Sexual violence and sexual harassment can occur between two children of any age and sex. It can also occur through a group of children sexually assaulting or sexually harassing a single child or group of children' (DfE, 2018a, p6).

- *Rape*: 'A person (A) commits an offence if— (a) he intentionally penetrates the vagina, anus or mouth of another person (B) with his penis, (b) B does not consent to the penetration, and (c) A does not reasonably believe that B consents' (Sexual Offences Act 2003, chapter 42, part 1).

- *Assault by penetration*: 'A person (A) commits an offence if— (a) he intentionally penetrates the vagina or anus of another person (B) with a part of his body or anything else, (b) the penetration is sexual, (c) B does not consent to the penetration, and (d) A does not reasonably believe that B consents' (Sexual Offences Act 2003, chapter 42, part 1).

- *Sexual assault*: 'A person (A) commits an offence if— (a) he intentionally touches another person (B), (b) the touching is sexual, (c) B does not consent to the touching, and (d) A does not reasonably believe that B consents' (Sexual Offences Act 2003, chapter 42, part 1).

- *Sexual abuse*: 'When someone is forced, pressurised or tricked into taking part in any kind of sexual activity with another person' (Childline, 2019).

- *Consent*: 'About having the freedom and capacity to choose. Consent may be given to one sexual activity but not another and it can be withdrawn at any time. Sexual intercourse without consent is rape. The age of consent is 16. A child under the age of 13 can never consent to any sexual activity' (DfE, 2018a, p8).

Sexual harassment involves a similar set of behaviours to those we looked at earlier in this chapter when we explored sexist language and sexist bullying in schools. Sexual harassment can also encompass physical behaviour such as brushing against someone or interfering with their clothes, or sharing sexual images and videos, as well as sexual exploitation, coercion and threats. This can occur online or offline, or between the two (DfE, 2018a).

In 2018, the National Society for the Prevention of Cruelty to Children (NSPCC) Childline service reported that it had provided over 3,004 counselling sessions to children who had been sexually abused by a peer. Almost half were aged 12–15 years and 114 were aged 11 years or under (NSPCC, 2018). These incidents can happen in many different settings, including school. Research by the NEU and UK Feminista (2017) found that 17 per cent of primary school teachers had witnessed sexual harassment in their school. In mixed-sex secondary schools, they found:

- 37 per cent of girls and 6 per cent of boys had personally experienced some form of sexual harassment at school;

- 24 per cent of girls and 4 per cent of boys had experienced unwanted physical touching of a sexual nature at school;

- 58 per cent of girls had experienced or witnessed sexual harassment at school;

- 36 per cent of teachers witnessed sexual harassment termly, 26 per cent on a weekly basis, and 6 per cent witnessed it daily at school.

Data published in September 2015 showed that 5,500 sexual offences, including 600 rapes, were recorded in UK schools over a three-year period (WEC, 2016). It is thought that these figures are well below the number of actual incidents because schools and pupils under-report incidents. In the case of pupils this is mostly due to fear a teacher will not take the report of an incident seriously or they are ashamed and afraid of the consequences of telling a teacher. Under-reporting in schools is also attributed to lack of effective policies and inertia (NEU and UK Feminista, 2017).

In 2016, the Women and Equalities Committee (WEC), a UK Parliament Select Committee, launched an inquiry into the scale and impact of sexual harassment and sexual violence in schools in England. They reviewed findings from several large-scale surveys and received 92 submissions of evidence from individuals and organisations. They held five oral sessions with schoolchildren aged 13–18 years, one with experts working with young people, a session with Ofsted, the National Education Union, the National Council of Police Chiefs and Welsh Women's Aid, a session focusing on boys and young men, and a session with government ministers.

## WHAT DO WE KNOW FROM RESEARCH?

### Evidence that was considered by the Women and Equalities Committee (WEC, 2016)

- Girlguiding reported that 22 per cent of girls aged 7–12 experienced sexualised jokes by boys.

- UK Feminista reported that 25 per cent of girls aged 11–16 said concerns over potential sexual harassment make them consider whether or not to speak out in class.

- End Violence Against Women reported that 29 per cent of girls aged 16–18 had experienced unwanted sexual touching in school and 28 per cent had seen sexual pictures on mobile phones at school a few times a month or more.

- The NASUWT reported the findings of a survey with teachers, which listed issues such as pupils filming themselves masturbating and sharing images, girls taking nude photographs of themselves and sending those to older boys, and regular incidents of the photographs being forwarded on to other boys.

*(Continued)*

(Continued)

Qualitative research considered in the inquiry added support to survey findings. Brook, a sexual health and wellbeing provider for under-25s, was one of the organisations that submitted evidence to the inquiry. They reported that children's experiences of sexual harassment in primary and secondary happens 'quite a lot' and for some children it occurs 'multiple times a day'. They reported that sexual harassment 'definitely happens in primary school, especially in Years 5 and 6'. Typical activities among that age group of children included 'lifting up skirts and pulling down pants'. They reported that because of this, some children were 'scared to wear skirts' (para 16). They commented that sexual harassment and violence in schools varies in severity, but the consequences are far-reaching and serious for victims and others in the environment, since it normalises behaviour.

Similar findings were reported to the Women and Equalities Committee by Public Health Bristol City Council (para 17). Children aged 13-16 said sexual bullying, sexism and sexual harassment is an everyday occurrence, but incidents are rarely reported because they are passed off as a joke. They attributed the problem to pressure on boys to prove their masculinity by objectifying and teasing girls. This might explain why the Anti-Bullying Alliance National Children's Bureau said that girls are less likely to 'do anything that will make them stand out and attract attention' and are self-conscious about appearance 'and not appearing too geeky'. They also reported that sexual harassment was 'taking up a lot of teacher time'.

The Women and Equalities Committee concluded: 'Sexual harassment and sexual violence in schools is a significant issue which affects a large number of children and young people, particularly girls, across the country' (para 45).

While it was found that boys are the main perpetrators and girls the victims of abuse, the committee pointed out it is essential that the negative impact on all parties is recognised and addressed. Not surprisingly, this is having an impact on pupils and school life. Teachers reported spending considerable time dealing with problems, but complained that they lack guidance, training and structures to deal with incidents. It might be for this reason that school staff and leaders often fail to consider incidents seriously (para 55).

The inquiry recommended: 'The Government and schools must make tackling sexual harassment and sexual violence an immediate policy priority' (para 48).

## REFLECTION

- In what ways has your understanding of sexism, sexual harassment and sexual assault changed as a consequence of reading this chapter?
- Pause to reflect on action you can take in your practice.

All schools should have a policy to counter sexism, which includes the use of sexist language. While many schools have such policies, research suggests that teachers are not fully aware of school policy. One action you can take after reading this chapter is to read the policy in your practice setting. It is also important to understand your legal duties. Advice from the Department for Education on sexual violence and sexual harassment between children in schools (DfE, 2018a) is cross-referenced with other sources of advice, aligned with statutory guidance on keeping children safe in education (DfE, 2018b), working together to safeguard children (HM Government, 2018) and legal obligations, such as the Human Rights Act 1998 and the Equality Act 2010, and contained within this the Public Sector Equality Duty. This advises on how to minimise the risk of sexual violence and harassment occurring, as well as what to do if it does occur or is alleged to have taken place. We will look at legislative frameworks and guidance for schools in more depth in Chapter 12.

## ACTIVITY

The Intervention Initiative is a free resource for universities and further education institutions, developed in 2014 by the University of the West of England with funding from Public Health England. It is an evidence-based educational programme for the prevention of sexual coercion and abuse in university settings; however, many of the activities could be used or adapted for use in primary or secondary educational settings with staff and/or students as the main goal is to empower individuals to act as prosocial citizens (Fenton et al., 2014).

Aim to identify at least one activity to complete yourself and consider how you might apply or adapt that for use in your practice context. Read more at: **http://socialsciences.exeter.ac.uk/research/interventioninitiative/toolkit/**

# CHAPTER SUMMARY

As this chapter has shown, gender stereotyping is at the root of many issues affecting children and young people at school.

- We explored evidence of sexism and the way this can manifest as sexist language and sexist bullying in schools. We looked at what you can do to prevent this and how you can respond when it happens.

- We looked at the growing problem of sexual harassment and sexual violence in schools. Failure to take appropriate action on your part could be considered a breach of contract and duty of care.

# FURTHER READING

**Institute of Physics (IOP)** (2015) *Opening Doors: A Guide to Good Practice in Countering Gender Stereotyping in Schools.* Available at: www.iop.org/education/teacher/support/girls_physics/reports-and-research/opening-doors/page_66438.html#gref

**SecEd** (2019) *Handling Incidents of Sexual Assault in Schools.* Available at: www.sec-ed.co.uk/best-practice/handling-incidents-of-sexual-assault-in-schools/

# REFERENCES

BBC News (2018) *School Teaches Pupils about Impact of Sexist Language*. Available at: www.bbc.co.uk/news/uk-42652967

Benokraitis, N.V. (1997) *Subtle Sexism: Current Practices and Prospects for Change*. Thousand Oaks, CA: SAGE.

Childline (2019) *Sexual Abuse*. Available at: www.childline.org.uk/info-advice/bullying-abuse-safety/abuse-safety/sexual-abuse/

Department for Children, Schools and Families (DCSF) (2009) *Guidance for Schools on Preventing and Responding to Sexist, Sexual and Transphobic Bullying. Safe to Learn: Embedding Anti-Bullying Work in Schools.* Nottingham: DCSF.

Department for Education (DfE) (2018a) *Sexual Violence and Sexual Harassment between Children in Schools and Colleges: Advice for Governing Bodies, Proprietors, Headteachers, Principals, Senior Leadership Teams and Designated Safeguarding Leads.* Available at: www.gov.uk/government/publications

Department for Education (DfE) (2018b) *Keeping Children Safe in Education*. Available at: www.gov.uk/government/publications/keeping-children-safe-in-education--2

End Violence Against Women (2010) *YouGov Poll Exposes High Levels Sexual Harassment in Schools*. Available at: www.endviolenceagainstwomen.org.uk/yougov-poll-exposes-high-levels-sexual-harassment-in-schools/

Fenton, R.A., Mott, H.L., McCartan, K. and Rumney, P. (2014) *The Intervention Initiative*. Available at: http://socialsciences.exeter.ac.uk/research/interventioninitiative/about/about/#2v1KBvGgOpsKh0TR.99

Girlguiding (2018) *'We See the Big Picture': Girls' Attitudes Survey 2018*. Available at: www.girlguiding.org.uk/globalassets/docs-and-resources/research-and-campaigns/girls-attitudes-survey-2018.pdf

Glick, P. and Fiske, S.T. (1996) The ambivalent sexism inventory: differentiating hostile and benevolent sexism. *Journal of Personality and Social Psychology*, 70(3): 491–512.

Glick, P. and Fiske, S.T. (2001) An ambivalent alliance: hostile and benevolent sexism as complementary justifications for gender inequality. *American Psychologist*, 56(2): 109–18.

HM Government (1998) *Human Rights Act 1998*. Available at: www.legislation.gov.uk/ukpga/1998/42/contents

HM Government (2003) *Sexual Offences Act 2003*. Available at: www.legislation.gov.uk/ukpga/2003/42/contents

HM Government (2010a) *Equality Act 2010*. Available at: www.legislation.gov.uk/ukpga/2010/15/contents

HM Government (2010b) *Public Sector Equality Duty*. Available at: www.legislation.gov.uk/ukpga/2010/15/section/149

HM Government (2018) *Working Together to Safeguard Children*. Available at: www.gov.uk/government/publications/working-together-to-safeguard-children--2

Kelly, L. (1988) *Surviving Sexual Violence*. Cambridge: Polity.

Merriam-Webster (2019) *Misogyny*. Available at: www.merriam-webster.com/dictionary/misogyny

National Education Union (NEU) and UK Feminista (2017) *'It's Just Everywhere': A Study of Sexism in Schools and How We Can Tackle It*. Available at: https://neu.org.uk/sites/neu.org.uk/files/sexism-survey-feminista-2017.pdf

National Society for the Prevention of Cruelty to Children (NSPCC) (2018) *Childline Sees over 3,000 Counselling Sessions about Peer Sexual Abuse*. Available at: www.nspcc.org.uk/what-we-do/news-opinion/childline-sees-over-3000-counselling-sessions-peer-sexual-abuse/

Swim, J.K. and Cohen, L.L. (1997) Overt, covert, and subtle sexism. *Psychology of Women Quarterly*, 21(1): 103–18.

Swim, J.K., Aikin, K.J., Hall, W.S. and Hunter, B. (1995) Sexism and racism: old fashioned and modern prejudices. *Journal of Personality and Social Psychology*, 68(2): 199–214.

Women and Equalities Committee (WEC) (2016) *Sexual Harassment and Sexual Violence in Schools: Third Report of Session 2016–17*. Available at: https://publications.parliament.uk/pa/cm201617/cmselect/cmwomeq/91/91.pdf

# 12

# A WHOLE-SCHOOL APPROACH

## KAREN JONES

## KEYWORDS

- **WHOLE-SCHOOL APPROACH**
- **SAFEGUARDING**

- **STATUTORY GUIDANCE**
- **LAW/LEGISLATION**
- **PARENTS**

- **LEADERS**
- **GOVERNORS**
- **COLLEAGUES**

### THIS CHAPTER

- explores your legal duty to safeguard and promote the welfare of children, as well as statutory guidance on what schools must do to comply with the law;
- sets out recommendations for a whole-school approach, as well as how collaboration between school leaders, staff, pupils and parents can act as a catalyst for change;
- provides examples of best practice and activities to transform practice.

## INTRODUCTION

As this book has shown, research suggests that most parents, teachers and school leaders believe in gender equality but may inadvertently or subtly reinforce gender stereotypes. Research in schools also suggests that teachers and school leaders often believe they don't have a problem with gender equality, and are therefore reluctant to initiate change. This means that those advocating change may face resistance. If you find yourself in that position, remember you have a professional duty of care. We will begin this chapter by looking at your statutory and legal duties to identify children at risk of harm and take action to protect them. We will then explore guidance on best practice in dealing with the issues we have examined in this book, such as sexism, sexist language, sexist bullying, sexual harassment and sexual violence. We will examine how communication and collaboration with parents, colleagues and school leaders can act as a catalyst for change. You will also be supported in this chapter with specific tangible actions taken in school settings. Pragmatic examples that we will look at in this chapter include a project to tackle gender stereotypes in education. The project includes activities that can be used by you with colleagues and school leaders to raise awareness of gender stereotypes and initiate change.

## UNDERSTANDING YOUR STATUTORY RESPONSIBILITIES

In the four nations that make up the UK, there are different child protection systems and legislative frameworks to protect children:

- *England*: The Department for Education (DfE) is responsible for child protection.

- *Northern Ireland*: Northern Ireland Executive and the Department of Health.

- *Scotland*: Scottish Government.

- *Wales*: Social Services and Well-Being (Wales) Act 2014 (in force from 2016).

All work on similar principles to identify children at risk of harm and take action to protect them. Legislation to protect the rights of children and young people against abuse and harm include the Human Rights Act 1998, the Equality Act 2010 and the Public Sector Equality Duty, which requires public bodies to have due regard to the need to eliminate discrimination, advance equality of opportunity, and foster good relations between different people when carrying out their activities. Schools and colleges have a statutory duty under the Education Act 2002 to safeguard and protect the welfare of children at school. The Education (Independent School Standards) Regulations 2014 apply the same principles to proprietors of independent schools, academies and free schools. The Non-Maintained Special Schools (England) Regulations 2015 set out similar obligations. The United Nations Convention on the Rights of the Child (UNCRC) is a legally binding international agreement.

Schools have a legal duty to identify and take action to protect children from harm. This includes the issues discussed in this book, such as gender stereotyping, sexism, sexist language, sexist bullying, sexual harassment and sexual violence.

## HOW ARE YOU PROTECTED?

If you are working in an environment where gender stereotyping and sexism is prevalent, you might find you are sometimes the target of sexist language, such as sexualised remarks, or you may be exposed to offensive sexual material, gestures or graffiti, or experience unwanted physical attention.

You are protected from sexual harassment by the Equality Act 2010. It does not matter what type of contract you are employed on or your gender; you are still protected by law. Your employer is required to take action to prevent and deal with sexual harassment (and other forms of harassment), whether this is caused by a third party, such as a pupil or group of pupils, a parent or colleague, or someone else. If your employer has been informed of the harassment, they may be liable if they do not take reasonable steps to prevent it from reoccurring. This means it is important that you report any incidences which might be considered sexual harassment to your employer in writing, as well as requesting that they record it. You can get further advice and guidance on this from your union, the National Education Union or Acas.

## BEST PRACTICE: A WHOLE-SCHOOL APPROACH

There is widespread agreement among researchers, education experts, policymakers and government bodies that the best practice for tackling gender stereotypes, as well as all of the related issues we have examined in this book, such as sexism, sexist language, sexist bullying, sexual harassment and sexual violence, is a *whole-school approach*. This involves all stakeholders working together and being committed to a plan of action that is supported by a written strategy and policy, driven by leadership and mapped to initiatives to support staff, students, parents and carers.

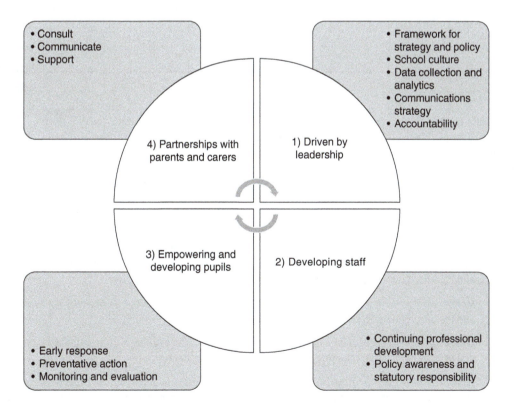

*Figure 12.1  A whole-school approach*

We will look at each segment of Figure 12.1 in turn, starting with segment 1, 'driven by leadership'.

## 1. A whole-school approach: driven by leadership

A whole-school approach is driven forward with leadership. Many people think that to be a leader, you must possess unique traits or characteristics. However, perspectives have changed, and nowadays leadership is generally viewed as the ability to engage in certain practices, to learn, reflect and be sensitive to the context in which you work in order to respond to issues. This means *you* may be called on to exercise leadership. In other words, you don't need to be a head teacher or in a formal leadership position to take the lead challenging gender stereotypes!

Most of what has been written about a whole-school approach refers to it as an institutional framework that encompasses school strategy and policy. A *strategy* sets out in a written document the school plan of action to achieve a set of long-term goals and is supported through *policy*. This is underpinned by the principles upheld by the school and includes rules and guidance to help everyone achieve long-term strategic goals. Guidance on how to deal with gender stereotypes and related harmful behaviour is relatively new to education and may not be included in existing strategy or policy documents, so these may need to be amended.

As illustrated, leadership of the whole-school approach involves sensitive consideration of school culture (i.e. the attitudes, norms, traditions, beliefs and ways of doing things). You will already have an opinion about this. An audit can help you understand how others view the culture. You may be surprised when you see the results!

---

### ACTIVITY

Audits involve a few simple steps or large-scale evaluation. We will focus on a few simple steps you can take to gather the views of a cross-section of staff, pupils, parents and carers:

1.  Distribute a short survey.

2.  Use sticky notes to gather views of staff and pupils. Use responses to prompt discussion of whether the school/organisational culture supports gender equality.

3.  Audit the physical environment. Make a note of artefacts displayed and the messages they convey about what is valued, who is celebrated and respected, and why. Are female and male alumni celebrated in equal numbers? Is there a cross-section of professions?

4.  Monitor the behaviour, attainment and attendance of children affected by harmful behaviour and the perpetrators to establish if interventions are needed.

5.  Where appropriate, collect data on subject selection and student progression to establish if girls and boys are restricting their choices to certain subjects or careers.

6.  When you have gathered this evidence, discuss it with colleagues and pupils. Building strong student-teacher relationships is an essential part of a positive school culture.

---

Driven by leadership, a *communications strategy* can help everyone understand the values of the school, its strategy, policy and rules of conduct.

Figure 12.2 includes a set of questions to guide the development of the communications strategy.

- Consider why you are communicating and what you want to achieve. Is the purpose to share your vision, launch a new initiative or event, or communicate changes in policy to staff? Are you trying to persuade your audience, inform them or grab their attention?

- Different audiences have their own unique information needs, at different time points. Carefully crafted messages tailored to the needs of each audience work best. Consider the different channels of communication available (e.g. website, email, social media, letter, leaflets, posters, notices and displays, presentations, training activities).

- We live in a world with information overload, so take care not to overload people with unnecessary information or alarm them by the way the message is framed, or its tone and language. For example, tweeting that the school has a new policy for sexual harassment and sexual violence could easily prompt widespread fear and panic among parents, pupils and people in the community! Always assess if the content or channel of communication has the potential to cause distress and/or damage relationships or reputation. Seek a second opinion on this.

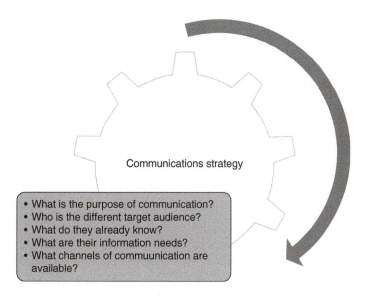

Communications strategy

- What is the purpose of communication?
- Who is the different target audience?
- What do they already know?
- What are their information needs?
- What channels of commuunication are available?

*Figure 12.2   Communications strategy*

Leaders also drive forward the notion that everyone is *accountable* for achieving the goals of the whole-school approach. People won't know this if they are not told. Even then, they may not feel accountable for achieving goals with which they do not agree. This can happen if staff don't think gender stereotyping is a problem or sexist language is just a bit of 'banter'. This brings us nicely to developing staff.

## 2. A whole-school approach: developing staff

A whole-school approach involves building capacity among staff. Information and training for staff should provide the following:

- Information about the whole-school approach – what it is and how it relates to the school strategy and policy.

- Clear messages to promote gender equality and prevent harmful behaviour. The message should be clear that there is a zero-tolerance policy and everyone is responsible.

- Clear guidance on what constitutes harmful behaviour, definitions of key terms, and how to explain harmful behaviour to children in an age-appropriate way.

- Opportunities to reflect on practice to understand how our own language, curriculum content and the learning environment might reinforce gender stereotypes.

- Practical guidance and activities to prevent gender stereotyping and promote respectful relationships to support gender equality.

- Opportunities to review schemes of work and lesson plans, as well as auditing the learning environment to identify where gender stereotypes might be generated and where they can be challenged and discussed with pupils.

- Practical steps to manage children's behaviour in the learning environment (e.g. practical advice on how to stop sexist language and gender stereotyping).

- Action to take if the welfare of a child is of concern or in the event of an incident. This should include how to report incidents and definitions of the terms used by the school for recording incidents. Many children do not report incidents because they fear the teacher will not believe them; therefore, training should include how to respond to and support a child who reports an incident.

- Provide information about further training, resources and support available for practitioners, children and parents.

Additional sources of information and advice on harmful sexual behaviour are available on the NSPCC website (**www.nspcc.org.uk**). Critical factors to consider include the stage of development of the children concerned. The Brook Sexual Behaviours Traffic Light Tool explains sexual development and age-related sexual behaviour (Brook, 2020). Other specialist advice is available from Brook, Rape Crisis, the Survivors Trust, the National Education Union and UK Feminista (see the useful websites section at the end of the chapter).

Statutory guidance is contained in the following government documents:

- *Working Together to Safeguard Children* (HM Government, 2018);

- *Keeping Children Safe in Education* (DfE, 2018);

- *Child Abuse Concerns: Guidance for Practitioners* (DfE, 2015a).

# TRANSFORMING PRACTICE

The following activities are adapted from a project developed at the University of Reading to help staff understand the impact of gender stereotypes on pupils.

## Session contents

- Three cartoon strips with scenarios.
- Role-play scenarios.
- Action planning and feedback.

## How the session works

The session facilitates active participation in a series of activities: first, to raise awareness of gender stereotypes in the classroom, so participants are better able to notice and challenge issues; then to consider the cumulative impact of gender stereotyping.

## Cartoon strips

The characters in the cartoon strips include a single dot and a group of asterisks in a class. They illustrate how one sex can be outnumbered by the other in class, and how that can shape people's behaviour. The dot tries to fit in with the asterisks but is rejected by them (see Figure 12.3).

*Figure 12.3   Cartoon strips*

## Questions to prompt reflection and discussion

- What is the scenario depicting? Does it really matter? Why?
- If the same dot experienced these scenarios regularly, what might the impact be?

*(Continued)*

(Continued)

- Why do we notice differences between groups as opposed to what people have in common? In what ways are the characters similar?

Consider each group (asterisks and dots) in the scenarios and reflect on the following questions:

- Do I feel positive (e.g. warmth, affection, compassion, pity) or negative emotions (e.g. anger, humiliation, apathy, shame, guilt, fear, tension) in connection with that group?
- Have my emotions arisen out of an affinity with one group (e.g. asterisks, dot)?
- Does my opinion resemble my response to similar situations in my practice context?
- Does my reasoning involve my own unchecked thoughts on gender stereotypes?

## Role play

Prepare scenarios or ask participants to prepare examples of situations where they have encountered gender stereotypes or sexist language. Ask participants to role-play the scenario. Follow that with discussion of the incident and how they could respond. Questions to prompt discussion include:

- How does that make you feel?
- Have others experienced similar situations?
- What explanation can you give for the behaviour?
- What would be an appropriate response?
- What action would you take following this incident?

## Action planning and feedback

Ask participants to create a plan for action that they can take into their practice. Give participants time to generate their own ideas. Use examples from this book if they need inspiration. Discuss the challenges that they may face implementing the action plan, as well as what they can do to overcome resistance. Provide feedback and follow up at a later date to monitor progress and share best practice.

## WHAT DO WE KNOW FROM RESEARCH?

### Supporting children

Ensure that children (as well as teachers, parents and carers) know what do if they experience or witness harmful behaviour or are concerned about the welfare of another child. Provide clear information, in an age-appropriate way, on how to report incidents or concerns. Ensure that this is visible (e.g. use posters or leaflets, wall displays, notices on the doors of toilet facilities). If an incident is reported or suspected, the Department for Children, Schools and Families advises that you *listen* to the child; take care with the language you use as this could give the impression that you doubt them or are judging them (DCSF, 2009). *Reassure* the child that your priority is their welfare and safety. Provide reassurance about reporting the incident to dispel any anxieties about how other staff, friends or family will react. Take prompt *action*, following school policy and guidance. Help the child to report the incident. Provide reassurance to parents/carers and advise on further support available. Provide additional support where needed. This may need to be sourced externally. *Monitor* behaviour, attendance and achievement to assess if children may need further support. Hold review meetings. Follow up with interventions to reduce the risk of further incidents. Gather feedback on how effectively the incident was dealt with; this could be in an anonymous survey or question sheet with smiley/sad face response options, depending on the age of the children.

## EVIDENCE FROM PRACTICE

The Wigan Analysis Window can help you to analyse the incident so that you can follow it up with appropriate action. It was developed by Professor Chris Gaine predominantly to analyse incidents such as sexist, sexual and transphobic bullying in schools, but can be used to analyse other harmful behaviour in order to identify the best course of action. Figure 12.4 illustrates the four main steps of the Wigan Analysis Window.

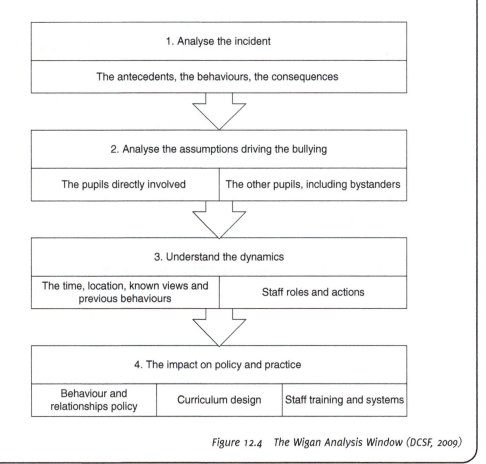

Figure 12.4   The Wigan Analysis Window (DCSF, 2009)

## 3. A whole-school approach: empowering and developing pupils

Turning to the third segment of a whole-school approach, empowering and developing pupils, first we will look at how to support early response to incidents, as well as action to take following incidents, then we will look at examples of preventative education to transform practice.

This brings us to *preventative* education, which should always be incorporated in curriculum planning, regardless of whether there has been an incident. The aim of preventative education is to empower and enable children to discuss and learn about harmful behaviour, as well as promoting gender equality and respectful relationships. This can form part of the curriculum for personal, social, health and economic education (PSHE) and relationships and sex education (RSE). Embed topics for discussion, such as those in Figure 12.5, in lesson planning, and ask children to suggest topics too! *Support* children to promote and take the lead on gender equality and be activists for change. Ask if there are campaigns or interventions they would like to lead. Take part in events such as the following:

- International Women's Day (**www.internationalwomensday.com**);

- International Day for the Elimination of Violence against Women (**www.un.org/en/events/ endviolenceday/**);

- Anti-Bullying Week (**www.anti-bullyingalliance.org.uk**);

- International Day Against Homophobia, Transphobia and Biphobia (**https://may17.org/**).

Get children involved in creating posters, notices and leaflets to promote positive relationships and communicate messages about the damaging effects of gender stereotypes. Ensure that children know where to go for further support if they are worried about their own safety or the welfare of another child, and know how to report incidents or concerns. The NEU and UK Feminista (2017) found that 'teachers are ill equipped to address sexism, and female students in particular feel unsupported in the face of normalised sexism and sexual harassment' (p19). Make sure you know how to support children, as well as what specialist support is available to them.

*Monitor and evaluate* initiatives so you know if they work, as well as providing important evidence of what has been accomplished.

## 4. A whole-school approach: partnerships with parents and carers

As the previous case study illustrates, working with parents and carers is important so that everyone feels committed to the same goals. Let's look at some additional ways you can work in partnership with parents and carers:

- Discuss the policy on equality with parents and carers. Show this to them at open days or enrolment visits, as well as involving them in the development of the equality policy when it is reviewed.

- Ensure that parents and carers understand the procedure for making a complaint and reporting an incident, as well as providing further sources of information and support.

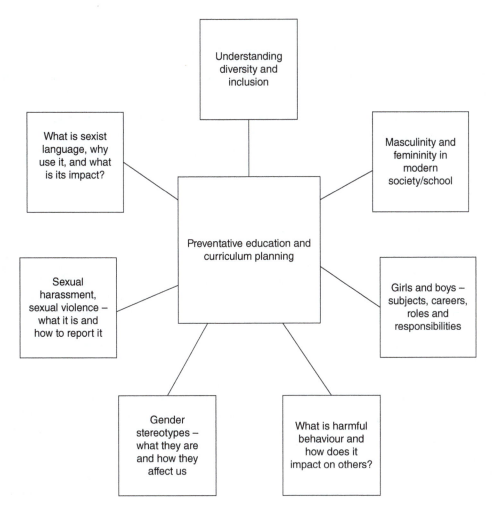

*Figure 12.5   Preventative education and curriculum planning*

- Consider the best way to communicate with parents and how to deal with possible misconceptions, such as the notion that gender inequality only affects females or that it results in males being worse off. Discussing issues with parents can help to correct misconceptions and defuse resistance.

- Use posters to showcase the work you are doing to challenge gender stereotypes and communicate why this is important. Display these where parents can see them, such as entrance doors or windows.

- Create postcards for children to take home.

- Include homework and projects that use exemplars of counter-stereotypes (e.g. female scientists, mathematicians).

- Involve families in events such as International Women's Day.

- Create volunteering opportunities for fathers and mothers.

- Source resources and learning materials that challenge gender stereotypes for parents and carers.

- Run workshops or information sessions with parents and carers. Consider how children can also be involved in these. Talk about what families can do to neutralise gender stereotypes and why this is important. Be passionate about gender equality and the empowerment of children and young people.

## CASE STUDY

This case study comes from the research of Joanna Leach (2019). She worked on a research project centred around girls' perceptions of gender stereotypes and professions. Her findings are interesting because they show that perceptions of traditional stereotypical views of professions can be broken down, and the case study provides a good example of how this can be achieved when schools and parents work together and share the same values.

The research project took place in an all-girls preparatory school that has a very strong ethos of gender equality and strives to empower girls. The school provides the girls with an exceptional platform to develop self-belief and confidence to succeed, which is summed up by the school's key aim to develop a love of learning through an exciting and stimulating education. Lesson planning and curricular activities are designed to challenge gender stereotypes associated with occupational roles, especially leadership roles. The head teacher was interested in whether this work was having an impact on girls' views, so, with the approval of the school governors, as well as consent from parents, pupils and teachers, the research project took place. The research had two areas of inquiry:

1.  Some 102 girls aged 5-11 completed a drawing of a doctor, an astronaut, a nurse and a head teacher; 64 of those girls aged 7-11 (Years 3-6) added keywords on what makes a good head teacher. The activity took place in the normal classroom setting with the class tutor. This was inspired by *Drawing the Future* (Chambers et al., 2018), where children's drawings were used to collect data on children's career choices, as well as other researchers who have used children's drawings to capture children's perceptions, feelings and beliefs (Prosser and Burke, 2008; Procter and Hatton, 2015). Rose (2013) suggests that drawings are one of the most straightforward and revealing ways to collect data from children.

2.  The data collected from the drawings were analysed and reoccurring themes and salient points were presented as a stimulus for discussion with 14 teachers, who were split into four focus groups. Harding (2018) defines this method of focus group research as 'a way of collecting qualitative data, which usually involves engaging a small number of people in an informal group discussion, "focused" around a particular topic or set of issues' (p45). The focus groups were audio-recorded, transcribed and analysed to identify key themes.

The findings revealed that overall, the girls drew 77 per cent of doctors as female, 65 per cent female astronauts, and strikingly 95 per cent female nurses and 97 per cent female head teachers. However, this varied across year groups. For example, the reception class drew more male doctors than female. The percentage of female doctors decreased from 87 per cent in Year 5 to 60 per cent in Year 6 (examples are shown in Figure 12.6). This raises the question of whether as girls grow older and are more aware of social norms, they are inclined to conform to gender stereotypes.

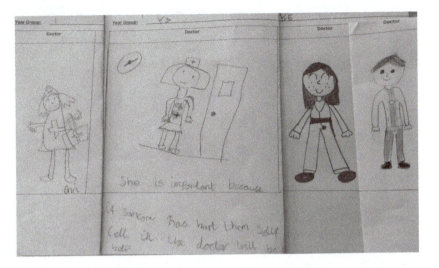

Figure 12.6   A selection of girls' drawings of a doctor (Years 1, 3, 5 and 6)

Years 1 and 4 drew more male astronauts, whereas it was the opposite in reception and Years 5 and 6. One startling result was the Year 2 class, where 88 per cent of astronauts were female (see Figure 12.7).

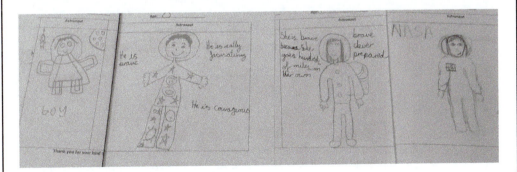

Figure 12.7   A selection of astronaut drawings (Years 2, 4, 5 and 6)

The most noticeable element of drawings of nurses was the stereotypical way that they were illustrated. For example, the majority had long hair and wore a dress and hat (see Figure 12.8).

(Continued)

(Continued)

*Figure 12.8    A selection of nurse drawings (reception and Years 2, 4 and 6)*

Finally, 95 per cent of the girls drew a female head teacher. Again, there are some hyper-feminine elements in the drawings (e.g. skin-tight skirt, hearts, frills, big lashes), unlike the head teacher of the school (see Figure 12.9). Some 304 words were written by the 64 older girls asked to describe a good head teacher. The five most popular words were 'kind', 'helpful', 'smart'/'clever', 'caring' and 'happy'. Most of these words are associated with females.

*Figure 12.9    A selection of head teacher drawings (reception and Years 2, 4 and 6)*

In viewing what the girls had drawn, the majority of teachers felt the prevalence of women drawn was not surprising as staff 'spend a long time talking about gender stereotypes and crushing those stereotypes … parents and teachers are quite aware of female empowerment'. The number of female astronauts drawn was of great interest as a female astronaut had featured in a STEM week research project, which suggests the girls had been influenced by that. However, there was a consensus that the girls' drawings of a head teacher were influenced by their own experience and relationship with their current head teacher.

In conclusion, the findings suggest that the environment in which a child is taught can break down perceptions of stereotypical views of professions in society. However, as noted by the teachers, the influence this will have is also shaped by role models the child is exposed to at home, as well as the values of the family.

## TRANSFORMING PRACTICE

Ideas from this study could be applied through action research in other educational settings, varying in size, location and gender composition.

## REFLECTION

- As you near the end of this chapter, think sensitively about situations in your practice setting to which you could respond.
- What can you do to take forward ideas from this chapter into your practice setting?

Many of the issues we have looked at in this book can be deeply harmful to children's sense of safety and wellbeing, not only at the time of the incident, but long into the future. Children can withdraw from subjects and school life to avoid being the target of hostility. This can isolate children and place arbitrary restrictions on their behaviour and aspirations. There is a great deal that you can do to eradicate harmful behaviour by working with school leaders, colleagues, parents, carers and pupils.

# CHAPTER SUMMARY

- Teachers and practitioners working with children and young people have a duty of care that requires them to take measures as are reasonable in the circumstances to protect and promote the welfare of children in their care.

- A whole-school approach is considered best practice to create the overarching framework for action to tackle harmful behaviour in education. It includes the school strategy and policy, and while it is driven by leadership, everyone is involved – that includes you!

# USEFUL WEBSITES

Acas: **www.acas.org.uk/index.aspx?articleid=6078**

Brook: **www.brook.org.uk**

Rape Crisis: **https://rapecrisis.org.uk**

The Survivors Trust: **www.thesurvivorstrust.org**

National Education Union: **https://neu.org.uk/advice/its-just-everywhere-sexism-schools**

UK Feminista: **https://ukfeminista.org.uk**

# REFERENCES

Brook (2020) *Brook Sexual Behaviours Traffic Light Tool.* Available at: https://legacy.brook.org.uk/our-work/the-sexual-behaviours-traffic-light-tool

Chambers, N., Kashefpakdel, E., Rehill, J. and Percy, C. (2018) *Drawing the Future Survey.* London: Education for Employers.

Department for Children, Schools and Families (DCSF) (2009) *Guidance for Schools on Preventing and Responding to Sexist, Sexual and Transphobic Bullying. Safe to Learn: Embedding Anti-Bullying Work in Schools.* Nottingham: DCSF.

Department for Education (DfE) (2015a) *Child Abuse Concerns: Guidance for Practitioners.* Available at: www.gov.uk/government/publications/what-to-do-if-youre-worried-a-child-is-being-abused--2

Department for Education (DfE) (2015b) *Non-Maintained Special Schools (England) Regulations 2015.* Available at: www.gov.uk/government/publications/non-maintained-special-schools-regulations-2015

Department for Education (DfE) (2018) *Keeping Children Safe in Education.* Available at: www.gov.uk/government/publications/keeping-children-safe-in-education--2

Harding, J. (2018) *Qualitative Data Analysis: From Start to Finish*, 2nd edn. London: SAGE.

HM Government (1998) *Human Rights Act 1998.* Available at: www.legislation.gov.uk/ukpga/1998/42/contents

HM Government (2002) *Education Act 2002.* Available at: www.legislation.gov.uk/ukpga/2002/32/contents

HM Government (2010a) *Equality Act 2010.* Available at: www.legislation.gov.uk/ukpga/2010/15/contents

HM Government (2010b) *United Nations Convention on the Rights of the Child.* Available at: www.gov.uk/government/publications/united-nations-convention-on-the-rights-of-the-child-uncrc-how-legislation-underpins-implementation-in-england

HM Government (2010c) *Public Sector Equality Duty.* Available at: www.legislation.gov.uk/ukpga/2010/15/section/149

HM Government (2014) *Education (Independent School Standards) Regulations 2014*. Available at: www. legislation.gov.uk/uksi/2014/3283/schedule/made

HM Government (2014) *Social Services and Well-Being (Wales) Act 2014*. Available at: www.legislation.gov. uk/anaw/2014/4/contents

HM Government (2018) *Working Together to Safeguard Children*. Available at: www.gov.uk/government/ publications/working-together-to-safeguard-children--2

Leach, J. (2019) *Is Leadership Engendered at a Young Age, Particularly in Girls, and Is This a Barrier Why Proportionately, Fewer Female Teachers Pursue Educational Leadership Roles in the Primary Sector?* Unpublished MA dissertation, University of Reading, UK.

National Education Union (NEU) and UK Feminista (2017) *'It's Just Everywhere': A Study of Sexism in Schools and How We Can Tackle It*. Available at: https://neu.org.uk/sites/neu.org.uk/files/sexism-survey-feminista-2017.pdf

Procter, L. and Hatton, A. (2015) Producing visual research with children: exploring power and meaning making. In E. Stirling and D. Yamada-Rice (eds), *Visual Methods with Children and Young People: Studies in Childhood and Youth*. London: Palgrave Macmillan.

Prosser, J. and Burke, C. (2008) Image-based research: childlike perspectives. In J.G. Knowles and A.L. Cole (eds), *Handbook of the Arts in Qualitative Research: Perspectives, Methodologies, Examples, and Issues*. London: SAGE.

Rose, G. (2013) On the relationship between 'visual research methods' and contemporary visual culture. *The Sociological Review, 62*(1): 24–46.

# 13

# EMPOWERING WOMEN FROM THE BOTTOM TO THE TOP: PARENTS, COMMUNITY AND PARTNERSHIP

## CAROL FULLER, MARIA KAMBOURI-DANOS AND CECILIA MULDOON

## KEYWORDS

- **DIVERSITY**
- **COMMUNITY**

- **PARTNERSHIP**
- **INCLUSION**

- **PARENTS**

### THIS CHAPTER

- highlights how a focus on aspiration and attainment-raising among students from under-represented communities fails to address the significant importance of trust;

*(Continued)*

(Continued)

- considers the role of parents in shaping and supporting the aspirations of their children and the importance of working with them in any initiatives;
- considers the importance of partnership with parents, as well as the value and significance of connecting with community groups, when seeking to empower and support the development of women and girls.

# INTRODUCTION

It makes sense that aspirations matter when we think about educational success. Not only do aspirations drive ambition as well as educational engagement; aspirations can also have an important impact on achievement more formally, in terms of educational attainment in exams as well as further educational plans. It is reasonable to assume, then, that if we want to raise the rates of exam success for some of our more poorly performing students, we will also need to – among other things – raise the ambitions and aspirations they have for themselves. The evidence is clear: when aspirations are high, students perform better in their exams (Khattab, 2015).

Yet raising aspirations among our students – and by this we mean their 'hopes and ambitions of achieving something' (Lexico, 2020) – is not that straightforward. The dreams and expectations of young people do not develop in a vacuum, but instead are shaped, influenced and reinforced by their family and the community in which they live. A plethora of research, for example, has indicated the important role that parents play in the aspirations of their children (Goodman and Gregg, 2010), with a number of large-scale studies highlighting strong correlations between parental expectations and student outcomes (e.g. Fan and Chen, 2001). What is significant about the research is that it clearly highlights it is parental *expectations*, not their involvement, that is key to this area. To illustrate, a study by Grinstein-Weiss et al. (2009) looked at data from more than 12,000 students aged between 5 and 17 and found that parental self-reported expectations were very closely linked to outcomes. This suggests that what parents hope most for their children will form a strong basis for the hopes that children have for themselves. However, we cannot ignore the role of gender in these aspirations. As Jezierski and Wall (2019) found in a meta-analysis of Canadian research and news items, it is the mother who is increasingly significant in the education and aspirations of children. Intuitively, this makes sense. If we are to raise the aspirations of our children, we will need to do so by working in collaboration with the children's families, and in particular with their mothers.

As well as the importance of families, we also need to explore the ways that aspirations are not just the outcome of our particular – and individual – preference, but are those that are also shaped and influenced by our exposure to particular experiences and attitudes from our surroundings. According to some writers, such formative forces are not always overt or obvious, yet they create a subconscious framework – a framework that Pierre Bourdieu, a well-known sociologist, refers to as habitus, which is fundamental to why we make the choices we make and think the things we think (Bourdieu, 1988). A good way to illustrate this idea is to ask your students why more boys than girls study maths. We are confident that they will offer a wonderful array of suggestions about why this may be so, yet when asked why they think the way they do, it will become much harder for them to articulate their rationale for the views they have. This is a clear example of how ideas are often obscure, in terms of why we think the way we do. In relation to gender inequality in STEM, we can look to children's books, films and the classroom for just a few examples of repeated exposure to gender bias in these subjects, the point being that the message is subtle and very rarely direct. So, when we look at aspirations, we need to understand them within the social context in which they have developed.

Social background is important to consider, then, in thinking about aspirations, particularly those of young people coming from much poorer areas. As our social world has an unequal economic distribution, differing social spaces become structured to reflect the differences in socio-economic status of those that live there. This means that families and their children will often grow up and go to school in communities with families who are very similar to them, in terms of their social background. Communities are therefore extremely important to the hopes, ambitions and expectations of the people that live there, because they too are a collective source of messages and ideas.

## WHAT DO WE KNOW FROM RESEARCH?

When thinking about the role of families and communities in the aspirations and ambitions of young people, the term 'social capital' becomes very useful for summing up some of the key ideas that frame this area. While it is a theoretical term, with nuanced distinctions to its meaning, depending on the academic discipline, broadly, the Organisation for Economic Co-operation and Development defines it as a network of relationships (with organisations, institutions and individuals) that has specific benefits and encompasses shared values, norms and understandings (OECD, 2007). For the purpose of this chapter, James Samuel Coleman's ideas about social capital are particularly useful. This is because for Coleman (1988), social capital was very much about the social connections and trust between groups and individuals, and could therefore essentially be summarised as the value of 'community.' In his seminal work theorising his understanding of the concept, Coleman (1988) highlights three ways that social capital works: (1) as a medium to transmit the social obligations and expectations of its members; (2) as a source of information-sharing; and (3) as a means to convey the social norms of the group. To emphasise his point empirically (i.e. by using evidence from research), he demonstrates how school dropout rates are lower among students who attend faith schools, largely because families and practitioners know each other as they live and worship in the same community. Thus, the social expectations and obligations of students are reinforced over multiple sites (e.g. church, school, community). He argues that social connections are strengthened in this way, and this creates relationships of trust. However, for Bourdieu (1988), social communities, while often built on these bonds of trust, are also structured and closed. What this means in practice is that they are hard to get access to if you do not belong, or at least if you do not belong from the perspective of its members. A consequence of this is social closure, where young people cannot get access or exposure to the networks that might develop and/or support their aspirations. Practitioners also struggle to get access to the families that are so crucial to supporting their work. As Fuller (2009, 2014) noted in her work on the aspirations of a group of young, poor girls, trust is a prerequisite to developing the social capital that supports aspirations, not an outcome, as most theory suggests.

Despite the importance of parents and the communities in which young people live, both are often omitted in the educational policies and initiatives that focus on young people. When they are factored in, how best to reach them is not addressed. In the rest of this chapter, we talk about working in partnership with parents, as well as the communities in which they live and work. We highlight with an example one way we have been working to try and create greater social equality by developing relationships of trust, by taking a more bottom-up approach. Instead of focusing on the students, we demonstrate how by supporting the mothers in their aspirations, we can support the aspirations of these children, but in a more sustainable and lasting way.

# THE IMPORTANCE OF PARTNERSHIPS AND HOW TO DEVELOP THEM

A partnership can be described as a continually evolving and mutually supportive relationship between parents and professionals working with the family, but also members of the community, which has at its core the promotion of successful outcomes for the children through active dialogue between all parties. Research suggests that the quality or the relationships which parents develop with the professionals that work with their children can have positive long-term benefits for all involved (Pirchio et al., 2013). We also know that children learn many things from their families, especially how to live in the society in which they are growing up and the aspirations they are expected to have. Families share experiences together, and these experiences are what will form the basis for children's values, attitudes, beliefs and life goals, shaping the identity of each child and young adult. Much of these experiences are developed within the community and the children's educational settings. Field (2010) reports that those working with children need to be in partnership with a child's family in order to ensure that children are able to make the most of the opportunities presented to them.

Working in partnership has a solid theoretical background that is supported both rhetorically and by Department for Education (DfE) legislation by in the UK. From a legislation point of view, working in partnership with parents is considered to be an essential part of an educator's role, with the overarching principle that children learn and develop best when they are part of an enabling environment that provides to their rich experiences and is in line with their individual needs, as well as an environment in which there is a strong partnership between the parents and the professionals that work with children (DfE, 2017). The White Paper *Every Parent Matters* highlights that a parent's active interest in their child's schooling is strongly linked to academic success (DfES, 2007, p2), confirming the government's perspective that working in partnership with parents can support the improvement of outcomes for all children involved (Driessen et al., 2005). What is also important to highlight is that working in parentship with the parents can have a positive impact on the whole family, not just the child, and can be more important in the development of a child's education and learning than the family's circumstances (e.g. background, family size, education level).

The importance of working in partnership with parents is also acknowledged by Ofsted; working with parents is a current Ofsted requirement and part of the Ofsted inspection handbook (Ofsted, 2015, 2018). Listening to parents, gathering their views and understanding their needs is an important aspect of developing partnerships, while it is also something that Ofsted inspectors can easily refer to when judging the quality of the partnership. Therefore, it is important for professionals to remember to keep records of the different methods they use to communicate with parents, as well as gathering their views and the methods they employ to develop their partnership with parents.

## REFLECTION

Gathering information about the families you work with, as well as their views and values, is very important, especially when aiming to work in partnership with them. What do you know about the families you work with? What ways can you use to find out more about them? Have you considered using a survey, face-to-face meeting, feedback box, email, and so on? For example, administering an online survey can give you the opportunity to anonymously collect the views of parents on specific issues such as the kinds of activities they like to do with their children. However, a face-to-face meeting can offer the opportunity for a more private and personal conversation. The right approach should be chosen depending on the situation and the parent/family.

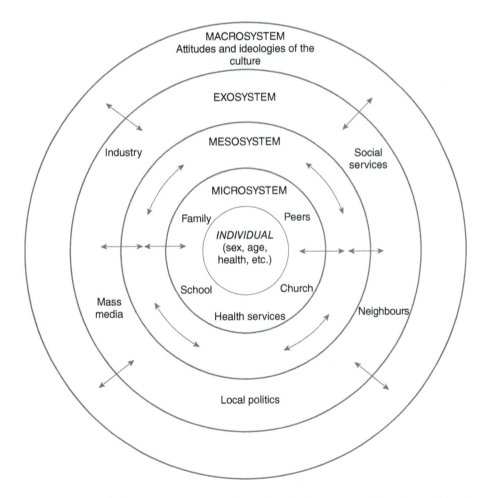

*Figure 13.1*   *Bronfenbrenner's ecological system theory (Bronfenbrenner's ecological theory of development by Hchokr is licensed under CC BY-SA 3.0)*

From an ecological human development point of view (Bronfenbrenner, 1979), children and young adults develop in the context of five environmental systems with which they interact (see Figure 13.1). According to Bronfenbrenner's (1979) theory, the meso-system is created by the links between the child's closest social contexts, home, school and community. Children actively engage with the different systems around them, and they are 'reflexive, moral agents' (Brannen et al., 2000, p10). Children are born with great observational skills. They learn about life, how to socialise, talk, behave and treat others. They also learn what is of value, as well as what attitudes and beliefs are accepted and expected in the society, by observing those around them, both those who are family members and those they meet in educational and community settings. Therefore, when the adults around the child work in partnership, they can facilitate the child's development. Such partnerships would support enhancing continuity between children's life contexts and providing a coherent environment within which to learn and develop.

Zhang (2015) notes that for any partnership to be considered meaningful, it should first be desirable (i.e. by everyone involved – the parents, the professionals, the child). We would add that it is also important for everyone involved in a partnership to have a shared vision and clear objectives and goals that are developed and formed collaboratively, not imposed from one to the other. In order to do this, it is important to be aware of the child's and the family's context, cultural norms and expectations, and the best way to do this is to communicate and listen to parents and their needs. Parents should be treated and recognised as the child's first educator, and their expertise should be acknowledged and taken into account in the partnership equation.

Sometimes initiatives, either from schools or communities, to involve families assume that all families follow a strict and traditional family model. Such assumptions of how a family should be may result in excluding those families that do not follow this model, either as a result of a lifestyle choice or because of specific circumstances that might be out of the family's control (Knowles and Holmstrom, 2013). As Chamber (2001) points out, family refers to 'a variety of living arrangements ... being experienced in western nations, including some complex multiple occupancy households that have not, as yet, been given a satisfactory label' (p1). In reality, a family can take any form. What is important is to remember that whatever form the family has, it will still need to be listened to, understood, valued and appreciated.

## REFLECTION

What types of families do the children you work with come from? For example, in today's society we have: nuclear families - two parents and child(ren), traditionally a mother and a father; single-parent families - one parent and child(ren); extended families - two or more adults who are related either by blood or marriage, with child(ren) living in the same household; stepfamilies - blended families of two separate families merging into one, with step-parents and stepchild(ren) in the same household (or moving between two households); and grandparent families - grandparents raising their grandchild(ren) when the parents are not present.

What could be the different challenges that these different families might face? How can you understand their needs more in order to develop relationships of trust and work in partnership with them? How can you ensure that you involve the female, male and LGBT+ members of your parent population?

## TRANSFORMING PRACTICE

The best way to develop an effective partnership with parents is to first invest in developing relationships of trust. Parents and families need to feel that they are listened to, understood, respected and valued. They need to feel that they and their children are welcome and safe when they are with you, and that although you are the expert in child development, they are the experts when it comes to their children.

Developing relationships of trust will not happen overnight. It takes time and effort and is a two-way relationship. Let parents know how important they are and that they hold the key to their children's learning and development. Help them to build their confidence, which enables them to participate and contribute in the partnership, by listening to them and understanding their values, priorities and needs. Share with them the benefits of working in partnership with you. Part of the journey is to help parents and families understand how important they are, and that because of their key role they also need to invest in this partnership for the benefit of their children.

This chapter has already discussed the importance of schools fully engaging with parents to inform effective partnerships, as well as the ways in which they can do this. By highlighting relevant research, we will also see how relationships between schools and families can be further developed by incorporating the wider local community, specifically community groups. This may be especially useful in less advantaged and diverse areas, where partnering with community groups can help build trust and support relationships with schools and families, which ultimately encourages children's learning and fosters educational aspirations.

# WHAT IS A COMMUNITY?

When we think about a community, we often think about geographical location, one that relates to the children and parents living in the local area. Depending on your catchment area, the children you teach may have very similar characteristics and social backgrounds, or they may be more diverse and represent different communities, based on economic, social or cultural differences. You may teach in an affluent area or have large numbers of children from less advantaged backgrounds. It is therefore important to recognise diversity within your teacher setting, as well as thinking carefully about how to include and support all children and their families. Our knowledge and understanding of others are shaped by our own past experiences, and so it is important to be aware of any preconceptions or stereotypes we may have.

The term 'community' can also include individuals, community groups and organisations not automatically associated with your school setting. When developing community partnerships, it is therefore important to recognise the wider community and the relationships you may be able to build to better support your teacher setting, as well as the children and families of those who attend it.

# THE BENEFITS OF COMMUNITY PARTNERSHIPS

The assumption in some government literature is that certain communities lack educational aspirations and that individual children and/or poor parenting is viewed as the central reason for educational failure (e.g. DfE, 2011a). This 'deficit model' (Centre for Research on Families and Relationships, 2017), however, does not consider structural inequalities around things such as class or family circumstances, and research has shown that children in less advantaged areas do have high ambitions, but not always the means to meet them (Wheeler, 2017).

Building trusting relationships between schools and families helps to break down any stereotypes (from school to home, and vice versa) and promotes positive relationships that can support children's learning and aspirations (McCaleb, 2013). Any parental engagement strategy, therefore, should be a whole-school approach rather than an individualised or 'bolt-on' approach, and, in addition, partnership and multi-agency collaborations can also help to facilitate successful parental engagement (DfE, 2011b). While there are a range of agencies that can help to support collaborative working, it may be particularly useful to consider local community groups in any partnership as they often already have a direct understanding of the needs of a particular group within your local area, as well as established relationships with them. This can be an effective way to initiate trust and further develop relations between the school and home environment. Research has shown that where there is less equality in a society, there is less trust, yet trust is essential for effective collaborative working (Wilkinson and Pickett, 2010). By establishing effective partnerships based on trust, we can empower individuals and strengthen communities, which will benefit everyone in all areas of life.

While parental engagement activities and community initiatives should be open to all parents, it is notable that while parenting is often depicted as gender-neutral, it is typically mothers who have the most involvement in their children's schooling, both in terms of emotional investment and practical support (Reay, 2017). It is also important to be aware of how gender intersects with class and ethnicity, as well as how this may influence the experiences and needs of your children and families. With this in mind, it is important to recognise the diversity in your teacher setting and useful to identify specific community groups who may be willing to work with you.

We set up a project in a small urban community where a teaching institute and a local community centre came together to support less socially advantaged mothers by running a programme aimed at building these women's self-confidence. Partnering with a community centre these women already trusted, and by working with the women to develop the content of the programme together, we were able to foster relationships built on respect, trust and understanding, and subsequently deliver sessions directly tailored to the mothers' identified needs (such as creating a CV and learning about interview techniques). This allowed the women involved in the programme to develop their confidence and identify and realise their personal goals and potential, which enabled them to better support their children. It also empowered them to foster and encourage the ambitions of their children, and subsequently to support other mothers more generally in the wider community. Working from a bottom-up community-driven initiative empowered these women from a strong base to build lasting support networks that then benefited many aspects of these women's and their families' lives.

# THE CHALLENGES OF COMMUNITY PARTNERSHIPS

Developing any community partnership can take a long time to establish, and this can pose problems for all those involved in terms of available time and resources. However, including local community groups who already have associations with families in the area can help to facilitate the trust required to form, and subsequently underpin, long-lasting and strong relationships that can benefit schools and families, and ultimately support children's educational attainment and aspirations.

## REFLECTION

- Do you think community partnerships could benefit your teacher setting?
- Would your leadership team and other work colleagues support any community partnerships?
- Can you identify any community groups within your local area that may be willing to get involved?
- To what extent are any new initiatives driven by time and resources?

**TRANSFORMING PRACTICE**

Ways to address the issues raised here include:

- speak to work colleagues (to gauge interest) and your leadership team (to generate support and identify available resources);
- contact other local teacher settings in your area to find out if any partnerships have already developed;
- identify local community groups that you could approach to discuss your ideas;
- research what can be done in the short term and what longer-term strategies could be put in place.

# CHAPTER SUMMARY

Working in partnership and building relationships based on trust and respect allows individuals and communities to challenge gender, class and ethnic stereotypes, which subsequently helps to make the school community stronger, and ultimately supports children's learning and ambitions. However, and perhaps more importantly, empowering individuals from the bottom to the top allows hope for a fairer and more equitable society, one where success and potential are not hampered by where you live or the family that you come from.

# FURTHER READING

**Bourdieu, P.** (1988) The forms of capital. In A. Halsey, H. Lauder, P. Brown and A. Stuart-Wells (eds), *Education, Culture, Economy, Society*. Oxford: Oxford University Press.

**Brannen, J., Heptinstall, E. and Bhopal, D.** (2000) *Connecting Children: Core and Family Life in Later Childhood*. Florence, KY: Routledge.

**Field, F.** (2010) *The Foundation Years: Preventing Poor Children Becoming Poor Adults – The Report of the Independent Review on Poverty and Life Chances*. London: Cabinet Office.

**Montacute, R. and Cullinane, C.** (2018) *How Parents Use Financial and Cultural Resources to Boost Their Children's Chances of Success*. Available at: www.suttontrust.com/wp-content/uploads/2019/12/Parent-Power-2018.pdf

**Wilkinson, R.G. and Pickett, K.** (2010) *The Spirit Level: Why Equality Is Better for Everyone*, rev. edn. London: Penguin Books.

# REFERENCES

Bourdieu, P. (1988) The forms of capital. In A. Halsey, H. Lauder, P. Brown and A. Stuart-Wells (eds), *Education, Culture, Economy, Society*. Oxford: Oxford University Press.

Brannen, J., Heptinstall, E. and Bhopal, D. (2000) *Connecting Children: Core and Family Life in Later Childhood*. Florence, KY: Routledge.

Bronfenbrenner, U. (1979) *The Ecology of Human Development*. Cambridge, MA: Harvard University Press.

Centre for Research on Families and Relationships (2017) *Can We Put the 'Poverty of Aspiration' Myth to Bed Now?* Available at: www.era.lib.ed.ac.uk/bitstream/handle/1842/25787/CRFR%20briefing%2091%20-%20Treanor.pdf

Chamber, D. (2001) *Representing the Family*. London: SAGE.

Coleman, J.S. (1988) Social capital in the creation of human capital. *American Journal of Sociology*, 94, Supplement: Organizations and Institutions: Sociological and Economic Approaches to the Analysis of Social Structure: S95–S120.

Department for Education (DfE) (2011a) *Positive for Youth: A New Approach to Cross-Government Policy for Young People Aged 13 to 19*. London: The Stationery Office.

Department for Education (DfE) (2011b) *Review of Best Practice in Parental Engagement*. Available at: https://assets.publishing.service.gov.uk/government/uploads/system/uploads/attachment_data/file/182508/DFE-RR156.pdf

Department for Education (DfE) (2017) *Statutory Framework for the Early Years Foundation Stage*. London: DfE.

Department for Education and Skills (DfES) (2007) *Every Parent Matters*. London: DfES.

Driessen, G., Smit, F. and Sleegers, P. (2005) Parental involvement and educational achievement. *British Educational Research Journal*, 31(4): 509–32.

Fan, X. and Chen, M. (2001) Parental involvement and students' academic achievement: a meta-analysis. *Educational Psychology Review*, 13(1): 1–22.

Field, F. (2010) *The Foundation Years: Preventing Poor Children Becoming Poor Adults – The Report of the Independent Review on Poverty and Life Chances*. London: Cabinet Office.

Fuller, C. (2009) *Sociology, Gender and Aspirations: Girls and Their Ambitions*. New York: Continuum.

Fuller, C. (2014) Social capital and the role of trust in aspirations for higher education. *Educational Review*, 66(1): 131–47.

Goodman, A. and Gregg, P. (2010) *Poorer Children's Educational Attainment: How Important Are Attitudes and Behaviour?* York: Joseph Rowntree Foundation.

Khattab, N. (2015) Students' aspirations, expectations and school achievement: what really matters. *British Journal of Educational Studies*, 41(5): 731–48.

Knowles, G. and Holmstrom, R. (2013) *Understanding Family Diversity and Home–School Relations: A Guide for Students and Practitioners in Early Years and Primary Settings*. London: Routledge.

Grinstein-Weiss, M., Yeo, Y.H., Irish, K. and Zhan, M. (2009) Parental assets: a pathway to positive child educational outcomes. *Journal of Sociology and Social Welfare*, 36(1): 61–83.

Jezierski, S. and Wall, G. (2019) Changing understandings and expectations of parental involvement in education. *Gender and Education*, 31(7): 811–26.

Lexico (2020) *Aspiration*. Available at: www.lexico.com/definition/aspiration

McCaleb, S.P. (2013) *Building Communities of Learners: A Collaboration among Teachers, Students, Families, and Community*. New York: Routledge.

Ofsted (2015) *Common Inspection Framework: Education, Skills and Early Years*. London: Ofsted.

Ofsted (2018) *Early Years Inspection Handbook*. London: Ofsted.

Organisation for Economic Co-operation and Development (OECD) (2007) *What Is Social Capital?* Paris: OECD.

Pirchio, S., Tritrini, C., Passiatore, Y. and Taechmer, T. (2013) The role of the relationship between parents and educators for child behaviour and wellbeing. *International Journal about Parents in Education*, 7(2): 145–55.

Reay, D. (2017) *Miseducation: Inequality, Education and the Working Classes*. Bristol: Policy Press.

Wheeler, S. (2017) The (re)production of (dis)advantage: class-based variations in parental aspirations, strategies and practices in relation to children's primary education. *Education 3–13: International Journal of Primary, Elementary and Early Years Education*, 46(7): 755–69.

Wilkinson, R.G. and Pickett, K. (2010) *The Spirit Level: Why Equality Is Better for Everyone*, rev. edn. London: Penguin Books.

Zhang, Q. (2015) Defining 'meaningfulness': enabling pre-schoolers to get the most out of parental involvement. *Australian Journal of Early Childhood*, 40(4): 112–20.

# 14

## WHAT NEXT?

## KAREN JONES

## KEYWORDS

- **WOMEN LEADERS**
- **GENDER PAY GAP**
- **SUICIDE**

- **EATING DISORDERS**
- **SELF-HARM**
- **ASSAULT**

- **BODY IMAGE**

## THIS CHAPTER

- reviews key topics and lessons learnt from the book;
- considers a world without gender stereotypes;
- prompts action planning in your practice context.

## INTRODUCTION

This final chapter provides a review of the topics covered in each chapter in the book. It then looks ahead to the future to consider where education might be in five to ten years if gender stereotyping is addressed. The chapter sets out a series of questions to aid the reader with action planning. Embedded within the chapter is guidance from the Department for Education (DfE) to support teachers to introduce ideas about differences, stereotypes and expectations based on gender, as well as best practice recommendations from the National Union of Teachers (NUT). The reader is supported with links to further reading and resources to supplement learning and aid action planning. This will include, for example, *Opening Doors: A Guide to Good Practice in Countering Gender Stereotyping in Schools*.

# REVIEW OF THE BOOK

The book set out to explore the highly topical issue of gender stereotyping in education. We started this book by exploring different meanings and understandings of the term 'gender'. Drawing on evidence from research, we looked at when and how gender stereotypes form, the different ways that gender stereotypes can be perpetuated in school, and the consequences for children and young people. In Chapter 3, we explored *non-binary gender identity*, then in Chapter 4 we looked at the influence of *social background in developing educational identities*, as well as how this can affect educational confidence, engagement and aspirations. In Chapter 5, we considered the economic implications of *subject choice and career decisions that arise, in part, because of gender stereotyping*.

The next four chapters focused on how gender stereotypes manifest at different stages of education and subjects. In Chapter 6, we explored *early years learning through play*, focusing on how play choices can be both influenced by gender stereotypes and perpetuated by them. We learnt that even when children share the same play area, they often use it in different ways. Ultimately, play choices can disadvantage children because they may miss important learning opportunities. In Chapter 7, we looked at *gender stereotypes in mathematics education*, then in Chapter 8 *gender stereotypes in history*, followed by *ICT* in Chapter 9. Taken together, these chapters provide important insights into how common gender stereotypes result in myths that often shape children's confidence to engage with certain subjects within and beyond their education. For example, we explored research which shows that gender stereotypes influence the development of a mathematical identity among young female mathematicians, and we saw how the *history curriculum in primary and secondary schools* is dominated by the actions of men, thus presenting a stereotypical view of the past in relation to gender.

In Chapter 10, we examined *gender and dyslexia*, notably the issue of gender differences in the diagnosis of dyslexia and under-diagnosis of girls with autistic spectrum disorder (ASD). It is thought that one reason for this is that girls develop compensating strategies to mask identifying signs in their behaviour. This chapter provided examples of best practice to help identify the signs of reading difficulties in the classroom.

We then moved on to the serious issue of *gender stereotyping, sexism, sexual harassment and sexual violence in schools* in Chapter 11. In that chapter, we examined the findings of a study on sexism in schools and how we tackle it (NEU and UK Feminista, 2017). We explored specific pressures facing children and young people in school, such as the impact of everyday sexist language. We then looked at evidence from a UK government inquiry, conducted in 2015, into the scale and impact of sexism, sexual harassment and sexual violence in schools. This was followed by Chapter 12 on the *whole-school approach* (about advocating good practice with parents, colleagues and school leaders), then Chapter 13, focusing on *the empowerment of women through community work and partnerships* as a way to support the aspirations and attainment of children from socially and economically deprived communities.

Let us consider next what the world might look like without gender stereotypes.

# IN A WORLD ~~WITH~~ *WITHOUT* GENDER STEREOTYPES . . .

## BOYS . . .

Feel less compelled to live up to **unachievable hypermasculine ideas.** They can **show emotions, be sensitive and cry without the fear of appearing weak.** When they are struggling, **boys seek support.** This **increases detection rates for depression** and other mental health issues to ensure they are managed effectively. **Male suicide statistics** plummet. The **incidence of violent crime**, injury and death among male adolescents **falls. Aggressive behaviour** and other damaging behavioural problems **become less frequent** in schools and **fewer boys are expelled from school.** Boys enjoy **healthier relationships** with their peers. When they grow up, they **take a greater role in childcare** and **other caring roles and professions.** In a future without gender stereotypes it is common to see men working in childcare, teaching nursery and primary age children. This results in **more diverse role models for young children.**

## GIRLS . . .

Are **more confident**, they **worry less about body image**, there are fewer cases of **eating disorders, reduced rates of self-harm** and less anxiety about personal safety. **Women appear in equal numbers** as scientists, mathematicians, computer programmers and software developers, engineers and in trades such as plumbing and electrics. Women represent **a greater number of Prime Ministers**, political leaders, Judges, Police Chiefs, Head Teachers or Principals of schools, Vice Chancellors of Universities, Chief Executive Officers (CEOs), to name just a few examples. **There is no gender pay gap.** Men take on a greater role in childcare. In consequence of this, **women are better supported pursing their careers.** The combined effect of these changes results in **families being better off financially too**, so child **poverty is reduced.**

---

**REFLECTION**

- Jot down your own thoughts on what the world would be like without gender stereotypes.
- Now compare your ideas with those below.

---

# A WORLD WITHOUT GENDER STEREOTYPES

---

## WHAT DO WE KNOW FROM RESEARCH?

### The effect of gender stereotypes on males

A wide body of evidence shows that gender stereotypes have a profound and wide-ranging impact on boys and continue to shape perceptions of appropriate roles and behaviour for men (and women) through adolescence and into adulthood. Next let us look at a snapshot of some of the ways gender stereotypes shape boys and men's lives:

- A study with 577 adolescent boys examined the longitudinal association between gender role attitudes and physical violence in dating. Traditional gender stereotype attitudes were found to be associated with increased risk for dating violence perpetration 18 months later (Reyes et al., 2016).
- Research by the Children's Society (2018) found that friendship groups which emphasise traditional gender stereotypes had lower overall wellbeing.
- Research with 116 high school children in Canada (70 female and 46 male) explored sexual coercion among adolescents. The findings suggested that both female victims and male perpetrators had more sexist attitudes compared, respectively, to other females and males. The female victims also had lower self-esteem than other female participants (Lacasse and Mendelson, 2007).
- The findings of a large-scale survey examining career aspirations of children aged 7-11 found that compared with girls, over four times more boys wanted to become engineers and nearly double the number of boys wanted to become scientists (Chambers et al., 2018).
- Statistics show that boys were 78 per cent of permanent exclusions and 74 per cent of fixed period exclusions in state-funded primary, state-funded secondary and special schools in England from 2016 to 2017 (DfE, 2018).
- It is estimated that males constitute approximately 25 per cent of people who experience an eating disorder (ED) at some point in their lives. However, figures are difficult to calculate and

---

vary across studies, in part because the problem is under-diagnosed in males. It is thought that the prevalence of EDs is increasing, but cultural stereotypes construct ED as a female issue, so males suffering with this problem are portrayed in ways that tend to stigmatise them. Males typically struggle to get appropriate support and treatment (Sweeting et al., 2015).

- In the UK in 2018, there were 6,507 deaths by suicide, and three-quarters of those were men. This is a sensitive issue and there are many different and complex reasons for these statistics; however, experts think one explanation is that boys/men are conditioned to 'bottle up' their emotions, and so they are less likely to seek help for mental health issues when they need it and not admit they are struggling (Wylie et al., 2012; Seidler et al., 2016; Wong et al., 2017; Mental Health Foundation, 2019).

In a world without gender stereotypes, boys feel less compelled to live up to unachievable hyper-masculine ideals. They can show emotions, be sensitive and cry without the fear of appearing weak. When they are struggling, boys seek support. This increases detection rates for depression and other mental health issues to ensure they are managed effectively. Male suicide statistics plummet. The incidence of violent crime, injury and death among male adolescents falls. Aggressive behaviour and other damaging behavioural problems become less frequent in schools and fewer boys are expelled from school. Boys enjoy healthier relationships with their peers. When they grow up, they take a greater role in childcare and other caring roles and professions. In a future without gender stereotypes, it is common to see men working in childcare, teaching nursery and primary-age children. This results in more diverse role models for young children (see Figure 14.1).

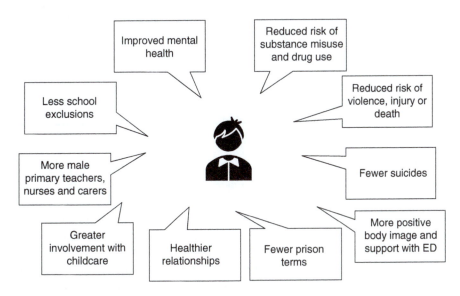

*Figure 14.1  Boys growing up in a world without gender stereotypes*

## WHAT DO WE KNOW FROM RESEARCH?

### The effects of gender stereotypes on females

- Findings from a study by Girlguiding (2018) show that just over half (51 per cent) of girls aged 7-10 are 'very happy' about the way they look, but this drops to 16 per cent for 11-16-year-olds and 13 per cent for girls aged 17-21. In fact, 41 per cent of 17-21-year-olds said they were 'not happy' with the way they look. Focusing on girls aged 11-21, the study found that 50 per cent had been on a diet, 33 per cent skipped meals to lose weight, 30 per cent would consider cosmetic procedures such as Botox to improve their appearance, and 29 per cent would consider cosmetic surgery.

- Some 67 per cent of 11-21-year-old girls in the Girlguiding survey knew other girls who had experienced self-harming, although this figure had dropped from 73 per cent in 2014 (Girlguiding, 2018).

- Eating disorders are more common among females than males, although this varies across different types of disorders. For instance, binge eating has been reported as affecting males and females equally (Sweeting et al., 2015). Some 52 per cent of girls aged 11-21 who took part in the Girlguiding survey knew other girls with an eating disorder (Girlguiding, 2018).

- According to the Girlguiding survey, 52 per cent of girls aged 11-16 had experienced or knew someone who had experienced street harassment (33 per cent stalking, 11 per cent upskirting). Among girls aged 11-21, 30 per cent said they knew another girl who had been raped or experienced sexual assault (Girlguiding, 2018).

- According to the World Economic Forum women represent 34 per cent of managerial positions globally, and less in the top roles (WEF, 2018). Many different studies have demonstrated gender bias in the selection of leaders. This is because the characteristics associated with leaders are highly congruent with stereotypes of masculine traits, not feminine traits (Eagly and Karau, 2002).

- The UK gender pay gap stood at 8.6 per cent among full-time employees in 2018 (ONS, 2018). However, this varies considerably across professions, and many women remain stuck in low-paid jobs with poor working conditions.

In a world without gender stereotypes, girls are more confident, they worry less about body image, and there are fewer cases of eating disorders, reduced rates of self-harm and less anxiety about personal safety. Women appear in equal numbers as scientists, mathematicians, computer programmers and software developers, engineers, and in trades such as plumbing and electrics. Women represent a greater number of prime ministers, political leaders, judges, police chiefs, head teachers or principals of schools, vice chancellors of universities and chief executive officers (CEOs), to name just a few examples. There is no gender pay gap. Men take on a greater role in childcare. In consequence, women are better supported in pursuing their careers. The combined effect of these changes also results in families being better off financially, so child poverty is reduced (see Figure 14.2).

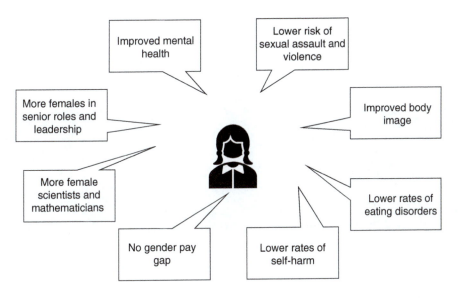

Figure 14.2   *Girls growing up in a world without gender stereotypes*

## REFLECTION

- Do you feel differently about the issue of gender stereotyping now compared to when you started this book? If so, in what ways? Why do you feel differently?
- What has been the most difficult part of this book? Why?
- What has been your most significant learning point from this book?
- What will you do as a result?

# ACTION PLANNING

As you have seen throughout this book, we can all do something to neutralise the damage of gender stereotypes. As you finish reading this book, we suggest you spend some time reflecting on what you can do to transform practice. Is there a problem or behaviour you want to change? Use Figure 14.3 to work through different stages of action planning for change. For example, after reading this book, you might want to update the policy for dealing with sexist language with colleagues, or you might want to do more to engage children in International Women's Day or encourage them to think of ways to counter gender stereotypes. During this process, consider if the current problem or offending behaviour you want to change might be related to other underlying problems. For example, if sexually offensive language is very prevalent, it might be related to lack of training in classroom management or weak policies for dealing with offensive language, or a combination of factors. Reflect on the skills you might need to take action and who you can turn to for support with this. Write down what the perfect success scenario will look like if you succeed.

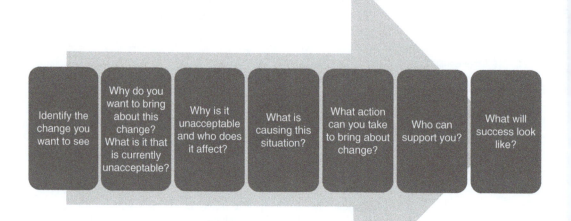

*Figure 14.3 Different stages of action planning*

## TRANSFORMING PRACTICE

As this book draws to a close, let's revisit key messages from the book on best practice for challenging gender stereotypes (DfE, 2018; National Union of Teachers, n.d.):

- Find opportunities to challenge the assumptions made by children, parents and carers, and colleagues. Question assumptions when you see or hear them. Be explicit when talking about why seeing people in a particular role is viewed as surprising.

- Initiate discussions about why some people believe girls/boys cannot do certain things or are not good at some tasks, subjects and jobs. Use these discussions to challenge gender stereotypes.

- Talk about how life for women and men has changed over time, as well as the way that attitudes have changed towards the roles that each can perform. Ask children to imagine how different life would have been for them in the past.

- Use books that challenge stereotypes and discuss why some characters hold or deviate from stereotypical views (e.g. *The Paper Bag Princess*, *The Different Dragon* for younger children).

- When possible, invite counter-stereotypical role models to talk to children about why they chose their career and how they achieved career success. Don't just incorporate these talks in lessons about gender stereotypes; invite speakers to a range of lessons, such as science, computing/technology, mathematics, English, and so on.

- Embed the work of counter-stereotypical figures across the curriculum. In history, the suffragettes, Catherine the Great and Queen Elizabeth I. In science, Emilie du Chatelet, Marie Curie, Caroline Herschel and Mary Somerville. In mathematics, use the work of Maryam Mirzakhani, Katherine Johnson, Dame Mary Lucy Cartwright and Marjorie Lee Browne, an African American who was the first black woman to earn a doctorate in mathematics. Then in computer science, to name just a few examples, Ada Lovelace, Grace Hopper, Ida Rhodes, Sophie Wilson and Aminata Sana Congo.

- Celebrate diversity events such as International Women's Day, LGBT History Month and Anti-Bullying Week.

- Use books with examples of counter-stereotypes, as well as using positive examples in learning materials, handouts and wall displays.

- Consider the subtle way that marketing materials and school hall of fame/alumni photographs can reinforce gender stereotypes.

- Present subjects equally to students in terms of their relative difficulty, and refrain from making remarks about how difficult or easy children might find a particular subject because of their sex.

- Reflect on whether you speak differently to boys and girls, interact differently, or offer different levels of praise or help.

- Encourage all children and staff to participate in activities, not just activities that are traditionally for males or females.

- Organise groups in ways that avoid emphasising differences between girls and boys (e.g. the way children line up, 'helping' tasks you assign to children).

- Consider how your own language, your way of questioning and the way you respond to children might inadvertently reinforce gender stereotypes or lead them to think you are expecting a particular response. For example, in a lesson where children write a story about what they did during the holidays, you might inadvertently lead children with gender-stereotypical examples of what they might write about.

- Instead of using the terms 'boys and girls' and 'mums and dads', use words such as 'children' and 'families'.

- Ensure that all staff know how to respond to gender stereotypes and sexist language. Explain why it is not acceptable and why it is harmful. Encourage children not to use offensive language against others.

- Ensure that the school equality policy is highly visible, both on the school website and as a hard copy, where parents, carers and visitors can see it. Use posters to reinforce key messages about equality around the school/premises.

# CHAPTER SUMMARY

We hope that the reading and activities in this book, along with the additional reading and resources listed, has helped you to consider how you can act to bring about change in the context in which you work. We saw early in the book that this issue has received little, if any, attention from teacher training courses or education courses, and practitioners generally feel unprepared and lack confidence taking action to deal with gender stereotypes in their practice context. This book is a unique resource for understanding gender stereotypes in education for those working with or aspiring to work with children and young people, and we hope that you have found it helpful to have a resource that links theory with practice and provides research-informed pragmatic solutions to improve practice and transform the school environment.

We have now reviewed the key messages from each chapter in this book, imagined a world without gender stereotypes, and helped you to think about how to plan action to transform your practice.

## FURTHER READING

**Education Scotland** (2019) *Improving Gender Balance and Equalities 3–18*. Available at: https://education. gov.scot/improvement/learning-resources/Improving%20gender%20balance%203-18

**Institute of Physics (IOP)** (2015) *Opening Doors: A Guide to Good Practice in Countering Gender Stereotyping in Schools*. Available at: www.iop.org/genderbalance

## REFERENCES

Chambers, N., Kashefpakdel, E., Rehill, J. and Percy, C. (2018) *Drawing the Future Survey*. London: Education for Employers.

Children's Society (2018) *The Good Childhood Report 2018*. London: Children's Society.

Department for Education (DfE) (2018) *Permanent and Fixed Period Exclusions in England: 2016 to 2017 National Tables*. Available at: https://assets.publishing.service.gov.uk/government/uploads/system/uploads/attachment_data/file/731413/national_tables_exc1617.xlsx

Eagly, A.H. and Karau, S.J. (2002) Role congruity theory of prejudice toward female leaders. *Psychology Review, 109*(3): 573–98.

Girlguiding (2018) *We See the Big Picture: Girls' Attitudes Survey 2018*. Available at: www.girlguiding.org. uk/globalassets/docs-and-resources/research-and-campaigns/girls-attitudes-survey-2018.pdf

Lacasse, A. and Mendelson, M.J. (2007) Sexual coercion among adolescents: victims and perpetrators. *Journal of Interpersonal Violence, 22*(4): 424–37.

Mental Health Foundation (2019) *Mental Health Statistics: Suicide*. Available at: www.mentalhealth.org. uk/statistics/mental-health-statistics-suicide

National Education Union (NEU) and UK Feminista (2017) *'It's Just Everywhere': A Study of Sexism in Schools and How We Can Tackle It*. Available at: https://neu.org.uk/sites/neu.org.uk/files/sexism-survey-feminista-2017.pdf

National Union of Teachers (n.d.) *Stereotypes Stop You Doing Stuff*. Available at: www.teachers.org

Office for National Statistics (ONS) (2018) *Gender Pay Gap in the UK 2018*. Available at: www.ons.gov. uk/employmentandlabourmarket/peopleinwork/earningsandworkinghours/bulletins/genderpaygapin theuk/2018

Reyes, H.L.M., Foshee, V.A., Niolon, P.H., Reidy, D.E. and Hall, J.E. (2016) Gender role attitudes and male adolescent dating violence perpetration: normative beliefs as moderators. *Journal of Youth and Adolescence*, *45*(2): 350–60.

Seidler, Z.E., Dawes, A.J., Rice, S.M., Oliffe, J.L. and Dhillon, H.M. (2016) The role of masculinity in men's help-seeking for depression: a systematic review. *Clinical Psychology Review*, *49*: 106–18.

Sweeting, H., Walker, L., MacLean, A., Patterson, C., Räisänen, U. and Hunt, K. (2015) Prevalence of eating disorders in males: a review of rates reported in academic research and UK mass media. *International Journal of Men's Health*, *14*(2): 1–27.

Wong, J.Y., Ho, M.R., Wang, S.Y. and Miller, I.S.K. (2017) Meta-analyses of the relationship between conformity to masculine norms and mental health-related outcomes. *Journal of Counselling Psychology*, *64*(1): 80–93.

World Economic Forum (WEF) (2018) *The Global Gender Gap Report 2018*. Available at: www3.weforum. org/docs/WEF_GGGR_2018.pdf

Wylie, C., Platt, S., Brownlie, J., Chandler, A., Connolly, S., Evans, R., et al. (2012) *Men, Suicide, and Society: Why Disadvantaged Men in Mid-Life Die by Suicide*. Available at: https://media.samaritans.org/documents/Samaritans_MenSuicideSociety_ResearchReport2012.pdf

# INDEX